Under the Western Skies: Lu Vason: Dreamer to Visionary, Visionary to Pioneer

By Anton Cunningham
Edited by Kai El Zabar
Interviews by Gordon Jackson
Published by Kaja Publishing, LLC
Foreward by Glynn Turman

Copyright © 2025 By Bill Pickett Invitational Rodeo & Kaja Publishing, LLC. All rights reserved. No part of this publication may be reproduced, distributed, or transmitted in any form or by any means, including photocopying, recording, or other electronic or mechanical methods, without the prior written permission of the publisher, except in the case of brief quotations embodied in critical reviews and certain other noncommercial uses permitted by copyright law. For permission requests, email to the publisher at anton@kajapublishing.com

TABLE OF CONTENT

Foreward

Introduction

Chapter 1:   The Vision   9
Chapter 2:   Out of the Chute   16
Chapter 3:   California, Here I Come   29
Chapter 4:   I'm In the Army Now   34
Chapter 5:   California Dreamin'   44
Chapter 6:   When the Stars Start to Align   71
Chapter 7:   From California to the Mile High City   95
Chapter 8:   The P-FUNK Bet   103
Chapter 9:   Getting Up and Back On the Horse   110
Chapter 10:   The Great Epiphany   120
Chapter 11:   Folklore of the West in Back   138
Chapter 12:   Bill Pickett Rodeo: In Full Stride   155
Chapter 13:   Valeria and the Secret Wedding   176
Chapter 14:   Serious as a Heart Attack   196
Chapter 15:   Unapologetic Blackness   204
Chapter 16:   The Feyline Connection   215
Chapter 17:   We are Family   222
Chapter 18:   This is My Rodeo   233
Chapter 19:   Roped Into History   242
Chapter 20:   Riding Into the Sunset   252

Epilogue

FOREWARD

The Bay Area of California has long been known for its creativity, cultural vibrancy, and, above all, its rebellious spirit. It's no surprise that Lu Vason found his voice, and his calling, in this exact environment.

It was here that he carved his path as a bold and intuitive entertainment promoter, connecting with people from all walks of life.

If you ever felt uncomfortable around Lu, the truth is, you were probably the problem. He made everyone feel seen, heard, and part of something greater.

Lu didn't just ask the hard questions, he acted on the answers. That fire, that relentless pursuit of justice, purpose, and celebration of Black excellence, was not only his style, but it was in his blood.

When word hit Black Hollywood that the All-Black Bill Pickett Invitational Rodeo was coming to our backyard, the excitement was electric. For too long, we had been erased from the stories of the untamed West, left out of the movies and the mythologies. So, when Lu invited us not just to witness, but to participate in the opening ceremonies, it wasn't just special, it was powerful. It was restorative.

I remember his big smile, it was infectious, as he greeted me and Danny Glover, ushering us from venue to venue. And oh, the food, Lu made sure we loaded up on catfish, barbecue chicken, greens, and mac & cheese. Well, you get the picture.

All of this, against a backdrop of Motown classics blaring through the loudspeakers, and proud Black cowboys and cowgirls dressed in their finest boots, buckles, and boldness. What Lu was building wasn't just an event, it was a movement, it was a cultural phenomenon.

Lu, his wonderful wife Valeria, and their dynamic team were placing a pin in American history, redefining one of the country's oldest traditions. I can't begin to count the number of times I've sat on horseback during the chaos and excitement of a grand entrance, flooded with memories of my eight-year-old self.

I'd flash back to the white neighborhood kids on my block, the ones who tried to deny my identity, taunting me with the words, "There's no such thing as a Black cowboy." Those were fighting words. And believe me, we went to blows over it, because I wasn't raised to ever be a victim or back down from truth.

Lu's vision silenced that lie. His work, his legacy, and this book stand as living proof: we have always been here. This is our history, too. Lu's story is not just a memoir, it's a blueprint. It reinforces the resilience of the American dream and the people who dare to reshape it.

His life was a song, a harmony of justice, chaos, passion, and purpose. I am a believer in the saying "one is a crowd." What started in a small arena in Denver Colorado now plays over national television airwaves. His vision has taken on a life of its own. His life is a testimony to perseverance and "dogged" determination. It's only fitting that his legacy continues in this book.

I'm honored to write this foreword for a man whose life exemplified what it means to walk with purpose, lead with courage, and build with love.

To my friend Lu, I miss you and we all miss you deeply. But your voice still echoes, your impact still expands, and your legacy lives on in every hoofbeat, every spotlight, and every dream sparked by your unwavering vision.

Glynn Russell Turman

PREFACE

"History is not the past. It is the present. We carry our history with us. We are our history." – James Baldwin

They'll tell you the West was wild, but they won't always tell you who helped build it. They'll talk about sheriffs, cowboys, and Indians, cattle drives and six-shooters, but you won't often hear about the Black men and women who rode harder, worked tougher, and carved out a legacy in silence. Well, I ain't never been one to stay silent.

Let me tell you something straight: this ain't just a history book, and it sure ain't a pity party. This is a ride. A ride through dusty plains, crowded arenas, smoky clubs, and meeting rooms where I was often the only Black man in the building, but never the quietest. This book is the story of how I went from cutting heads to turning heads. From being underestimated to becoming a founder, promoter, and the heartbeat of something bigger than myself.

See, I wasn't raised on a ranch. I came up in the city. My hustle didn't start on a horse. It started with pressing combs and a head full of ambition. I was a stylist first, then stepped into the world of music and entertainment, promoting acts like Prince and the O'Jays, rubbing shoulders with greatness before I ever built my own stage.

But then I saw a rodeo in Cheyenne, Wyoming, and everything changed. Not because of what I saw, but because of what I didn't see. No Black cowboys. No recognition. No representation. It didn't sit right with me. And when something doesn't sit right with me? I will do something about it.

I dug into history and found out what school never taught me: that one out of every four cowboys was Black. The names like Bill Pickett, Nat Love, and Bose Ikard weren't just footnotes, they were pioneers. Legends. And I made a decision right then and there: I was going to shine a light on these stories the world had ignored.

That's when I became a historian, not the kind buried in stacks of books, but the kind who puts boots on the ground and truth on the stage. I didn't just study our past, I gave it a mic, a spotlight, and a sold-out crowd.

I took our history out of the shadows and rode it right into the center of the arena where it always belonged.

The Bill Pickett Invitational Rodeo was born not just out of vision, but out of frustration, out of pride, and out of love for our people.

In 1984, I didn't just organize a rodeo, I kicked open a door that had been shut for far too long. And for many years, we've been touring the country, letting the world know: we've always been here.

So what's this book really about?

It's about legacy. Not the kind written in marble or bronze, but the kind etched into dirt arenas and rodeo banners and the hearts of young Black boys and girls who saw a cowboy that looked like them for the first time.

It's about risk. I didn't have a blueprint. I had a gut, a grind, and a God-given gift to connect dots where other people saw dead ends.

It's about history, not the one you read in textbooks, but the one you feel in your bones when you know your people helped shape the very land that tried to erase them.

It's about entrepreneurship. I built this thing from scratch, with no safety net. I brokered deals, made calls, pulled favors, and sometimes, slept in my car. But I kept going, because I knew the mission was bigger than me.

It's about community. I didn't do this alone. Along the way, I found warriors, riders, dreamers, believers, and stubborn souls like me who wouldn't let our history disappear.

It's about Black excellence. Period. On horseback. In business. On stages. In boardrooms. Wherever we go, we bring brilliance, and I wanted to make sure the world saw it under the bright lights of the rodeo arena.

Now let me warn you, this story ain't linear. It's not some tidy little tale with a neat beginning and end.

My life's been a winding trail of sharp turns, fast gallops, and hard falls. I've made mistakes. I've trusted the wrong folks. I've had to fight to be heard, and fight harder to stay true. But through it all, I've held tight to one thing: my purpose.

So as you turn these pages, I want you to feel like you're riding beside me. Hear the crackle of a microphone before showtime. Smell the dirt as a bull kicks off the chute.

Feel the weight of what it means to carry a legacy forward with no guarantee of applause.

You'll meet legends, some living, some long gone. You'll learn how I took a forgotten truth and turned it into a movement. You'll see how faith, stubbornness, and just enough "crazy", can push a man past every obstacle standing in his way.

Whether you're a young hustler trying to find your lane, a student of history hungry for the full story, or someone who's just curious how a Black man pulled off some many things, hair stylist, model, writer, promoter, actor, entrepreneur ending with a rodeo, a **national rodeo tour** in a world that didn't think he belonged, this book is for you.

And don't worry, you don't need to know anything about the rodeo world to ride with me. Just bring your open mind, a little curiosity, and maybe a little swagger.

By the end of this journey, you won't just know about Black cowboys and black cowgirls, you'll understand why their story matters now more than ever.

I didn't write this book for the history books. I wrote it for the future, for the little girl in the front row with braids and boots. For the grandson of a sharecropper who's learning he comes from strength. For every person who's been told they don't belong in a space and decided to show up anyway.

This is *Under the Western Skies*. This is my story, but it's also our story.

Our heritage. Our hustle. Our hope.

Now turn the page. The ride's just getting started.

Lu Vason

Chapter 1: THE VISION

In the summer of 1977, the stretched out plains of Cheyenne, Wyoming, transformed into the vibrant epicenter of cowboy culture during the Cheyenne Frontier Days Rodeo. Among this grand spectacle of traditional rodeo contests, bull riding, steer wrestling, and saddle bronc riding, there I sat with friends in the sun-drenched stands, immersed in the excitement and raw energy that filled the arena. As they indulged in the thrill of the competition, a moment of stark realization washed over me.

Watching the sea of cowboys showcasing their skills, not a single participant was Black. The absence was not just noticeable; it was eye-opening.

Turning to my mentor, Tom Foster, among the roar of the crowd, I leaned in and whispered, driven by a sudden spark of inspiration, "Man, you know, we can do this." Foster, caught off guard, responded with a puzzled expression, *"Do what?"*

My reply came with a visionary's clarity, "Produce a rodeo, but we'll make it all Black, Black cowboys and Black cowgirls.

The idea, bold and unprecedented, hung heavily in the air. Foster's silence was real, a mix of disbelief and contemplation. This wasn't the usual pitch I would make as a concert promoter; this was something entirely different, something revolutionary.

I was there primarily to discuss business with country music legend Charlie Pride, hoping to organize a concert in Denver. Yet, here I was, contemplating diving into the world of rodeos, a field far removed from my expertise in concert promotions. To my friends, the idea seemed as crazy and wild and unpredictable as the bucking broncos in the arena.

Despite the initial shock and skepticism from many people, my entrepreneurial spirit was unfazed. I also shared the vision with my assistant, Linda Motley, and despite all of their reservations, they knew one thing for certain about me: when I set my mind to something, I would pursue it with relentless determination.

Even without all the details fleshed out, my past successes had been built on my incredible ability to turn my dreams into visions, and my visions into reality, to see beyond the doubts and hurdles that would have stalled many.

Anthony Bruno, a seasoned Black cowboy and Trail boss from Houston, once shared with me that, *"The rodeo world was going to be a tough nut to crack. To get a foot in the door, you needed an invitation from two existing members, and those doors weren't exactly wide open to people like us."*
But knowing where we come from gives us the vision to see where we can go. Our ancestors were not just cowboys; they were the original horsemen and cattle herders whose skills shaped the American frontier. This heritage, rich and tough, has always been a part of us, even if history books have been slow to acknowledge it.

I envisioned the rodeo not just as a sporting event, but as a cultural festival that would celebrate and reclaim the heritage of Black cowboys and cowgirls. My vision extended far beyond mere entertainment; it was about education, enlightenment, and empowerment. I imagined an event where families, children, parents, and grandparents could all come together, not just to watch, but to engage and connect with a part of their history that had been largely unrecognized.

It's about showing that Black cowboys have always been around, as integral to the cowboy culture as were their White counterparts, yet so many in our community don't even know this part of American history.

The more I spoke about the vision, the more detailed it became. I could see fathers and sons, fathers and daughters, and mothers with their children all in the bleachers. Grandparents, teenagers, young adults, seriously, people of all ages would come to the rodeo and love it! And once I saw it, I mean, everything.

The venue, the horses, the cattle, the bulls, the cowboys, the cowgirls, the procession of dignitaries, the vibrant parades, and the gravity of the Black National Anthem sung by celebrities who stood in solidarity with my cause.

I saw the competitions, the awards, the joy, and the community, all coming together in a grand spectacle that was as much a reunion as it was a revelation. I saw the rewards and benefits! I saw it all and I knew that my vision was a reality.

When asked why I thought that it would work, the feasibility of my vision, I confidently responded, The reality is, Black cowboys have been a part of America's fabric as long as cowboys have ridden across its plains. However, unless you were raised alongside them, their presence has largely been invisible.

There have always been communities of Black cowboys, particularly in the Southern and Western regions of the country, where societal constraints often stifled their dreams and ambitions.

Landowners and businesses traditionally dictated their roles, restricting their advancement opportunities. Those who harbored greater aspirations often felt compelled to leave these regions in search of broader horizons.

Let me take you on a quick history lesson for a second. In the vast expanses of what was once the Texas Territory, a significant number of Black cowboys lived, developing a distinct culture that persists to this day. In the early 19th century, white settlers driven by the pursuit of inexpensive land and the evasion of debts moved into what was then Spanish and later Mexican territories. Despite the Mexican government's opposition to slavery, these settlers brought enslaved Africans to work the lands and establish cotton farms and cattle ranches.

By 1825, enslaved people made up 25 percent of the settler population in Texas, a figure that surged to over 30 percent by 1860. When Texas joined the Confederacy in 1861, many white Texans joined the Civil War, leaving their ranches in the hands of enslaved workers.

These workers not only maintained the land but also refined critical skills in cattle herding and horse breaking, which became indispensable to the Texas cattle industry after the war.

There was a delay in the emancipation of enslaved people in Texas, Although President Abraham Lincoln issued the Emancipation Proclamation in 1862, it wasn't until June 19, 1865, that the enslaved in Texas were finally informed of their freedom, two and a half years later.

This day, known as Juneteenth, marks a pivotal moment in history, reflecting a long-delayed promise of freedom and the enduring spirit of the Black community in Texas.

We all have an idea on some of the harsh realities of the South and Southwest. The culture there had a way of crushing a man's spirit and vision. Black men often saw only white men in charge of rodeos, with little hope for themselves to participate significantly.

Their best prospects were limited to small, local competitions or working behind the scenes as handlers. The thought of competing on a national stage for recognition and financial success seemed implausible, a distant dream.

Those Black individuals who did grow up with rodeos and horses, ingrained in their daily lives, were predominantly from these southern regions. Yet, the reality today is that the majority of modern-day Black Americans reside in urban communities across the country.

This demographic shift was largely due to the Great Migration, a massive movement of approximately six million African Americans from the rural Southern states to the urban North between 1916 and 1970, occurring in two phases around the time of the Great Depression.

This migration fostered the development of vibrant Black urban cultures in cities like Washington D.C., Detroit, Philadelphia, Pittsburgh, Chicago, Harlem, Watts, and Oakland. Seeking a new reality and better opportunities, these individuals left the rural South where the absence of farmland and cotton-picking jobs in urban settings compelled them to adapt to different lifestyles and opportunities.

The oppressive agrarian system of the South, often little better than indentured servitude under the appearance of sharecropping, forced many to leave. Sharecropping was supposed to involve wages for crops and leasing land, but the economic reality was such that sharecroppers rarely earned more than what was needed to cover the cost of their lodgings and utilities, keeping them perpetually indebted to landowners.

Many found new hope in the industrial opportunities of the North, factories like Ford Motor Company in Detroit and other manufacturing giants such as Abbott Laboratories, Walgreens, and Sears in Chicago, as well as steel mills in Pittsburgh. States like Pennsylvania, Ohio, Indiana, and Illinois became new homes for millions, offering jobs in industries that leveraged the natural resources of the Great Lakes region, such as the large steel mills in Gary, Indiana, and Cleveland, Ohio.

The Great Migration significantly drained the South of its able-bodied Black population and led to the emergence of a new class of Black Americans.

One of educated professionals, politicians, government workers, and entrepreneurs who contributed to a transformed social and economic landscape in the North.

This shift not only changed the demographic makeup of the United States but also enriched the cultural fabric of the Northern cities with new ideas, ambitions, and a resolute pursuit of a better life.

The myth had been challenged, blacks were not subhuman and when given the opportunity emerged skilled, able, and successful equal to their white counterparts.

As I learned this, my ambition was to dismantle the myths that confined Black cowboys to the margins of American history. The real history, as my knowledge grew, was much richer. Echoing through my plans were the voices of history like those of Glynn Turman and Reginald T. Dorsey.

Glynn Turman, is a distinguished Emmy Award winning American actor with a career spanning over six decades, but many people don't know about his passionate life as a real cowboy off-screen. He wasn't just playing a role when it comes to being a cowboy - it's been a genuine passion and lifestyle for him since the 1970s. Glynn became an accomplished rodeo champion, competing in team roping events. He founded and operated Camp Gid D Up, a free summer camp that introduced inner-city and at-risk youth to horseback riding and ranch life for over 25 years. Won the 1999 Regional Team Roping Finals. He was inducted into the Western Heritage Multi-Cultural Museum's Hall of Fame. In 2011, Turman was inducted into the Silver Spur Awards, honoring his contributions to Western heritage.

Reginald T. Dorsey, a Texas-born actor and producer deeply rooted in Western heritage, has embraced cowboy culture throughout his life and career. Not only has he portrayed cowboys in productions like "Return to Lonesome Dove," but he's also participated in my historic Bill Pickett Invitational Rodeo, the oldest Black rodeo in America. Dorsey actively advocates for recognizing the contributions of Black cowboys in American history, using his platform to highlight this often-overlooked legacy while working with initiatives that introduce horsemanship to at-risk youth.

I understood the historical context, but I also saw that it could be an incredible business opportunity. My background in the entertainment industry equipped me with the skills to package and market this vision, to create an event that would resonate with audiences on multiple levels. Yet, through my proposed rodeo, I aimed to bridge existing gaps.

I could envision the event as a platform for renewing ties to a historical legacy, for inspiring new generations, and for fostering a renewed sense of pride and identity among the Black community.

I was ready to ride off into the unknown, fearlessly pursuing a dream that would change the face of the rodeo forever.

But hold up now…

Before we dive headfirst into bulls, broncos, and spurs, let me back it up for a second. Let me take you to where it all started.

See, everybody sees the showman, the promoter, the pioneer. But before all that? I was just a kid with big dreams, sharp instincts, and a drive to do things my own damn way.

So come with me for a minute, not to the rodeo grounds, but back to the roots. Let me tell you who I am, where I come from, and how a city boy like me ended up rewriting cowboy history.

Are you ready? Good. Let's ride.

Chapter 2: OUT OF THE CHUTE

"You could see the 'For Colored Only' and 'For Whites Only' signs. As a youngster, you don't pay a whole lot of attention to that. It wasn't until I entered my teens before I realized what was actually happening during those times." - Lu Vason

My story begins from modest roots, much like many Black Americans. Born Lucious Augusta Vason, Jr. on April 6, 1939, in New Orleans, Louisiana, a city alive with brass bands, steamy sidewalks, and the smell of gumbo floating through screen doors. I was named after my father, Lucious Vason, Sr. My mother, Dollie Lee Lucas, worked as a domestic worker, and my father as a laborer. Their jobs reflected the limited opportunities available to them. Although I carry the "Jr." suffix, I rarely use my full name. Initially known as "Lucious," I adopted the name "Lu" when I began my career in modeling, and that marked the beginning of a new identity and chapter in my life.

Before I was born, my parents left Alabama for New Orleans, chasing better opportunities and hoping to carve out a life beyond the limits of the Jim Crow South. They stayed with my godmother and her sister, my aunt, I guess that would make them both my aunts, in a small house filled with warmth, gospel music, and the aroma of something always cooking on the stove.

Six months after I arrived in the world, we returned to Montgomery, Alabama. A city pulsing with Southern pride and segregation. This was the early 1940's, and Montgomery was still a place where the color of your skin dictated which doors opened and which ones stayed shut.

My mother soon left for Michigan to find work, leaving me in the care of my maternal grandmother. A tough, no-nonsense woman with hands worn from work and a heart full of quiet strength. That move meant I didn't get much time with my father, but that's a story I'll circle back to later.

Reflecting on my early years, a few powerful moments come to mind. At three, I unknowingly helped prevent a house fire. I didn't do much physically, but when I saw smoke curling up from the floorboards, I screamed like my soul was on fire. The adults came running, thinking I was hurt, but once they saw what I saw, they jumped into action and stopped that fire before it could do real damage.

By six, I was already dancing around the edges of show business. My grand uncles, my grandfather's brothers, owned the Little Harlem nightclub just outside Montgomery. In the daylight hours, while they swept and polished the floors, I'd sneak under the tables, wide-eyed and quiet as a church mouse, listening to the rehearsal sounds of legends. Count Basie, Ella Fitzgerald, Chick Webb.

They weren't just names back then, they were real voices, real smiles, real giants in shiny shoes just a few feet away. Sometimes they'd notice me peeking out and give me a wink or a laugh. I didn't know it then, but something about those moments penetrated my soul and stayed with me. That rhythm, that glow, that world, I would find my way back to it one day.

At seven years old, I didn't know the word "entrepreneur," but I was already becoming one. It started with dirt. Not just any dirt, Alabama dirt. The kind that sticks under your fingernails no matter how many times you wash your hands. Right outside my grandmother's house, she'd pour out her used dishwater, soapy, cloudy, full of food scraps, into the same patch of earth every evening. That dishwater turned our front yard into a worm paradise. And after a good rain? Man, those suckers came up like they had somewhere to be.

Naturally, I grabbed an old coffee can, scooped in some soft mud, and got to work. I'd be out there at sunrise, digging and snatching up worms before the sun dried the soil. There I was, Little Lucious, in hand-me-down overalls too big at the cuffs, crouched low like a soldier on a mission, scanning the ground like I was looking for treasure. And in reality, unaware to me then, I was.

The corner store down the block was my first client. I walked in like I had a million-dollar deal in my back pocket. Plopped that can of worms right on the counter and said, "These are fresh." The owner squinted at me, probably wondering what this skinny kid was up to. But when those worms started flying off the shelves as fish bait, we both knew we had something.

Next thing I knew, I had repeat customers. Not just one store, multiple. I had my own little supply chain. I dug, they sold, the fishermen bought, and everybody walked away happy.

I didn't know I was applying business principles. I just knew I liked the way it felt to trade effort for value. I liked that I created something out of nothing. And I loved that people were paying attention.

It was my first taste of ownership, of turning observation into opportunity, or an idea into cash money. And I'll tell you right now, that's all business really is. Seeing what other folks overlook and finding a way to make it work.

That coffee can full of dirt and worms? That was my first pitch deck. That corner store counter? My first boardroom table. That moment? The start of something that never stopped growing.

My maternal grandmother, the backbone of everything solid in my life, would let me go stay with my paternal grandmother during the summer months.

First, it was down to Pensacola, Florida, where the air smelled like saltwater and shrimp boats. Then later, Mobile, Alabama, where Spanish moss hung from the trees like nature's lace and the porch was a front-row seat to neighborhood storytelling.

For four years straight, I split those summers between the two. Two seasons in Pensacola. Two in Mobile. And every time I went, I carried with me the lessons, and the watchful eyes, of the woman who raised me right.

Now let me tell you something about my maternal grandmother. She wasn't loud. She didn't need to be. Her words didn't explode, they landed. Soft voice, firm spirit. She could shut down nonsense with a single look. No shouting, no slapping, just **truth**. But don't get it twisted, she wasn't afraid to deliver consequences. And I earned a few, trust me.

I remember one time in particular, like it happened yesterday.

I was out in the street playing baseball with some friends, you know, using a broomstick for a bat, bases made out of whatever we could find. Just as we were getting a good game going, my grandmother leaned out the door and said, *"Boy, put that ball in the house so I can get to town."* As she locked the door. *"Don't let me come home and find it outside. You hear me?"* Her voice was calm, but in that **don't-test-me** kind of way that made your spine straighten up.

Consequently, I did what she said, sort of. I put the ball up in the house. But then one of my so-called friends, who already had a reputation for being slick, leaned over and said, *"You wanna know how to break in and get it back?"*

I should've said no. I should've walked away. But I was seven, and he made it sound like a magic trick. To that reason, I let him show me.

He climbed up, slid the window open, reached through, and boom, bam, ball retrieved! Simple. But what I didn't realize was, my grandmother had eyes everywhere, and mamas like her always know when something doesn't add up.

She came home, saw me back outside with the ball, and stopped cold. She squinted, gave me that look like she was reading my soul, and said, *"Boy, now I know good and well you didn't. How did you get that ball out that house?"*

I froze. I tried to lie. I tried to shrug. She leaned in closer, arms folded, eyebrows raised. *"You best open your mouth and tell the truth 'fore I go looking for it myself."*

I cracked. Told her everything. Even told her the kid's name. Her face didn't change a bit, but Lord, her silence was loud. Then came the discipline. Not with fists, not with fury, but with words, wisdom, and just enough sting to make it stick. Let's just say, I never tried breaking into anything again. Not a house. Not a shed. Not even a locked cookie jar.

That day wasn't just about a baseball; it was about **character**. About consequences. About understanding that trust, once cracked, is hard to fix.

Now, don't get me wrong, my grandmother didn't raise me alone. As the saying goes, **"It takes a village,"** and trust me, my village didn't play. While she was the architect of my morals, others were more than happy to help lay the bricks, especially when I stepped out of line. One such moment? Whew, let me tell you about the last whipping I ever got. I was in third or maybe fourth grade. My memory's a little fuzzy, but my backside still remembers.

So here's the setup: My grandmother had sent me to the store after school to pick up a bottle of castor oil. She gave me strict instructions. *"Get the castor oil and come straight home."* You already know, Black folks in the South believed castor oil could fix anything. Headache? Castor oil. Cough? Castor oil. Sore feelings? Yep, castor oil. It was like Vicks VapoRub in liquid form.

Well, I got the bottle just fine. But on the way home, something in me said, *"What does this stuff actually taste like?"* Don't ask me why. I didn't sip it. I gulped it. Half the bottle. Right there on the sidewalk, like I was drinking a cold soda. Smooth. No orange slice. No chaser. Just straight castor oil like I was trying to impress somebody. But nobody was watching.

By the time I got home, I handed the bottle to my grandmother like everything was normal. She looked at it. She looked at me. She tilted it sideways and said, *"Where's the rest of it?"* I said with all the confidence of a kid who didn't fully grasp the gravity of his decision: "I drank it."

She didn't raise her voice. She didn't chase me around the house. She simply turned to my step-grandfather and said, *"Handle it."*

Now my step-grandfather was old-school. Quiet. Sharp-eyed. Barely said two words a day unless it involved fixing something or correcting someone. He called me over like I was being summoned to the gallows. I stood there, legs twitching, hoping maybe I'd get a long lecture and escape the belt.

Nope. He asked, *"What happened to the castor oil?"* I said, "I drank it." He blinked. *"You drank it?"* "Yes sir." *"You drank castor oil... with no orange?"*

"Yes sir. Neat." I replied.

He shook his head like he was trying to figure out if I was brave, dumb, or both. Then came the whipping, not out of anger, not because he thought I was lying.

He made it real clear: *"I'm not punishing you for drinking it. I'm punishing you because you disobeyed your grandmother. She gave you instructions, and you did something else."*

Now look, I didn't understand it then. I was just a skinny kid who had already been punished for breaking into the house to get my baseball, after I was told to leave it alone. You'd think I'd learned the lesson the first time, right? But nooo... Young Lucious had to test the limits. Whether it was baseballs or castor oil, I kept thinking *"I know better."*

But here's what finally clicked for me, that belt wasn't about pain. It was about protection. See, when you're a kid, you don't know what could go wrong. All you see is what you want. That ball. That taste. That shortcut. You don't see the house burning down. You don't think about glass slicing your arm or getting into a scuffle because you broke in. You definitely don't think about the possibility of drinking something that could mess up your stomach for days.

But grown folks? They've already seen the consequences. That's why they give instructions like maps, not to control you, but to guide you.

It took growing up, and later, raising kids of my own, to realize that those old-school rules were actually wisdom in disguise. It wasn't about obedience for obedience's sake. It was about safety. Discipline. Integrity.

And you best believe that castor oil episode, that was my final belt-worthy performance. From that day on, I started listening closely. Didn't mean I never made mistakes again, Lord knows I did, but it meant I began to understand the *why* behind the *what*.

Those lessons laid the foundation. They built the frame. They started shaping the man the world would one day call **Lu Vason**.

It was later explained that following the guidance of elders could save your life or prevent harm. Adults possess knowledge that children don't have yet. This realization struck a chord with me and underscored the importance of respecting and listening to our elders. There's always a reason to, even if it isn't immediately apparent. Reflecting on the time I broke into the house to retrieve my ball, after being specifically told to leave it inside and play outside, highlights this. As a child, my understanding of life was limited.

It didn't matter that I didn't grasp the reasons behind their instructions. I should have respected them, acknowledging that their experience and concern were for my welfare. Suppose I had accidentally started a fire inside; I could have succumbed to smoke inhalation before anyone realized, not to mention potentially burning down the house. Or consider the possibility of breaking a window or getting into an altercation over the ball. The lesson is that children should listen to adults, often for their own safety. Then we grow up, have children of our own, and the lessons truly resonate. These incidents were great lessons, setting the foundation that significantly shaped the man I would become.

But for all the lessons I learned from the grown folks around me, there was still one absence that echoed louder than any wisdom I received, my father.

For a boy, growing up without your daddy, and without anyone really telling you why, is a quiet kind of confusion.

It's a question that lives in your chest. A question you carry around like a weight is "What happened?", "Was it something I did?"

I remember asking, soft and hopeful, "Where's Daddy? When's he coming home?" The answers were always vague. *He's away working,* they'd say, like they were reading off a script meant to end the conversation. And for a while, I believed it.

It wasn't until much later, decades later, that I learned the truth. My father had been incarcerated. In 1954, he was locked up in Raiford Penitentiary, the Florida State Prison down in Bradford County. Back then, that name meant nothing to me. But it carried a heavy weight that no one in the family wanted to talk about.

One summer, while I was staying with my paternal grandmother in Florida, she and my stepsister, **Irma Jean**, told me we were taking a trip. No explanation. Just a long, hot drive, nearly five hours, through backroads and Southern heat thick enough to chew.

We pulled up to a place that didn't look like anywhere I'd ever visited. Barbed wire. Guard towers. A cold stillness in the air. I didn't ask questions. Back then, kids were taught to stay in a child's place. So, I stayed quiet. I didn't know why we were there. I didn't care. All I knew was that Daddy was on the other side of those gates. And I was going to see him.

I don't remember much about the visit, just the feeling. The electricity of being in his presence. The way I watched his every move like he might disappear again if I blinked. No one talked about why he was there, and eventually, I stopped asking. The silence became normal. Expected.

It wasn't until 2013, nearly sixty years later, that I finally got the full story. Irma Jean and I were talking, and out of nowhere she said, *"You know, Daddy was in Raiford for making and selling moonshine."* I just sat there, quiet. Moonshine?

Turns out, my father had been running liquor, trying to make ends meet. One hundred gallons of it, buried underground. He got caught after a police chase and, according to Irma Jean, tried to play it slick, ran home and jumped into bed, pretending he'd been asleep the whole time. But the law wasn't buying it.

Hearing that didn't make me angry. It just made things...clearer. My father wasn't a bad person. He was no different than Joseph Kennedy Sr., father of John F. Kennedy who was involved in importing alcoholic beverages in the United States, notably before prohibition ended. He never went to jail, instead he and James Roosevelt, son of Franklin Roosevelt eventually obtained exclusive rights to import certain brands from Great Britain. They later founded Somerset importers, which became the exclusive American agent for various brands. He also purchased spirits-importation rights from Schenley Industries.

The only real difference between what my father did and what Kennedy did was timing and paperwork. One was called illegal, the other called business. But at the end of the day, both men were hustling to feed their families and build something that could last.

My father wasn't missing because he didn't care. He was just a man trying to survive in a system that left folks like us with damn few options. And that hustle, misguided as it might've been, wasn't so different from what I'd come to understand later. Sometimes, when the doors won't open for you, you go looking for side doors. That revelation helped me forgive the silence, and it helped me understand the man I never really got to know.

I have to admit, some of my folks down in Florida are probably still cooking up moonshine. It wouldn't surprise me if they brought a few jars to my rodeo in Atlanta a couple years back. The truth is those jokers actually did.

Growing up around my father's side of the family in Alabama, I saw firsthand what real labor looked like. Most of them were skilled tradesmen, brick masons, plasterers, what we now call drywall installers. They worked with their hands, built things from the ground up, and took pride in it. As a boy, seven or eight years old, I'd tag along with them to job sites, swinging my own little hatchet like I was part of the crew. I'd help hang drywall in closets, sweating right beside them. Those were special moments, days when I felt like one of the men.

I especially looked up to my grandfather. In our family, he was *the man* when it came to drywall, nobody did it better. I wanted to be just like him. But he died too soon. Blood poisoning, they said, from holding nails in his mouth while he worked. It was one of those quiet tragedies you didn't question back then. Occupational hazards were a part of the job, especially for Black laborers who had limited access to proper medical care or safety advice. There weren't many Black doctors around, and white hospitals often didn't want us inside their doors. Therefore, folks endured pain in silence, until it was too late.

Even now, I see how valuable those experiences were, working alongside the men in my family, learning the rhythm of work, the dignity of doing something with your hands. It planted something in me.

My great-grandfather was a bricklayer, too. So yeah, working for yourself, carving your own lane, that ran deep in our bloodline. Maybe that's where my entrepreneurial spirit first took root. Now, my father? He wasn't about that hammer-and-nails life. He was what they called a "slickster." Always dressed sharp, always had a scheme in motion. I guess that's where my love for fashion developed. He didn't mind hard work, but he preferred to outthink it.

I remember wondering how he always had money in his pocket. He never seemed strapped for cash. At the time, I just figured his side of the family was wealthy. I didn't ask questions, I was too busy being impressed.

Looking back, I get it. He liked knowing he had money. It wasn't just about having it, it was about what it meant: comfort, options, control. In that way, we were alike. We didn't want to punch a clock or work a job just because it was safe. We weren't built for factory lines or post office counters. Oddly, I ended up taking a job at the post office for a couple months, but I'll get to that later.

We were built to carve our own way, even if it was the harder road. We needed to love what we were doing or at least like it. And looking back now, I can say this with certainty: ***"I wanted to do it my way."***

RACIAL CLIMATE AWARENESS

Although I didn't fully understand the racial climate of Alabama in the 1940's, it was all around me. I just didn't have the language or perspective to name it. I was a child, wide-eyed and mostly focused on comic books, cornbread, and catching worms. In our small rural community, tucked away in red clay and pine trees, things felt simple. Right next to our house stood EJ's Grocery, a store run by a kind Jewish man who treated Black families with fairness. He even gave my grandmother a line of credit. I didn't know what that meant back then, but I knew I could walk in, grab what she needed, and walk out like a big man. She'd settle-up later. That kind of dignity was rare, and I now know how precious it was.

But when we crossed into downtown Montgomery, it was a different world. I still remember the moment, standing at a newsstand, flipping through a comic book when my mother rushed over, leaned in close, and whispered, *"Put that down."* Her tone was soft but sharp. At home, reading was praised, even encouraged. Thus, her urgency for me to put the book down didn't make sense to me until much later, when I learned the unspoken rule. Black folks weren't allowed to browse magazines unless they intended to buy them. Our touch was seen as contamination. Just handling a comic book was enough to provoke a scolding or worse.

Truth is, I was blind to the racial lines that hemmed us in. I never questioned why we sat at the back of the bus. The adults did it, so we did too. Segregation wasn't explained, it was simply performed, like the morning routines of the South. You didn't ask. You just followed.

But everything changed for me in the summer of 1953.

By then, we had moved to California, however I returned back to Montgomery to visit. That's when I saw Black folks standing up, literally fighting for the right to sit where they chose to on public buses. I saw policemen in stiff uniforms and white helmets holding snarling German Shepherds like leashes were optional. I watched those dogs attack peaceful protesters…and then, they turned on me.

Two of them charged at me, one clamped onto my lower leg, the other dug into my thigh. I still carry the scars today. An older Black woman shouted for me to stand still, to stop running, but fear had already taken the reins. That moment was more than terrifying, it was transforming. It showed me what hate looked like when it had a badge. And it happened before Rosa Parks ever refused her seat. Before the Montgomery Bus Boycott made history.

That was the first time I felt the world shift under my feet. Downtown Montgomery was covered in signs, "Whites Only," "Colored Section," reminders posted like streetlights to direct our place in society. As kids, we didn't grasp what it meant. We just knew we weren't welcome everywhere. But as we became teenagers, we started to realize that these weren't small inconveniences; they were signs of a deeper sickness.
Still, it wasn't until California, "The Wild Wild West," that I truly started waking up.

The West was a different kind of wild. California didn't look like Alabama, and it sure didn't feel like it either. It was fast, loud, and free-spirited. The culture was louder, and the rules…well, they bent more than they snapped. Back in Montgomery, I was Lucious, a respectful, soft-spoken boy raised to keep his head down and follow the rules.

But in Oakland? That place challenged me to lift my head and find my voice.

I'll never forget the day I met **Bobby Seale** at a friend's house. He started breaking things down, Malcolm X, the Panthers, *The Ballot or the Bullet*. He spoke with fire in his chest and truth on his tongue. It cracked opened something within me. It made me realize I didn't have to apologize for being Black. I didn't have to shrink. I could stand tall, be proud, and speak loudly.

That moment didn't just wake me up, it set me free.

California was a long ride from the red dirt roads of Alabama. It was a different range, a new frontier, a land full of risk and promise. But that's where I learned how to create and walk my own trail. That's where I learned to ride with vision.

And that's where **Lucious became Lu…Under those Western Skies.**

Chapter 3: CALIFORNIA, HERE I COME!

By the time I turned ten, my mama had come back from Michigan. She had already divorced my father a few years earlier, something I didn't fully understand at the time. What I did know was that a man we called Tootsie out West had sent for her. Not long after that, we packed our things and headed to Berkeley, California, a place I couldn't even visually imagine until I saw it with my own eyes. That opened the door to a brand new chapter of my life, my West Coast trail.

Coming from the South, California felt like stepping into a different world. The first thing I noticed? Space. Everything felt bigger, wider streets, taller trees, fewer bugs (thank God), and a breeze that didn't stick to your skin like Southern heat did. Back in Alabama, the air was thick, slow, and heavy with rules. Out west, it felt like the air itself had more freedom. More room to breathe.

As a 10-year-old boy who'd spent his life under the shadow of segregation and whispers, California was thrilling. Everything was so different. The buildings looked different, the air smelled different, the food tasted different, the people moved fast, and they talked like they weren't afraid of being heard. I didn't have the words for it yet, but something in me knew this place could shape a whole new kind of me. This wasn't just a new location, it was a new mindset. A new range. And I was ready to ride.

When we first got to Berkeley, we moved into Codornices Village, a military housing project that became the backdrop of my early West Coast life. We were in Apartment E, and right next door in Apartment F lived the Seales. Yeah, that Seale family. And back then, before Bobby was a founding Panther, he was just another neighborhood kid with a sharp tongue and a loud laugh.

Me and Jon, one of the Seale boys, used to hustle together. Before grocery carts were a thing, we'd walk folks home from the store carrying their groceries for a quarter, 25 cents a block.

Let me tell you something: that change added up quickly when you had energy and no shame asking strangers if they needed a hand. That was one of my first real West Coast hustles.

The first person I met after we got settled, aside from family, was **Herbert Mims**. Now, by marriage, he's my cousin. My stepfather's sister married Herbert's uncle, which made us something like cousins-once-removed-with-a-side-of-in-law, but to me, Herbert was like a big brother. We've kept that bond through the years: phone calls, Thanksgiving visits, and swapping stories like the best of friends.

Herbert was a musician, smooth with the saxophone. Watching him play lit a fire in me. I figured I'd try my hand at it, too. At first, I wanted to blow the trumpet, wanted to be like Louis Armstrong, till I found out Satchmo didn't even play the trumpet, he played the cornet. It sounded close enough, but trust me, it wasn't.

The cornet's got a warmer, rounder tone than a trumpet. Trumpets cut through a band like a blade; cornets glide, like smooth butter on hot cornbread. It's kinda like the flugelhorn, that big, mellow cousin that whispers while the trumpet shouts.

Now, before I ever picked up that cornet in junior high, I actually started out banging on the drums. Yeah, I was the one in the back of the band keeping rhythm and acting like I was leading the whole parade. I eventually joined the school's marching band as a cornet player, but those drums...That's where I first found my groove. Quite the musical journey, huh?

Now let's talk about how I first started making my own money, California-style. My entrepreneurial spirit didn't take long to kick in full throttle once we hit the West Coast. I was flipping through one of my comic books, I was a comic book junkie back then, and I saw this little ad on the back page: **"Earn money selling Chlorine Salve!"**

I didn't even know what salve was, but that ad spoke to me like it had my name on it.

Next thing I knew, I was walking the housing projects with a little box of tins, pitching miracle cream to anyone who'd listen. Folks would buy it too. Probably more because of my hustle than the product. That experience taught me early: **every ad, every word in print, every message on a wall is an opportunity**, if you've got the eye to see it and the will to work it.

That was just the beginning. Over the next few years, I took on all kinds of odd jobs. I cut grass around the complex on the regular. Those apartments were labeled A to G, and I knew every blade between them. We lived in Apartment E, right next door to Bobby Seale's family in Apartment F. Bobby's younger brother, Jon, was my running partner, my ace boon coon. Me and Jon? We were like the Bobbsey Twins with better sneakers. We dressed alike, ate alike, finished each other's sentences, and if you saw one of us, you knew the other wasn't far behind.

Our hustle? Hauling groceries. Before grocery carts were even a thought in somebody's head, we'd walk folks' home from the store carrying their groceries for a quarter, 25 cents a block. We worked like little CEOs, customer service, logistics, and marketing, all rolled into two skinny kids with quick feet and sharp mouths.

Eventually, I moved up to a paper route. Delivering newspapers felt like leveling up. I was out there early in the morning with a sack full of headlines, feeling grown, like I was really making my way in the world.

Me and Jon also got into some harmless mischief here and there. I remember we "liberated" a couple of Mickey D's T-shirts, you know, the ones from the Mickey Mouse Clubhouse, from the Army surplus store.

We thought they were just some fly gear. Took 'em home, dyed 'em pink and black, the fashion heat of the moment, and wore 'em to school like we were the coolest kids in the Bay. No one could tell us nothing.

I got close to the whole Seale family. Bobby, who'd later go on to shake up the entire country with the Black Panthers, was just Bobby back then. Sharp, serious, and always thinking. Their older sister, Betty, was like family to me too.

When I joined the military, me and Jon lost touch. We weren't big on writing letters, but Betty and I stayed close. She eventually moved to Denver, and we remained lifelong friends.

The transition from Alabama's school system to California's was a rough ride initially. When I arrived, they placed me in a lower grade than I should've been in. I wasn't too thrilled about that. But instead of pouting, I listened when my school counselor in Berkeley suggested summer school to catch up. That's one thing about me, even back then, I knew when opportunity knocked, you didn't just open the door...you kicked it wide open.

I hit the books hard, and sure enough, my grades shot up. I climbed back to the right grade level. The next year, that same counselor told me, *"Lu, if you do one more summer session, you can graduate early."* That was all I needed to hear. I took the recommendation and ran with it. I graduated from Berkeley High School in January 1956, a whole semester ahead of schedule. Go Jackets!

That's something I've always believed: If you see an opportunity that's legal, ethical, and lines up with your goals, you take it. I never waited around for life to hand me anything. If there was a chance to level up, I took it. Every single time.

After high school, I enrolled at Contra Costa Junior College in San Pablo, California. I had every intention of staying focused...but let's be real: the books weren't the only thing calling my name. Me and a group of classmates would meet up in the parking lot every day, where we played Bid Whist like it was a varsity sport...and we were on a scholarship. Man, we'd be out there talking trash, slamming cards, and schooling each other like champions, except none of that showed up on my transcript.

After about a year and a half, the school showed me the door, with a friendly little academic probation notice. I knew if I went home with grades like that, my folks were gonna raise holy hell. I needed a plan. Fast.

That's when I thought about my cousin, **Emma Vaiton.** Emma was a boss before we even used the word. She had joined the Air Force back in 1953, worked as a nurse, and was stationed at Travis Air Force Base in California. In our family, Emma was a hero. She walked with confidence, wore that uniform with pride, and everybody respected her. If Emma could do it, I figured so could I.

Finally, I made my decision. No more Bid Whist in the parking lot. I was trading in my deck of cards for a pair of combats boots and a uniform. It was time for the next chapter. And just like that, I was off, to serve, to grow, and to figure out who I really was becoming.

Chapter 4: I'M IN THE ARMY NOW

"It was in Germany where my experiences would help me start thinking about what I was going to do when I got out of the Army." - Lu Vason

Truth be told, I didn't join the Army out of some deep patriotic calling, I joined because I needed to get ahead of the storm.

After spending more time playing Bid Whist in the parking lot than cracking open textbooks at Contra Costa, my grades tanked. And I knew one thing for sure: if my stepfather saw that report card, the fallout was going to be legendary. That man didn't believe in second chances when it came to responsibility. So, I did what any fast-thinking, future-focused young man would do, I beat him to the punch. I marched myself right into the Army recruiter's office and said, "Sign me up."

And just like that, it was settled. I was headed for the U.S. Army, and surprisingly, I wasn't even mad about it. What made it even better? I wasn't going alone. My good friend **Glenn Daniels**, who lived just five houses down from me, signed up with me under the Army's Buddy Plan. That meant we'd go through basic training together, two East Bay boys taking on the military world side by side. At the time, it felt like the right move. And looking back now? It wasn't just an escape plan. It was a launch pad.

I did my basic training at Fort Ord, right off the beautiful coast of California in the Monterey Bay area. The views were nice, but they didn't ease the sting of drill sergeants barking in your face before sunrise. Still, I got through it. Which is amazing to me, because everyone knows that I am not a morning person; I am a night owl.

After basic training, they shipped me off to Fort Sill, down near Lawton, Oklahoma, flatlands and artillery country. That place had a rhythm all its own: marching boots, field drills, and the never-ending boom of training exercises echoing across the horizon.

Then came the real surprise. My next assignment took me across the Atlantic to Germany. Specifically, **Camp Dachau.** Now, let me tell you why this story hits different for me.

During my time in the U.S. Army, I was stationed in Germany, and one of the posts I served at was Camp Dachau. The same site where the Nazis ran their first concentration camp during the war. That place carried weight. The air itself seemed to hold on to sorrow. I wasn't some wide-eyed kid walking into history, I was a young Black man standing on the soil where unthinkable pain had happened.

But here's the twist…What most people don't know, and what some still deny, is that the 761st Tank Battalion was part of the U.S. forces that helped liberate Dachau in 1945. I stood where they stood. I breathed the same air. Walked those same roads. Looked at those same gates, but I got to walk back out. That realization never left me.

It was one thing to read about the 761st in a history book, but to be stationed in a place they helped free, as a Black soldier myself, that put everything into perspective. These men weren't just brave; they were bold in the face of a world that tried to erase them. And they still came out fighting.

The Army didn't talk much about the 761st when I was serving. Their legacy wasn't part of the training manuals. No plaques. No parades. But I knew better.

And I made it my mission to make sure other people did, too.

See, stories like the 761st matter not just because they're history, but because they remind us that Black excellence has always been there, fighting, building, surviving, and leading. And too often, it gets left behind when the cameras stop rolling.
That's why I did what I did. Why I told the stories I told. Why I created stages, not just in salons and theaters, but in rodeo arenas too. Because we deserved more than the scraps of recognition. We deserved to own our legacy, just like those brothers in the 761st did, even when the world tried to deny it.

So here's the story. Even if the paperwork doesn't tie every loose end, I know one thing for sure, Black soldiers were there, fighting and dying in Europe, even while being denied basic rights back home. There were entire units of Black excellence in the war - **the Tuskegee Airmen, the Montford Point Marines, the 92nd Infantry, and yes, the 761st.**

During World War II, while most people still believed that Black soldiers weren't fit for frontline combat, the U.S. Army quietly put together a unit that would blow those lies out of the water. That unit was the **761st Tank Battalion**, better known as the **Black Panthers**. And let me tell you, they didn't just show up, they showed out.

These men were the first Black armored unit in U.S. military history to see combat. Activated in 1942, right in the thick of Jim Crow and military segregation, they were part of what the government called an "experiment." You see, at that time, the Army didn't think Black troops could handle combat leadership or tank warfare. But the 761st wasn't there to fit the mold. They were there to shatter it.

They trained longer than white units, two full years, down in Louisiana and Texas, facing racism from outside and inside the ranks. They were riding M5 Stuarts and M4 Sherman tanks, mastering their craft while being told they didn't belong. The unit even had **Jackie Robinson** in its ranks during training, yes, that Jackie Robinson. He stood up to a segregation incident on a military bus in 1944, foreshadowing the courage he'd later show breaking baseball's color line. Their motto? **"Come Out Fighting."** And they lived it.

In October 1944, they landed in Normandy and were attached to General George S. Patton's Third Army. Now Patton, he was tough. Didn't mince words. *"I don't care what color you are as long as you kill the enemy,"* he told them. *"Everyone's watching you."*

They went into combat on November 7, 1944, and made history as the first Black tankers to fight in WWII. And from that moment on, they never looked back.

For the next 183 straight days, the 761st was in the fight, pushing through Northern France, the Rhineland, the Ardennes (Battle of the Bulge), and Central Europe. They liberated over 30 towns, breached the Siegfried Line, and were among the first U.S. troops to meet the Soviet Army in Austria.

Let that sink in: **Six countries. Four major campaigns. Nearly 200 days of non-stop combat.** They didn't just participate, they excelled. Their impact helped turn the tide of the war. And like in every war, there were heroes among them.

One name you need to know is **Staff Sgt. Ruben Rivers**. That man was a one-man army. He stayed in the fight even after being wounded, protecting his unit until the very end. He was killed in action, but it wasn't until 1997 that the U.S. finally gave him the Medal of Honor, decades overdue.

Another hero? Their commander, **Lt. Col. Paul L. Bates**. He defended his men against the Army's internal racism and never let anyone question their capabilities, not even superiors. That kind of leadership made all the difference.

And while Jackie Robinson didn't go to Europe with the 761st, his fight against segregation within the Army began right there, proving that the war these men fought wasn't just on foreign soil. It was here at home, too.

By the time WWII ended, the Black Panthers had earned:

- **11 Silver Stars**

- **Around 69 Bronze Stars**

- **Nearly 300 Purple Hearts**

That's not just impressive for a Black unit, that's elite by any standard.

But when they came home, America wasn't ready to salute them. No parades. No medals. Just back to the same segregated streets they had left. It wasn't until 1978, over 30 years later, that President Jimmy Carter awarded the 761st a Presidential Unit Citation for their "extraordinary heroism." And it wasn't until the 1990s that the Army started reviewing the records of Black WWII veterans and finally began awarding Medals of Honor.

The recognition came late, but it came. And let me be clear, this unit didn't just win battles overseas. They helped win a bigger fight against racism in the military. Their performance helped push the government toward desegregating the Armed Forces in 1948, when President Truman signed Executive Order 9981. That's right. The 761st didn't just fight Nazis, they fought institutional racism, and won.

They even got reactivated from 1947 to 1955 as an integrated unit. A symbol of the very change they helped force into reality.

Today, you'll find monuments and museum exhibits that honor the 761st Tank Battalion. But more than that, you'll find their fingerprints all over the story of American progress. These were men who fought on two fronts, one against fascism abroad and another against racism at home. And they never flinched.

During my time in the military, my love affair with jazz really took root. The seed had been planted long before, but it started to bloom during a leave back to Berkeley around 1959. And once again, it was my cousin Herbert Mims who lit the spark. Herbert wasn't just into jazz, he was a jazz man through and through. He knew the sound, the soul, and the science of it all. He introduced me to the cool, laid-back rhythm of West Coast Jazz, breaking down names like Ornette Coleman, Cal Tjader, and Dave Brubeck like he was reading from the Book of Jazz.

Herbert had a way of painting pictures with music, showing me how every region had its own sonic fingerprint. From the swing and stomp of New Orleans, where Satchmo made his name, to the cool breeze of the West and the hard bop grit of the East, jazz wasn't just music. It was a map of America's soul.

But let me tell you about the moment that took me from curious to committed and gave me a dose of humble pie.

Picture this: I'm back on base, hanging out in the rec room with a bunch of soldiers. We're swapping records, everyone showing off their prized collections. I'm feeling good, really good, as I reach into my case and pull out my best. Cal Tjader, Brubeck, that clean West Coast sound. I slide the record out, chest puffed out, ready to bless the room. But before the needle could drop, a few cats from Los Angeles looked over and just started chuckling. *"Man, you don't know nothin' about jazz!"* one of them laughed.

Then they went to work. Out came Dexter Gordon, Dizzy Gillespie, Thelonious Monk, Coltrane, Miles, Billie Holiday, Sarah Vaughan, Abbey Lincoln, Ella...It was like getting hit with a musical thunderstorm. Their records didn't just play, they preached. It was deep, rich, sometimes chaotic, sometimes smooth, but always alive.

At first, I was a little salty. But then...I leaned in. That moment flipped a switch in me. Their teasing wasn't cruel; it was a challenge. A dare to dig deeper. To listen wider. And that's just what I did. I went from being a casual listener with a couple of favorites to becoming a full-blown student of the sound.

I wanted to understand it all. The structure, the swing, the soul of it. Over my lifetime, I collected more than 5000 albums and records, including a few from my son Ralph, which he didn't know I had. What started as a rivalry became a revelation.

By the time I left the service, I wasn't just a fan, I was a connoisseur, with ears tuned to the complexities and the beauty of a genre that spoke its truth in every note. Jazz became more than background music. It became part of how I moved, how I thought, how I improvised my way through life.

Now, what most folks don't know about me, and probably wouldn't guess, is that my modeling career actually began while I was still in uniform.

That's right, my first runway wasn't in New York or Paris, it was military bases across Europe. While stationed overseas, I got recruited by a French-based company called Stateside Styles. Their hustle was sharp: on payday, they'd show up on base with racks of stylish clothes, dress up a few of us servicemen, and send us out like walking billboards.

Next thing I knew, I was strutting across barracks in tailored outfits, feeling like James Brown in combat boots. It wasn't just fun, and it wasn't just for show.

That experience opened my eyes to how powerful image and presence could be, especially when tied to timing and environment.

That was my first real lesson in marketing. Not in theory, in practice.

You've got to meet people where they are, speak their language, and then lead them somewhere new. Whether I was modeling, doing hair, booking talent, or building a rodeo brand, that principle stayed with me. And it all started with a uniform, a paycheck, and a sharp suit in post-war Europe.

From those early fashion fits to the bright lights of the arena, I learned that sometimes the path to purpose starts where you least expect it. And for me? It started with a pose, a pitch, and a little Parisian hustle.

Looking back, I had a pretty smooth run in the service, racially speaking, but there was this one peculiar incident that still sticks with me. It involved a white kid from New Orleans who, for reasons beyond our comprehension, couldn't stop calling us Black enlisted men 'niggers.' It was like he was stuck on repeat, and it earned him a regular beatdown every weekend.

You'd think he'd learn his lesson, but no, he was like a record that kept skipping back to the same offensive spot.

It was 1959, a somber year for us, as we lost the legendary blues and jazz singer Billie Holiday. One day, out in the field, this kid dropped the N-bomb again. True to form, he received a thorough ass beating, which led to an intervention from the First Sergeant. We were all hauled into his office, including the bruised instigator.

The First Sergeant, with a mix of bewilderment and frustration, finally asked him, "*Son, why on earth do you keep stirring trouble? Aren't you tired of getting beat up every time?*" The boy's answer was as simple as it was shocking, "*That's what my parents taught me.*" Turns out, he claimed the Blacks back in New Orleans tolerated it, so he figured we were the odd ones out for reacting. Despite his skewed views, outside of this habit, he was actually a decent guy, just parroting the prejudices ingrained in him by his parents, without grasping the hurtful impact of his words.

Miraculously, that was the extent of my direct encounters with racial prejudice in the army, which is something of a minor miracle. Aside from that blip, my stint in the U.S. Army was pretty solid. My time in Germany was pivotal, shaping my thoughts on my future and what I would pursue after my military service.

As my time in the service was winding down, something unexpected happened. My stint in Germany, which had already opened my eyes to jazz, culture, and history, also introduced me to the world of hairstyling, though I didn't realize it at first.

It all started on a day trip to Munich with my buddy **Robert Bachelor**. We were just strolling the streets, soaking in the city. Its cafés, its music, its rhythm, when we spotted a group of women walking down the sidewalk.

Mini-skirts swaying, beehive hairstyles towering, confidence in every step. They looked like they had just stepped off a fashion runway.

Naturally, we followed.

They walked into a building, and curiosity pulled us right in after them. Next thing we knew, we were standing in the middle of what I can only describe as a high-fashion hive, full of stylists, hairspray, bold looks, and bold personalities. I was surrounded by style, and it hit me like a revelation.

I nudged Robert and half-joked, "That's it, I'm getting into hair when I get out."

But deep down, I wasn't joking at all. It was an epiphany. I wasn't just admiring the styles, I was imagining how I could bring them to life, how I could be part of that creative process.

And truth be told, I was also caught up in the beauty of it all. The women, the flair, the energy. Germany had style, and Germany had women. I was dating two German women at the time, and to say I was "involved" would be putting it lightly. Then life made things real.

In October of 1961, one of the women whose name was Angela, gave birth to a child, a son I can't say I know his name. I didn't stay in contact. And I never got the chance to find out the truth. It's one of my deepest regrets. At the time, I was young, overwhelmed, and unsure how to handle something so permanent and life-changing. I didn't have the tools or even know how to step into that responsibility. And I've carried that weight with me ever since.

But that period in Germany, that mix of discovery, style, and real-life consequences, was a turning point. It shaped the next version of me. I came out of the service not just as a soldier ready to return home, but as a man with a vision: to bring style, swagger, and creativity to a whole new stage, through hair.

With a proud grin and a glint in my eye, I often say, In 1961, I left the service and headed back to the States, unscathed. But before I could make it home, there was one memorable detour that still makes me laugh to this day.

My cousin **Emma Vaiton**, a decorated officer in the Air Force, was stationed in England at the time. As fate would have it, my ship had a layover there while coming back from Germany. I figured we'd dock, wave to the land, and stay put on the ship until clearance was given. But Emma had other plans.

"I had just gotten back from the States myself," Emma recalls with a chuckle. *"When I found out Lu's ship was in port, I went down to greet him. But they told us that no one was allowed off the vessel, not even for a quick hello."*

She shakes her head, laughing. *"I wasn't having that. I marched right up to the commander, had a polite but firm conversation, and worked a little magic. Sure enough, after a bit of persuasion, he agreed to let me take Lu out for a few hours."*

She still tells the story like it happened yesterday. *"You should've seen him. The moment Lu stepped off that ship and got in the car, he lit up like he was on stage. Sitting there in the passenger seat, waving back at everyone on the ship like he was the president riding through town. That was just typical Lu, always owning the moment, always adding a little flair to life."*

And she's right, I did feel special that day. I was honestly surprised they let me off the ship. But then again, knowing Emma, I shouldn't have been. She's always been bold, always had that take-charge fire in her. Watching her navigate military protocol like it was a minor inconvenience just confirmed everything I'd always admired about her.

That short visit turned into one of those unforgettable moments. We rode around, laughed, caught up, and just soaked in the joy of family, far from home, but close in spirit.

Emma and I still laugh about it to this day. It was one of those moments that perfectly captured who we were: **Emma, the fearless leader**, and me, the confident charmer, soaking it all in. That unexpected layover in England?
It became a memory for the books.

Chapter 5 : CALIFORNIA DREAMIN' RIDING THE WAVES OF INNOVATION - LU VASON'S CREATIVE ODYSSEY

When I returned stateside in 1961, fresh out of the Army, I landed in Oakland, California, and let me tell you, it felt like stepping into a whole new world. I'd traded my fatigues for civilian clothes, but my pace didn't slow for a second. I wasn't built for sitting still.

I was a **dreamer**, a **visionary**, and yeah I knew it. Like my father, I wasn't interested in working myself into the ground at a job that just paid the bills. Hard labor wasn't my calling. Creative movement was. But out of necessity, I started with a quick nine-month stint at the U.S. Post Office. It paid. It was steady. But the moment something more creative came knocking, I was gone like smoke in the wind.

I had no idea I was walking straight into a cultural revolution.

One day, I dropped by the house of a young lady I knew from back in the day, just a casual visit. But when I walked through that door, I stepped into something *different*. There, in the middle of the room, was Bobby Seale, Jon's brother, my childhood partner-in-crime back in Berkeley. But this wasn't the Bobby I remembered as a teenager. This Bobby had fire in his eyes and revolution in his voice.

And the soundtrack? Not jazz. Not Motown, but **Malcolm X.**

That's right, Malcolm X's speeches spinning on 45s, like they were chart-toppers. And in that room, they were. No A-side slow jams, no B-side fillers, just truth on vinyl, playing loud and proud through the speakers.

Now, 45s, those little 7-inch records spinning at 45 RPM, were known for blasting out the hottest singles of the day. But instead of Sam Cooke or Jackie Wilson, I was hearing Malcolm break down Black unity, power, and self-determination. It stopped me in my tracks.

This wasn't just a living room, it was a think tank. There were readers, organizers, researchers, and firestarters, all bouncing ideas, soaking in the urgency of the moment. I'd never experienced anything like it.

That day, Bobby introduced me to a speech that changed everything.

"**The Ballot or the Bullet.**" I'd never heard a man speak like that before. Malcolm wasn't asking for attention, he was demanding action. His voice carried a weight, a purpose, a boldness that named the truth others danced around. Systemic racism, self-defense, civic power, it was all there, stripped down and unapologetic. That speech didn't just make an impression; it rewired my thinking.

Bobby shared that he was raising funds for something he called the Black Nationalist Party. Before the world ever heard the name "Black Panther Party for Self-Defense," the spark was already lit, and Bobby Seale was one of the men striking the match. A vision that would later evolve into what the world would know as the Black Panther Party for Self-Defense. I didn't know then how far it would go, but I felt the ground shifting beneath me. The seeds of something powerful had been planted.

That afternoon in Oakland became a crossroad for me. Life has a way of creating so many of them.

It wasn't just about style or hustle anymore. It was about purpose. About using your platform, your presence, your gifts, for something bigger. That's when I realized: I didn't just want to create. I wanted to create with impact.

By 1962, Bobby had connected with a sharp-minded brother named Huey Newton at Merritt College in Oakland. Together, they joined the Afro-American Association (AAA), an intellectual powerhouse that became a training ground for critical Black thought. What started as conversations and campus activism would, by 1966, evolve into something revolutionary: **The Black Panther Party for Self-Defense.**

This name? It carried weight. It came from the heat of frustration, the speed of urgency, and the clarity of knowing we needed change. The climate at the time was so electric. Black youth were restless. The polite patience of peaceful protest was starting to feel like too slow a train. People respected Dr. King's nonviolence, but there was a growing hunger for something more assertive, something you could, as we used to say, **"take to the bank."**

Then came **Stokely Carmichael**, a name that carried weight and shook rooms. A veteran of the 1961 Freedom Rides with the Student Nonviolent Coordinating Committee (SNCC), led in part by powerful women like Diane Nash. Carmichael had been mentored by giants: Ella Baker, Bob Moses. Names that didn't always make the headlines but made the movement run. Women weren't just standing beside the movement, they were strategizing, organizing, and leading it from the inside out.

But by the mid-60s, Carmichael's patience had thinned. After watching the Mississippi Freedom Democratic Party get denied official recognition at the 1964 Democratic National Convention, something in him shifted. He began building independent Black political power, forming groups like the Lowndes County Freedom Organization, which bore the first Black Panther logo, before it became a national symbol.

He carried the torch lit by Malcolm X, refusing to water down his message. Carmichael spoke with heat, with edge, with a rhythm that made your bones sit up straight. His call for Black Power was loud, raw, and real, and not everyone was ready for it. But for many of us watching from the sidelines, it was a wake-up call.

Even the FBI took notice. J. Edgar Hoover, the same man who feared King's dream, secretly labeled Carmichael as the figure most likely to succeed Malcolm X as America's "Black Messiah." That's the energy we were living in. Revolution wasn't just a headline. It was happening outside your front door. And I was right there, eyes open, listening, learning, and slowly finding my place in it all.

The younger generation was stepping up, and I could feel it. You could see it in the streets, hear it in the barbershops, and feel it vibrating through Black communities. We weren't just marching anymore. We were moving, rethinking, reshaping what civil rights meant for us. And the Black Panther Party? Man, the respect for them was real. Even before they had national headlines, folks in the community looked at them with a kind of awe you don't fake. You could tell they were changing the game.

I remember listening to **Julian Bond** talk about those days with a smile and a little edge in his voice. He was one of the original soldiers in the Student Nonviolent Coordinating Committee, SNCC. That crew? They weren't your average suit-and-tie civil rights types. They were the rebels, the ones who went deep into the danger zones where even seasoned activists hesitated.

Julian used to joke that we had our own name for Dr. King. We'd see him coming and whisper, *"Here comes da lawd!"* It wasn't disrespect, it was love with a little side-eye. King was revered, no doubt, but we believed no single man was going to come down and save us. The movement was bigger than any pulpit. Leaders didn't descend; they rose up from the people. Julian lived that truth.

He got elected, three times, to the Georgia state legislature, but they kept denying him his seat. Why? Because he and SNCC stood against the Vietnam War. It took the Supreme Court to finally force Georgia to do the right thing. That's how bold Julian was, he had to go to the nation's highest court just to sit in the seat the people gave him.

And I'll never forget what he said about the evolution of SNCC's thinking.

"There came a time," Julian said, *"when we had to ask ourselves: Is nonviolence really a principle...or just a tactic?"* We were peaceful, yeah. But peaceful didn't mean passive. After getting spit on, beaten, thrown in jail, and paid damn near nothing for it, the question got louder. If someone comes at you in the street, are you supposed to just take it?

We were tired. Tired of being polite in the face of police dogs. Tired of being patient while policies crushed us. Tired of waiting.

And that's where the Panthers came in, with their black leather jackets, berets, raised fists, and **don't-even-try-it** energy. I remember Julian saying, with a little grit, *"Man, they shook the room."* He admitted it stung a bit, because SNCC had been doing community work for years, often in silence, and then the Panthers exploded onto the scene, grabbing headlines and hearts. But even Julian had to admit there was something magnetic about them.

They weren't just defending themselves; they were clapping back. And to a community that had been told to sit down, shut up, and wait for change, that kind of defiance felt like liberation. Julian never joined the Panthers, but he respected the hell out of them.

He once said something I never forgot: *"Good things don't come to those who wait. They come to those who agitate."*

That line. That's the spirit of our era. And whether you were marching, preaching, organizing, or posting up at a breakfast program with a Black beret, we were all part of the same storm. Looking back, I remember how Julian Bond described the shift that took hold in the Civil Rights Movement.

A shift away from nonviolence, not just as a strategy but as a belief system. In SNCC, things were changing. The pain, the beatings, the lack of protection, it made you start asking: At what point do you stop turning the other cheek?

Julian said it plain: *"If someone hits me, I'm going to hit back."* It wasn't about revenge; it was about dignity. Survival. A growing realization that real change might require more forceful assertion of our rights, especially in a country that often refused to hear us until we shouted.

Being back home in California, I found myself closely aligned with the energy of the Black Panthers. I never joined officially, but I understood them. **I got it.** I understood their philosophy, their rage, their discipline. I understood why they walked into the lion's den fully suited in leather and truth.

But if I'm honest, I stayed out of the direct line of fire, and a lot of that had to do with how I was raised. My grandparents, especially my grandmother, were strict, but they were protective. They made sure I understood what time to be home, how to carry myself, and how to move in a world that didn't always see me as human.

I always say: Being home before the streetlights come on will save your life.

That simple rule probably kept me out of situations that swallowed a lot of my peers. How you walk, how you talk, how you dress, where you go, it all sends a message. And in those days, the wrong message could get you stopped, harassed, or worse.

I'm grateful eternally, for the foundation my grandparents laid. They taught me self-respect. They taught me awareness. They taught me how to move smart, not scared.

So while my brotherfriend, Jon joined the Panthers and stood on the frontlines after Bobby and Huey were being arrested regularly, I chose a different route. But the Panthers were never far from my world. In fact, the day before Huey Newton's shooting of Officer John Frey on October 28, 1967, his girlfriend Lavern Williams was in my salon, getting her hair done. Huey had borrowed her Volkswagen Beetle that same day. It was supposed to be a normal afternoon.

Then everything changed. That traffic stop, over parking violations in Lavern's name, turned into a fatal shootout. Huey was wounded. Officer Frey was dead. The city was shaken. Just five months later, Bobby Hutton, the Panthers' first recruit and treasurer, was killed at 17 in another shootout with Oakland police.

We were mourning, marching, organizing, and boiling inside, all at the same time. The atmosphere in Oakland was electric, but it was also heavy. It felt like we were being hunted.

The police didn't feel like protectors, they felt like predators. And for young Black men trying to simply exist, it felt like every move was being watched, every mistake magnified. That tension lived in our bones. It lived in our music, our fashion, our whispers on the corner. And yet, we kept going.

You know...IT WAS HEAVY! I think about those days often, days when I was young, Black, and searching. Searching for purpose. For identity. For power in a world that constantly tried to strip what power I did have away. The pressure of that time, the marches, the funerals, the speeches, the rage, it was real. But in that heaviness, there was also an awakening. I was being refined. Pressured. Molded. And even when the world tried to box us in, my mind was opening.

I didn't always know where I was going, but I knew I couldn't stand still.

My grandparents had taught me to stand tall, to stay sharp, and to carry myself with purpose. They didn't just teach me how to stay safe, they taught me how to see. To see opportunity. To see the streets and the systems for what they were.

And most importantly, to see myself. And in that reflection, I saw a few paths open before me.

One led back to beauty and creativity, to the salon chair, to style, to expression.

One led to promotion and performance, spotlights, stages, and building something big. And one led to something deeper, a legacy project. Something that would honor our past while giving our people a future.

I didn't know it then, but all of it, every step, every turn, every conversation, was pulling me closer to something amazing. To my own kind of revolution.

One rooted in pride, history, and celebration. The path wasn't clear yet.

But the vision? Oh, it was starting to take shape.

BACK IN THE BAY: HUSTLE, HEART, AND HAIR SHOWS

Coming back to Berkeley after my military experience, life hit me like a fast-moving train, with no plans to slow down. Everything was in motion. I mean that literally, I was **all over the place.** I had a job at the post office that kept me grounded for about nine months, but I already knew it wasn't where I was meant to stay.

While delivering mail by day, I jumped headfirst back into the world of modeling by enrolling in a modeling school, even though, truth be told, I'd already done my walk through Europe's fashion scene. But I was serious about it by then. If I was going to make a name for myself in this space, I wanted to understand it all, from runway to business.

At the same time, I made good on a promise I had whispered to myself back in Germany, I enrolled in beauty college. I had seen something in those Parisian salons, in those high-rise beehives and carefully carved cuts, and I knew I had a gift for it. Hair wasn't just style, it was a statement. And I wanted to master that.

Somewhere between modeling, styling, and school, life happened in the most beautiful way. I met **Bobbie Walker**, who was pregnant with Lashelle at the time when I married her. She became Bobbie Vason, and together we built a family, raising three children: **Corey, LaShelle, and Sheri**. That part of my life grounded me in ways no runway ever could. There is a story here but no needs to know all that!

I also started working with Charmed Unlimited Finishing School in Berkeley. That place wasn't just about modeling, it was about movement, confidence, business, and poise.
I walked the runway, sure, but more importantly, I started learning how the business of beauty and presentation worked. It was food for my entrepreneurial soul.

Then came the acting bug.

When I signed with the Brebner Modeling & Casting Agency, I knew something had shifted. It felt like I had stepped out of the shadows and onto center stage. Suddenly, my modeling career was on fire. I was getting booked for print ads with Macy's, showing up in Ebony Magazine, and getting featured in local staples like The Post, The Sun Reporter, and The Tribune.

It wasn't just about posing, it was about **presence**.

I even had the chance to walk for San Francisco Fashion Week, one of the biggest stages in the game. To this day, that event still draws major attention, but back then, being a part of it felt like I had made it.

But as all this unfolded, the lights, the lenses, the glamour, I started to feel another spark inside me: I wanted to write. Not just bios or blurbs, I wanted to become a movie critic.
I was obsessed with film and media, and the cultural shift happening for Black folks during that time only fueled my fire. Every Black newspaper I could find, I devoured. I was drawn to the features of powerful entertainers, activists, and entrepreneurs, but something started to bug me.

Where were the everyday heroes? Why wasn't anyone writing about the Herbert Polks of the world? Regular folks doing extraordinary things in our communities? Herbert was a buddy from school, deeply rooted in uplifting people around him. But you'd never hear his name in the papers. The stories always seemed to circle the same groups, The Links, the Eastern Stars, the fraternities and sororities, the Jack and Jill crowd.

Meanwhile, folks like Herbert were doing the real work and getting zero recognition. I realized there was a whole segment of the community, whose stories were just not being told.
That realization lit a fire in me. This journey wasn't just about hair or fashion anymore. It was about voice. Platform. Truth. And I started thinking, maybe I could be the one to tell those stories.

At one point, I decided to get serious about becoming a movie critic, so I reached out to one of the top film critics in the Bay Area. I was hoping to get some deep insight, maybe some secret sauce, a framework, something to point me in the right direction.

His advice? *"You just go to the movies...and you write. You write about the movies."* That was it.

I remember sitting there thinking, That's it? That's the game? Part of me wondered if he was brushing me off. Maybe he thought I wasn't serious. Or maybe...that was the game. Just write. Write well. Write often. But it felt too simple to me at the time. Like a pianist being told, "Just press the keys."

I couldn't help but question it. Actors need training. Athletes need practice. Even if someone's gifted, they still need the fundamentals. I figured, surely the same went for critics.

A real critic doesn't just watch a film and jot down their feelings. You need to analyze, understand narrative structure, spot what's working behind the scenes, and communicate your thoughts clearly and creatively, and then take the heat when people disagree with you.

Ironically, for all that interest, I never officially became a movie critic.

But stay with me, I wasn't standing still.

At the time, I was still juggling multiple roles: modeling gigs, working part-time at the post office, writing for the Berkeley Post, and finishing up Beauty College. Somewhere in all of that, I started doing hair professionally too. Every day felt like a new scene in a movie I was starring in and directing.

Things were beginning to click. Not in some neat, orderly way, but in motion.

Real motion. I could feel momentum building. This rhythm, this flow, like all the threads of my life were starting to weave into something bigger.

It's funny how one introduction can change your whole trajectory.

One connection always seemed to lead to another, and before I knew it, I was finding myself in the company of people who would help shape the course of my life and career in ways I never could've imagined. These were the real ones, mentors, motivators, role models, and future business associates. Whether they knew it or not, they were pouring into me, and I was soaking it all up like a sponge.

One of the first was **Louise Skinner**, a powerhouse in the Bay Area fashion scene. Louise was known for organizing the kind of fashion shows that packed out the Continental Ballroom, and she was the first person to feature me as a model in one of her shows. That was a turning point.

Thanks to Louise, I earned the nickname **"Mr. Continental"**, and let me tell you, that name opened doors. It wasn't just a title; it was a calling card. Suddenly, people *knew* me. I went from "that new guy" to the guy you wanted on your runway.

It wasn't just modeling doors that opened, some opened wide, and others quietly closed behind me. One of those closing doors was my first marriage.

Bobbie was deep in the Church of God in Christ, and between her and her mother, there was a constant push, pressure that didn't fit the rhythm of my life. We were moving in different directions, and eventually, the marriage unraveled.

As fate would have it, another door opened around that same time, and on the other side was **Lillie Young**, a young fashion designer I met through Louise at one of her shows. Lillie would later become my second wife. Life has a funny way of blending business with the personal, and before long, we were sharing both worlds. Working as extras on film sets, building something creative together.

Modeling gave us the foundation, but the energy between us turned it into something more, another lane, another platform, another way to be seen. It was exciting, unpredictable, and just wild enough to feel like we were chasing something bigger together. When we married in 1967, Lillie already had two children**, Ralph and Karisse,** who became my children, too. I never liked the word "step." When you marry someone, you take on the whole package. That's just how I saw it. I knew the importance of a stepfather since I had one and Tootsie was a great man.

Meanwhile, I was still cutting and styling hair, building my name in that world too. That's when I met **Edith Austin**, a woman who saw something in me, not just the style, not just the show, but the business potential underneath it all. She was the force that motivated me and started pushing me from stylist to serious entrepreneur. She didn't just give advice, she gave direction.

One of the greatest gifts Edith gave me was an introduction to **Belva Davis**.

Now, Belva was already making moves. Back in the late '50s, she was a freelance correspondent writing for JET Magazine and a host of Black newspapers. But she wasn't just reporting the news, she was becoming the news. Belva would go on to become a media legend in California, but even then, she had a presence. Poise. A voice that demanded respect. She stayed rooted.

One of the many ways she poured back into the culture was through her work organizing pre-fashion shows for the Ebony Fashion Fair. Those shows weren't just warm-ups for the national tour, they were polished, powerful events that spotlighted local Black talent, style, and sophistication. Thanks to Belva, I got the opportunity to model in those pre-shows. That platform gave me visibility and experience, and more importantly, affirmation that we could create luxury and beauty our way.

Belva was also the visionary behind the Miss Bronze Pageant, a celebration of Black womanhood at a time when the mainstream refused to acknowledge our beauty. This wasn't some imitation of Miss America, this was a statement, our declaration, it was a movement. It honored grace, intelligence, and cultural pride, all wrapped in elegant gowns and Black excellence.

I was proud to support her with that event, not just behind the scenes, but in spirit. It wasn't just about helping, it was about learning. Watching Belva command a room, build a brand, and center our people in a world that constantly tried to erase us. That on-the-job training taught me more about media and messaging than any textbook ever could.

Belva Davis was more than just a media figure, she was a cultural force. She used her platform to disrupt the norms, to challenge perceptions, and to create space for the rest of us. And she did it all while sharing her truth.

I remember her saying, with quiet strength, *"In the 1960s, it was a well-known fact that a dark-skinned girl had no chance at the Miss America crown."*

She'd talk about the racism she had faced, how the few Black women who made it into those pageants were used as props or tokens. But instead of folding under that pressure, she used it as fuel, to lift others up, to redefine beauty, and to push boundaries with grace and grit.

Working with Belva gave me more than experience, it gave me clarity. It showed me the power of platform, purpose, voice, and owning your narrative.

"What distinguished Lu was his propensity to say 'yes', not in any derogatory way, but rather he was open to new ideas, taking risks, and trying new things. You could say he was adventurous, unafraid to venture out."

"I believe people who learn to say 'yes' early on often do so from a place of self-criticism. I include myself in that category, which is why I recognized it in Lu. People who say 'yes' take chances; that's what made Lu stand out. While many were focused on securing what they had, Lu was always open to exploring what else might be possible."

"Because I was older, I'd like to think I had a hand in helping him. When I first met Lu, he was always laughing. It's easy to misinterpret that if you're not paying attention. But if you really listened to him or watched his actions, you'd see he was serious about his commitments. That was huge. People often just talk, but Lu was a man of his word."

"I'm driven by adventure, not being academically educated but learning through experience instead. Lu picked up that same kind of incentive and enthusiasm along his path. Sometimes, we would do things we thought were impossible. Why not? There's no harm in trying. We even planned." – **Belva Davis**

I remember telling Belva on one occasion, Look, this can be a statewide effort. You take Southern California and I'll take Northern California. We'll produce two pageants and then bring them together in Los Angeles or Hollywood for a finale, and the big prize will be a screen test.

"For two Black people at that time, even talking about offering a screen test as a prize was practically unimaginable. There was a certain freedom in being Black that felt like breaking loose. Having had so much closed off to us, there was ample room for innovation because we had been held back for so long. When you were the first to do something significant, it wasn't necessarily because you were the first to think of it or the most qualified to do it; often, it was all about timing. Lu had a keen sense for good timing, which was one of his strengths."
"I remember Lu as a charming, handsome young man with a great smile, always open to doing new things. I can't precisely recall how or where we first met; it seems like we've been friends for most of our active adult lives."

"People were always looking to build their reputations, and artists often came to my home for parties, where Lu would meet up-and-coming stars, promoters, and agents. It was in this social environment that he met the Pointer Sisters at one of my parties, which was initially for Oscar Brown Jr. That meeting was crucial—they were ready to step out, and Lu was open to the opportunity. They naturally connected with him, and he with them. I only heard about their progress through others because Lu was quick to act."

"Being in the right place at the right time played a part in the equation, but it was more about the alignment of circumstances and Lu's willingness to say 'yes.' He hadn't managed musicians before, but he trusted himself and his instincts. It was all about his willingness to embrace opportunities, even though he hadn't done that kind of work before. I was merely a conduit, having worked in radio and having connections like the Johnson Publishing Company at a time when Black people were rarely seen on mainstream media. These were all growing experiences for us." **Belva Davis.**

That moment reminded me: it's not just what you do, it's who you're connected to. And more importantly, who believes in you enough to open a door.

Those early connections weren't coincidences. They were chapters in the story I was writing, real-time mentorship that helped guide my hustle, sharpen my instincts, and stretch my vision for what was possible.

Looking back, I can clearly trace how certain experiences set me on the path I was meant to walk. Working with the Miss Bronze Pageant under Belva was one of those defining moments. Being part of that production wasn't just fulfilling, it lit a spark.

It gave me an up-close view of what it meant to produce an event with style, purpose, and community impact. Watching Belva command an audience and orchestrate every detail made something click for me. That's when I first caught the bug for pageantry and promotions (P&P).

Inspired by that experience, I decided to launch my own production: **The Ram's Fleece Fashion Shows**. Now, the name wasn't random. I pulled it straight from my zodiac sign, Aries, the ram.

I wanted something bold, distinctive, and personal. And I wasn't just putting on fashion shows for the sake of fashion, I was creating a full experience. I intentionally scheduled those shows to align with major HBCU football games. The energy was already high, the crowds were already coming out, and I knew how to ride that wave.

It wasn't long before I found myself working alongside some serious heavyweights, **Henry "Champ" Winston** being one of them. Champ was a legend in the world of sports promotions. He was the man behind major boxing matchups and eventually became the manager of George Foreman. But Champ wasn't one-dimensional, he also owned East Bay Ambulance, which just showed how wide his vision stretched. From 1963 to 1966, we teamed up on multiple events, forming a strong partnership that blended sports, entertainment, and cultural pride.

One of our big strategies? Matchups between Southern University and Hayward State, or Prairie View A&M and Santa Clara. The matchups just random pairings, they were calculated moves. Take Santa Clara, for example. It wasn't known for having a strong Black alumni base, and that was *exactly* the point. We were intentional about choosing venues where we could build an audience, not just serve one.

So here's the thing: In promotions, knowing your audience is everything.

Who you're speaking to. Why they'll show up. And finally, what you're offering that speaks to them directly.
I was following trends, and more significantly, I was setting them. I was carving out spaces where fashion, culture, and entrepreneurship could connect and shine together. We took the Ram's Fleece shows on the road across California, turning each stop into a vibrant celebration, an appealing stylish experience that showcased Black creativity, culture, and limitless possibility.

It can't be reduced to just entertainment. It was a blended movement.

And I was just getting started.

"From the spirited excitement of those early days emerged the 'Miss Bronze Pageant.' It was through this platform that incredible talents such as Marilyn McCoo and Florence LaRue of the singing group, "The Fifth Dimension." Vonetta McGee, who placed second in 1962, went on to become a notable figure in the 1970s Black Cinema, starring in classics such as "Thomasine & Bushrod" and "Shaft in Africa." Vonetta, along with Pam Grier, Lonette McKee, and others, became iconic figures representing Black Hollywood's first wave of sex symbols, following in the footsteps of legends like Lena Horne and Dorothy Dandridge." - **Belva Davis**

Belva always said the Miss Bronze Pageant had depth not limited to the crowns and gowns, it created opportunities where none existed before. And she was right. That pageant didn't just celebrate Black beauty, it launched careers.

I remember **Margaret Avery**, who placed fifth back in 1964. She went on to shine in a big way, most folks remember her as Shug Avery in *The Color Purple*. But before that, she was out here making moves with **Richard Pryor** in *Which Way is Up?*, and later with **Martin Lawrence** in *Welcome Home, Roscoe Jenkins*.

To see her rise from our local circles to the big screen was powerful. It was proof that dreams do come true. It was real. And I'm almost certain **Beverly Johnson** came through our world too, before she broke barriers as one of the first Black supermodels to grace the cover of major fashion magazines. Her success was a signal that high fashion had to make room for Black excellence.

Another standout was **Carolyn Blakely**. Carolyn didn't just model, she took the stage and took it global. She became the first among us to lock in an international tour, performing as a vocalist all the way in Tehran. Yeah, the Middle East. She was out there singing her heart out, representing us with elegance and pride.

Carolyn's success didn't belong to her exclusively, it was a beacon shining our light. It demonstrated to young Black women, singers, artists, dreamers, that there was a world out there waiting for them, if they dared to reach.

Those weren't just moments. They were milestones in a movement that started with community and echoed across continents.

Riding the momentum from the pageants, I knew when it was time to elevate the game; and I launched the **Lu Vason Modeling Troupe**, my own platform, my own brand.

My modeling experience had evolved beyond runway work. I wasn't just walking in shows anymore, I was building them, curating talent, and shaping what Black excellence looked like on stage.

My modeling career reached a new level around 1964, when I made history as the first Black model to appear on the back covers of both *Newsweek* and *Time* magazines. It was a huge moment, not just for me, but for visibility in an industry that rarely let us be seen, let alone celebrated.

But that milestone came with its own set of challenges. Back then, the photography world hadn't figured out how to properly capture darker skin tones. The technology for color separation was still in its early stages, and most photographers weren't trained, or equipped, to shoot Black skin in a way that honored its richness.

When those covers hit the stands, I was proud... but I also had to laugh. I looked green. Literally. The image didn't reflect my real complexion at all. It was like they lit me for a spotlight I was never meant to be in. But still, I was there. On that cover. Proof that I belonged, better yet we belonged. Even when the industry wasn't ready to see us clearly, I made sure they couldn't ignore us.

Now remember, I had my hand in a little bit of everything during this time. Modeling, hair, writing, acting, and promoting fashion shows. And somehow, in the middle of all that motion, I still managed to complete Beauty College and officially started doing hair professionally. That was the beauty of that season, everything was falling into place, one domino knocking down the next. Life wasn't slowing down. If anything, it was picking up speed.

Thanks to Edith Austin, who was always in my corner, I landed a position as a society writer for the *Oakland Post*, a paper founded and published by the legendary **Tom Berkley**. But it didn't take long before I found myself shifting lanes. A new opportunity opened up, and I moved from society coverage into the role of entertainment editor.

Now that's where things got interesting. In that position, I started writing about folks I actually knew, friends, peers, community leaders, and social groups. Sometimes I wrote with admiration. Other times? I told it like it was. And I quickly learned that not everyone likes seeing themselves in print unless the light is flattering.

There's a funny thing about influence, people tend to uplift those within their line of sight. I used that insight to spotlight people I believed deserved recognition, folks like my friend Herbert Polk, who was doing real work in the community, even if he wasn't part of the usual "who's who" crowd.

Consequently, not all the feedback was positive.
I remember one article in particular that didn't sit well with Byron Rumpert and his wife, who were both prominent in The Links, Incorporated, which is an international nonprofit organization founded in 1946. As one of the oldest and largest volunteer service organizations in the United States, it is dedicated to enriching and sustaining the cultural heritage and economic well-being of African Americans and people of African descent around the world. Truth is the organization favored those of "high status". Mrs. Rumpert wasn't amused. She went straight to Tom Berkley, demanding a retraction.

Next thing I knew, I was being called into Tom's office. I walked in, cool but curious.

He looked me in the eye and asked, *"Did you write this?"* Yes, sir. *"Did you mean what you said?"* Yes, sir. That was it. He leaned back and said, *"You can go."* No scolding. No firing. No retraction. I think Tom respected that I stood behind my words. He didn't always have to agree with me, but he valued integrity.

I continued writing for the *Oakland Post* until around 1969. And throughout that time, I learned one of the most important lessons of my journalism career: there's a difference between reporting and commentary.

News is meant to capture and report factual information and, therefore, be neutral, but commentary? That's where you bring your perspective, your experience, your voice. And when you're telling *your* truth, you'd better be ready for the heat.

I never backed down from it. Because to me, telling the truth, even when it made people uncomfortable, was part of the job. By the late 1960s, I had established a solid reputation in writing, modeling, and community work, but there was still one more path I needed to explore before fully committing to my next interest and adventure: acting.

Now, my time in the film world was short, but it sparkled with its own highlights. In 1965, Lillie and I landed some bit parts in the film *Once a Thief*, starring French heartthrob **Alain Delon**, with **Ann-Margret** and **Jack Palance**.
You can catch me in a few scenes, just look for the clean-cut Black man, pipe in hand, pulling Ann-Margret out of a bar fight like I belonged on the cover of a noir novel. Lillie was there too, posted up in the background as one of the bar patrons, cool and composed, doing her thing.

But the most memorable project I ever worked on? **Sidney Poitier's** *Guess Who's Coming to Dinner*.

That film was a game-changer, a landmark in American cinema, not just for its plot but for what it stood for. I had two brief appearances: once when Sidney's character arrives at the airport from Hawaii, and another when he's picking up his luggage. I even had the honor of standing in for Sidney Poitier so the set directors could adjust the lighting before filming. That meant something to me. This was the man who, just two years earlier, had become the first Black actor to win the Academy Award for Best Actor for *Lilies of the Field*, and there I was, on set, even if only in the margins of history.

That same year, I also booked a Nabisco commercial that aired during the TV series *Bewitched*. That spot earned me steady royalties and residuals, which was my first real lesson in how money could keep flowing even after the work was done.

From there, I picked up a few more roles, small ones, but with big-name productions. I was in Lucille Ball's *Yours, Mine & Ours* (1968) and even had a quick moment in the cult-classic crime film Bullitt, sharing space with the likes of **Steve McQueen**, **Robert Vaughn**, and **Jacqueline Bisset**. Not bad for a kid from Berkeley just figuring it all out.

By 1968, my modeling and acting chapters were coming to a close. While I appreciated the doors those opportunities opened, and the connections they gave me, I eventually realized that acting wasn't my true calling.

But here's the thing, I left the film industry with something valuable. Being on set taught me about presentation, branding, and more importantly, money management in the entertainment world. I became fascinated with residuals, the idea that your work could keep paying you over time. That concept stuck with me and broadened how I thought about building sustainable income, long before the word "entrepreneur" became trendy. Acting gave me a glimpse into a different lifestyle, one built on visibility, timing, and knowing your value. And even though I left the silver screen behind, the business lessons stayed with me.

Now remember, I had already completed Beauty College and was officially in the game, doing hair with purpose and getting paid. After dabbling in just about every creative lane you can imagine, modeling, acting, writing, it felt good to have something that was hands-on, personal, and profitable.

My first real job in the industry came at an upscale, all-white beauty salon called **I. Magin**, tucked inside one of the major department stores in the area. On paper, it looked impressive. The environment was polished, the clientele was high-end, and I was surrounded by professionals. Sadly, the paycheck didn't match the polish.

I was bringing in $90 a week, plus commission, but even back then, I knew that wasn't going to cut it. Not for the vision I had. Not for the lifestyle I wanted to build. I looked around, realizing that I could do better.

That realization was the momentum that pushed me to strike out on my own and led me to Lee Gilliam's Salon, a place that contributed to a key part of my evolution. It wasn't just a stepping-stone; it was a proving ground. It's where I sharpened my skills, built my clientele, and gained the confidence to think bigger.

It was also during that time, right there at Lee's shop, that Belva Davis came calling again. By then, I'd already worked with her on the Miss Bronze Pageant, both styling and helping behind the scenes. But when she came a calling that next time, Belva had a new ask: *"Can you and the guys style the hair for all the pageant contestants?"* Of course, I was in. But I didn't stop at styling.

Belva also tapped me to be one of the pageant judges, helping select which young women would advance through the competition. I sat on that judging panel alongside **Lee Gilliam, Frank Gonder, and Al Young**, some of the hottest young stylists in the Bay Area. The four of us had been moving in step since 1962, and by the time the pageant rolled around, we had chemistry, credibility, and an eye for talent.

That work wasn't just about hair. It was about vision, taste, and influence.

We weren't just shaping styles, we were shaping futures.
By 1968, Belva's media career was taking off like a rocket, and she gracefully stepped back from her role in the pageant world. But even after she moved on, my world stayed the course, growing and expanding.

Edith Austin, always the connector, continued to send high-profile clients my way, people who trusted her taste and respected her referrals. One of the most memorable? **Bobby Freeman**, the singer behind those Top Ten hits like *"Do You Want to Dance"* (1958) and *"C'mon and Swim"* (1964). I had the opportunity to style his hair, adding another name to my growing list of celebrity clients.

That chapter marked a turning point. I wasn't just doing hair anymore, rather I was building a brand. And soon enough, it was time to launch a salon of my own.

"During that time, it was a blessing that Lu was so versatile; He did the hair for many of the contestants. We were all just starting out, building from the ground up with hardly any real money to work with. We were driven by our passion and did things our way. If everything had been organized, the unions would likely have excluded us, but we weren't going to let that stop us. We improvised as we went along."

"Then, as life often does, it took Lu and me in completely different directions. I transitioned into television and news, which led to me hosting several programs."
"This new path led me to become actively involved with the Black Filmmakers Hall of Fame. Our mission was to enhance the representation of Blacks in film and engage with Hollywood studios to ensure they were making genuine efforts. For the next 16 years, I dedicated myself to this cause, challenging Hollywood's practices."

"We became quite influential; by the time the 1989 movie "Glory," starring Denzel Washington and Morgan Freeman, was released, we had the clout to bring about 15 to 20 Hollywood insiders to Oakland for our program. We were recognized as a formidable force in the industry. Meanwhile, Lu had moved on to other endeavors." - **Belva Davis**.

"I remember those early days with Lu like they were yesterday," I say with a grin. "He came into my salon with a whole lot of ambition and just enough experience to get started, but what really stood out was how open and receptive he was. He didn't walk in acting like he knew everything. He was hungry to learn. And that made all the difference."

"As someone who had already been in the game for a while, I didn't just see myself as a boss, I saw myself as a mentor. I coached Lu quite a bit in those first months. Back then, the popular styles were press and curls, roller sets were everywhere, and perms were just starting to find their place. Lu, though?". Lee chuckles. He was never all that into press and curls. You could tell he was already thinking ahead."

"Then one day, right in the middle of the workweek, he turned to me and said", 'You know what, Lee? I'm done with pressing curls. From now on, it's perms for all my clients.' "Just like that. I laughed at first, but I'll be honest, I was impressed."

"That kind of boldness takes guts. I didn't fully grasp it then, but looking back now, Lu was ahead of his time. Not just with hair, but in how he moved through business and life. His decisiveness, that fearlessness, it was inspiring."

"In fact, it rubbed off on me. After watching him stick to his vision, I made a shift in my own salon. For almost ten years, we didn't touch a curling iron or hair roller. We went all in on perms and natural styles, and that pivot came directly from watching Lu do his thing. That's who he was, a forward-thinker, a trend-setter, a risk-taker. He made up his mind, and he moved. And the rest of us had to catch up." - **Lee Gilliam**

By 1967, I'd sharpened my skills, made my mark in the industry, and I knew it was time to plant something permanent. So I took a leap, a big one, and invested in a two-story building on Telegraph Avenue in Oakland, California.

That building became the foundation of my next chapter.
On the ground floor, I opened my first official salon: **Lu Vason Stylon.**

It wasn't just a place to cut hair, it was a place where style met culture. A place where everyday folks and entertainers alike could walk in and walk out transformed.

But I wasn't done. See, I'd always been thinking a step ahead. So I turned the second floor of that same building into **Lu Vason Productions**, a management and production company where I could book, manage, and promote the talent I was styling downstairs. That setup? It was genius. It became a one-stop shop where beauty met business, where glamour and gig bookings shared the same staircase.

Imagine this:

On any given day, you could walk into the salon and see someone getting their hair touched up before heading upstairs to sign a performance contract or map out a tour schedule. It was synergy in real-time, an engine running on creativity, style, and strategy.

The space quickly became a magnet for talent. My chair wasn't just a place to sit, it was a place to connect.
I'll never forget when **Tammi Terrell** came through. **Bobby Freeman** introduced us. Even now, it's hard to talk about her without emotion. Tammi had a voice that could melt steel; she was beautiful, and her duets with **Marvin Gaye** were pure magic. She passed way too young, just 24 years old in 1970, but during her time, she was a bright, blazing star. To have her in my space, to be part of her world even for a moment, was unforgettable.

Other legends followed. **Lena Horne**, always the epitome of elegance. **Patricia Harris**, who made history not once, but multiple times, first serving under Presidents Kennedy and Johnson, and later becoming a cabinet member under President Jimmy Carter.

And it wasn't just Black royalty.

I also styled white entertainers like **Gisele Mackenzie** and **Carol Lawrence**, who were performing at the Loews Grand Theater in Berkeley at the time. My salon welcomed everyone, but the experience was always rooted in Black excellence.

That blend of culture, creativity, and inclusion helped establish Lu Vason Stylon as one of the premier destinations for celebrity styling in the Bay Area.

As time went on, life had a way of quietly stirring beneath me, like shifting sand beneath steady feet, unsettling the ground I thought was solid and awakening something deep within my spirit.

By 1971, my heart was being pulled in a new direction. I was still styling, still producing, but more and more, my energy was moving toward promoting entertainers and special events. The urge became too big to ignore. The truth be told, the entertainment world was more lucrative, and more fulfilling. It gave me room to build, to connect, to create experiences that lived far beyond a mirror or a magazine.

Soon, I was managing acts like The Whispers, The Pointer Sisters, and working with comedy royalty like Richard Pryor. I wasn't just styling stars anymore, I was managing them. Promoting them. Watching them rise.

And little did I know that everything I had learned up to that point, every connection, every hustle, every runway and record, shaped me. Molded me. Trained me for what was coming next, because just up ahead, the two worlds I had been balancing, culture and creativity, identity and enterprise, were about to come crashing together in a Lu type of way.

Two stars. One destined collision.

Chapter 6: WHEN THE STARS START TO ALIGN

Back on Telegraph Avenue, my salon was in full swing, stylish, vibrant, and alive with energy. But just upstairs, something bigger was brewing.

I had set it up with purpose. Lu Vason Productions operated right above the salon, a move that allowed me to blend style and show business under one roof. It wasn't just convenient, it was intentional. A space where hair met hustle, and beauty intersected with business.

My office wasn't much to look at, I like to say. About 9' x 9', with a desk almost the same size as the room. It may have been small, but that little room had big dreams. On one side sat my assistant, **Joyce Reynolds**, sharp, organized, always one step ahead. On the other was me, phone in one hand, calendar in the other, piecing together opportunities like a puzzle only I could see.

And then there was **Beatrice Davis**, or as everyone called her, **Bea**. My salon manager. Bea was the heartbeat of the shop, keeping things moving when everything else was trying to pull us in ten directions. Between the three of us, we ran a tight operation, even if it sometimes felt like we were sprinting behind a train we had just set in motion.

We were busy. Always moving. Always building. And looking back, I sometimes wonder if Joyce and Bea really had any idea just how wild things were about to get.

Picture this, I'm downstairs in the shop, music playing low, Stevie Wonder or Aretha Franklin setting the vibe, my hands deep in a client's curls, the steady hum of a blow dryer filling the background. It's rhythm. It's flow. It's familiar.

Then the phone rings. I wipe my hands, nod to Bea, and take the stairs two at a time, heading up to see what the world wants this time. Next thing I know, I'm not just a stylist anymore. I'm booking The Pointer Sisters for their next big show.
From hairpins to headliners. From bobby pins to booking agents. One heartbeat, two worlds. And somehow, I was living both.

Not long after things started buzzing at the salon and upstairs at Lu Vason Productions, a new door opened, one I hadn't expected, but I was more than ready to walk through.

I got invited to the Fairmont Hotel in San Francisco to interview **Polly Bergen**, the Emmy award-winning actress and singer. Elegant, talented, and commanding, Polly performed that night with three Black background singers, **The Delights**, as they were called. What caught everyone's attention, even before they opened their mouths, was the charm, unity, and creative, expressive manner they brought to the stage. Their names? **Charlie, Paul, and Sonny.** And yes, those were the names they went by on stage, full of flair and mystery.

At that event, I was joined by **Lillie Young**, my second wife at the time. A gifted model and fashion designer in her own right. Lillie knew style, and The Delights saw it right away. The next day, they approached her with a request. They needed new gowns and a hairstylist to match their growing image.

Lillie, never one to miss a beat, told them, *"That man you saw with me at the show? That's my husband. He owns a beauty salon."* And just like that, the connection was made.

The Delights became more than clients, it formed into a great friendship. And not long after, they came to me with another request, *"Lu, will you manage us?"*

That was the moment everything shifted. Even though I had never officially managed talent before, I said yes. Why? Because I saw something in them, and more importantly, they saw something in me.

Managing The Delights, I often say, was about one thing: keeping them working. If they were booked and performing, we all ate. And if I didn't keep them working? Well, then I wasn't working either. Simple math. High stakes.

It was a new kind of pressure, exciting, nerve-wracking, and completely addictive. I continued styling hair. I was still writing. But now, I was also making calls, sealing deals, and opening doors across racial lines for a trio of talented performers who could light up any stage they touched.

And as fate would have it, The Delights had a "brother group" they often shared stages with down in Los Angeles. Their chemistry mirrored that of The Supremes and The Temptations, a musical harmony that just made sense. That "brother group"? None other than **The Whispers**. Yes, those Whispers.

When the opportunity came to manage them, I jumped at it. I had already gotten a taste of what it meant to represent talent. Now, I was ready to take it further.

And just like that, what started with an interview at the Fairmont turned into a full-on pivot into the entertainment world. The world really *is* small. But if you're paying attention, and ready to move when your name gets called? Small worlds can lead to big stages.

One of the small but sweet memories from that era was my friendship with **Wallace Scott**, lead singer of The Whispers. Wallace and I weren't just business, we were brothers in the grind, and we shared a lot of time over something simple: Casper hot dogs.

We'd meet at The Original Casper's on Telegraph in Oakland, just two guys talking music, dreams, and real life over a paper tray of mustard, onions, and snap-perfect beef. Man, I loved those hot dogs, I laugh now. Didn't realize back then how many of 'em I'd be paying for later, in cholesterol and doctor's visits.

But those moments? They meant something. Yes, we were creating a movement through music, but also building friendships, building trust, bonding over stories and greasy wrappers. That kind of connection doesn't come from a boardroom, it comes from shared tables and real conversations. Plus, it does help if you're making money together.

Around that same time, Belva Davis popped back into my orbit, just like she always did at key moments in my life. She invited me to a gathering at her home, one of those cultural salons where the guest list mattered. And she had someone she wanted me to meet: **Oscar Brown Jr.**

Now if you don't know Oscar, let me tell you, he was the real deal. A creative powerhouse from Chicago, Oscar first blew up when **Mahalia Jackson** recorded his song "Brown Baby." He later teamed up with **Max Roach** on the iconic album We Insist!, a bold, jazz-infused cry for Black freedom and justice. He didn't just write songs, he wrote movements. His touch was on classics like "Afro Blue," which **Abbey Lincoln** turned into a timeless anthem.

That night at Belva's was already special...but then two young women got up to perform, and the room just paused.

June and Bonnie Pointer.

Back then, they were performing under the name 'Pointers, a Pair', and the minute they opened their mouths, I could feel it; there was something there.

I didn't need a crystal ball, I like to say, just ears, instinct, and an office.

I invited them to come see me. We sat down in that small 9x9 space above my salon and sealed the deal. I signed a management contract with them that week. And just like that, we started making moves around the Bay Area, small venues, growing buzz, and undeniable talent.

As time went on, their sisters Anita and Ruth joined in, and together, they became the **Pointer Sisters**. That was the moment things shifted, not just for them, but for me too. Managing the Pointer Sisters gave me credibility, visibility, and momentum.

And yes, Belva tells the story a little differently, but that's how it went down. Because like I always say: It's not just what you know, it's who you know, and being in the right place at the right time." And I just happened to be sitting in the living room of one of the most connected women in the Bay when lightning struck. That night? That moment? It was more than luck; it was alignment. The stars were starting to line up. And this time, I knew exactly what to do with the light.

Not long after all that magic with the Pointer Sisters and The Whispers, I got a call that felt like a full-circle moment. **Oscar Brown Jr.**, yes, *the* Oscar Brown Jr., poet, songwriter, jazz man, activist, asked me to manage him.

I thought, Man, the same brother I just met through Belva...now he wants me in his corner? That was huge for me. Not just because of who he was, but because it marked a new chapter. I was no longer just managing groups on the come-up. This was a man who had shared stages with legends and put his fingerprints all over the jazz and civil rights movement. He was a legend. With Oscar in my corner, my reach in the industry expanded overnight.

One of the standout moments from that season was a show I booked where The Whispers and the Pointer Sisters shared the stage, same day, same lineup, at the Spokane County Fair in Washington State. And just when I thought the day couldn't get any better, the lineup dropped some jazz royalty right in my lap.

First came my favorite jazz vocalist, **Dakota Staton**, smooth, sultry, with phrasing that made you stop breathing for a second. Then came **Nancy Wilson**, just as graceful and fierce as ever. And following her set was the powerhouse herself, **Ernestine Anderson**.

Now hold up, let me take you back real quick.

You remember how back in the Army, I was just a young kid in Germany, getting my first real taste of jazz, trying to impress folks with my Cal Tjader and Dave Brubeck records before the LA cats humbled me with Miles, Coltrane, Monk, and the whole jazz alphabet?

Well, there I was now, years later, managing some of those same voices I once got schooled on. It was like my military playlist had walked out of the stereo and onto my stage. That day in Spokane? I started with hairpins in my hand and dreams in my head. From spinning jazz to giving out job titles, one day I'm in uniform overseas, the next I'm headlining with icons.

But it didn't stop there. Oscar Brown Jr., always the connector, introduced me to **Ernestine Anderson**, who later became one of my clients. And through Oscar, I also met the incomparable **Abbey Lincoln**. Now if you know anything about jazz or film, you know Abbey was a force. Actress, singer, activist, truth-teller. She starred alongside **Sidney Poitier** in the 1968 film *For the Love of Ivy*, and that shared connection with Sidney became an instant conversation starter between us.

What are the odds, I told her, that two kids from two different worlds both ended up standing in Sidney Poitier's shadow, on camera and in life?

Abbey and I hit it off. At the time, she was married to legendary jazz drummer Max Roach, and though she had adopted the name Aminata Moseka in the '70s, she still performed as Abbey Lincoln. The duality of her name reflected the depth of her artistry, always rooted in Black identity, always reaching beyond the expected.

Those moments, they were more than just career highlights, they were valuable personal and professional experiences. They were affirmations. Signs that I was right where I needed to be. Because in this business, it's not always about climbing a ladder. Sometimes, it's about **knowing the rhythm.** Being in the pocket. **Like jazz.**

You don't always know the next note, but when it lands just right…**you feel it.** And let me tell you, by that point in my life? I was playing my own melody, and the room was starting to listen.

Working with Abbey Lincoln was a different kind of honor. She was a creative soul. She was a voice cutting through a world that often tried to tell Black women how they should look, sound, or feel. Abbey rejected the "glamour girl" image that many Black female jazz vocalists were expected to uphold. She wasn't interested in just being beautiful or palatable. She was interested in being free.

Alongside artists like **Nina Simone**, Abbey embraced her natural hair and infused her music with the heartbeat of the era. Their songs were more than performances, they were statements, echoing the raw spirit of the Civil Rights Movement. Abbey once said she avoided singing about personal heartbreak because she wanted her songs to reflect **dignity, love, and strength**, not just sorrow.

"I want to sing about a Black woman's right to love and be loved," she told me. And that stuck with me. Her activism didn't stop at the mic either. Abbey was actively involved in community programs run by the Black Panthers, feeding the people and fueling the movement. I could relate to that.

While I was never officially a Panther myself, I'd been around their work, close enough to feel the fire.

This stage of my management career was about more than just booking talent. It was about walking alongside cultural disruptors.

Artists like **Jon Hendricks**, of *Lambert, Hendricks & Ross*, became part of my roster. Jon was a genius with vocalese and scat, the kind of stuff that took jazz to another level. **Ella Fitzgerald** may have helped bring scat into the mainstream, but Jon pushed the boundaries, turning vocal jazz into a full-on storytelling art. His style would later influence talents like **Kurt Elling**, but back then, Jon was already in a league of his own.

Managing artists like Abbey, Oscar, and Jon, these weren't just gigs. These were partnerships with revolutionaries. Every set, every show, every studio session, it all carried weight. These were voices that were reshaping culture in real time.
Oscar Brown Jr., in particular, inspired me in ways that went beyond business. He provoked, inspired, and informed people. His worldview was shaped by his father, a respected and outspoken attorney in Chicago. Some called his father a Communist, but really, he was just unapologetically Black and unafraid to say what others whispered behind closed doors.

Oscar carried that same fire. He brought art and activism together in a way that made people uncomfortable yet made them listen.

Being in that space, surrounded by voices that didn't ask for permission, I realized something. I was managing real talent. I was managing impact. I was helping artists find a stage, I was helping their stories shape the culture. Looking back now, it's almost surreal how quickly it all happened.

In just a few years, I went from standing in the fire of the Civil Rights Movement, feeling overwhelmed by the weight of change and unsure of where I truly fit in, to standing firm in my purpose, shoulder to shoulder with artists, activists, and culture-shapers who were doing the real work.

I found my place, not by marching down the most obvious path, but by using my gifts, style, vision, voice, and hustle to help reshape the culture from the inside out.

Whether it was helping artists like Abbey Lincoln, creating stages for acts like The Whispers and The Pointer Sisters, or building platforms through my salon and my pen, I realized I wasn't just watching history unfold. I was part of it. I was contributing to change, making history.

And once I understood that, everything changed.

One night that's stuck with me over the years was a quiet one, just me and Oscar Brown Jr. sharing a hotel room during a string of shows. We were both lying in our twin beds, winding down from the day, when Oscar suddenly asked me, *"What if I died? What would you do?"* I tried to keep it light and said, I'd try to get you a movie. But Oscar didn't let it go. He looked at me and said, *"Do it now."*

There was no performance in his voice, just truth. What followed was one of the deepest conversations I've ever had about legacy and recognition. Two things Oscar carried heavily. He started talking about Scott Joplin, how the man had created some of the most important compositions in American music history, and yet died broke, invisible, and unrecognized in 1917. Then decades later, Marvin Hamlisch comes along, arranges Joplin's music for *The Sting*, and walks away with two Academy Awards.

Oscar wasn't bitter. But he was heartbroken and determined. That night, between soft jazz playing in the background and Oscar's quiet voice cutting through the dark, I learned a truth I'd carry forever: You've got to claim your place. You've got to protect your work. Because the world won't always honor what you gave until it's too late.

Oscar taught me that with his words, his tears during performances, and the conviction in his voice when no one was watching.

That lesson stuck.

While I was having conversations about cultural legacy and artistic integrity upstairs, life downstairs was still in full swing. **Bea Davis**, who managed my salon, knew that rhythm better than anyone.

"Lu's business setup was quite dynamic; he managed his entertainment business from an office directly above the salon. This unique arrangement meant that I frequently encountered musicians and entertainers, some well-known and others just emerging in the scene. Lu was a whirlwind of activity, always on the move to meet someone or manage something for another. Because of his busy schedule, his mother would often visit the shop. Since Lu was often tied up, I became the go-between, ensuring that all messages from his mother reached him. I made sure he was aware of her requests or anything else she needed. He had a deep bond with his mother, and I did my part to keep that connection strong despite his hectic life." - **Bea Davis.**

Bea held it down. She was more than a business manager. She was like a little sister, and she kept the whole operation running smoothly while I bounced between meetings, the salon, and stages. And in the middle of all that? My mother, always present, always watching. When I couldn't step away to talk, Bea became the bridge. She made sure I got her messages, her reminders, her love. And for that, I'll always be grateful.

"I understood something important, something not everyone saw: That behind the artist manager, the entrepreneur, the cultural mover...Lu was still somebody's son." **- Bea Davis**

FROM SCISSORS TO SPOTLIGHTS: STEPPING FULLY INTO ENTERTAINMENT

By 1971, my salon was thriving, but something in me had shifted. I still loved the work, the energy, and the people, but I felt a deeper pull. The entertainment world was calling, and this time, I wasn't just tending to the looks of the stars, I wanted to shape their stages.

I was having fun. And more importantly, I was good at it. My client list was starting to sound like a who's who of the industry, from **The Whispers** and **The Pointer Sisters** to **The Natural Four** and **The Ballads**.

I was also producing shows and concerts for icons like the **Ike and Tina Revue**, **Barry White**, and the incomparable **Richard Pryor**. It was wild. One minute I was behind the chair, the next I was behind the scenes of a sold-out venue, making the whole thing happen.

While building momentum in the Bay Area, I often partnered with my dear friend **Mary Ann Pollar**, a powerhouse promoter who helped bring some of the greatest names in R&B and jazz to the West Coast. Together, we carved out real spaces for Black artists, before they were "mainstream."

This period also overlapped with the release of the film *Superfly* in 1972, which turned into a career-defining moment for **Curtis Mayfield**, who composed the film's unforgettable soundtrack. But here's the thing, before Superfly, I had already produced shows for **The Impressions**, where Curtis was lead singer. He was one of us. We had helped build him up.

Then came the twist: after *Superfly* blew up, Curtis was suddenly being managed by **Bill Graham**, a prominent white promoter who, until then, had never touched Black artists. And just like that, he was front and center. That shift didn't sit right with us.

Now let me ask you something. **Why is it that once some of our artists made it big with us by their side, got that mainstream shine, the first move they made was to switch over to white promoters?** I'm talking about folks who had been booked, supported, and elevated by Black promoters, Black radio, and Black audiences for years.

Where was the loyalty?

I mean, did they even have a Black manager? Who was there with them, city to city, when the rooms were half-full and the checks were light? We helped build their names.

We helped fill the seats. But once the money got long and the spotlight got bright, they started taking meetings with people who hadn't invested in their journey until the profits were guaranteed.

Isn't that interesting? You'd think they'd bring the people who believed in them from the beginning with them. But that's when I learned one of the hardest lessons in this business: **Success will test loyalty faster than failure ever will.**

And as tough as it was to swallow, I realized something else too, If we don't build our own tables, someone else will always decide where we get to sit.

I led a group of us, including Mary Ann and Dick Griffey, from Los Angeles to confront Bill directly. We laid it out plain and clear: "You don't run shows with Black artists in our community without including us. Period."

We had put in the work. We had promoted the shows. We had the local radio on our side. We knew the audience. And now, once the money got big, we were being pushed to the side. We were loud. We were clear. And we were fed up.

Still, Bill Graham went on to host major acts, Aretha Franklin at the Fillmore, among them. But those shows didn't come without resistance. Mary Ann Pollar, especially, was a fighter. Known as one of the **"Sistahs of the Sun,"** she was among the first Black women to proudly wear a natural hairstyle, and she rolled with cultural giants like Maya Angelou, Odette Beckford, and Ruth Beckford.

These women were warriors, unshakable in the face of inequality.

Their strength was contagious. James Brown was telling us, "I'm Black and I'm Proud," and we weren't just dancing to it, we were living it.

That time was full of tension, yes, but it was also transformational. It redefined my relationship with the industry. I was becoming more than just a promoter, I became a guardian of culture, a protector of the artists and communities we served. And despite the noise, the politics, and the pushback, I still had work to do.

1972 turned out to be a milestone year for me. My booking and management company hit its stride, and I produced a massive event in Oakland called *"The Black Quake."* Cities across the country were throwing these mega concerts to support the National Urban League and other grassroots movements. Ours featured **Barry White**, **The Pointer Sisters**, and a crowd that proved the power of Black entertainment, by us, for us.

That same summer, I met **Paul Mack**, **Landri Taylor**, and **Craig Malent**. We linked up our connections, power and strength and launched a two-year run of the Greek Jazz Festival, which brought some of the finest from the CTI Records (Creed Taylor Inc.) roster to the stage.

Names like **Grover Washington Jr.**, **Deodato**, **Hubert Laws**, and **Idris Muhammad** filled the lineup, creating one of the most vibrant jazz scenes the Bay had seen in years.

When I think about that time, I can't help but echo Lou Rawls, "1972 was a very good year."

FROM LOCAL LEGEND TO NATIONAL VISION

By 1972, things were moving fast, and all in the right direction. California had been good to me. The concerts, the talent, the relationships I built, it all felt like I was hitting my stride. I had grown from a local promoter into a regional force, and now, my sights were set higher. National tours started to feel not just possible, but inevitable.

That's around the time I met **Jim "Dr. Daddio" Walker**, a sharp, seasoned promoter and former owner of KDKO AM out of Denver. Jim had built a solid national presence with his company as his foundation. **J Mack Production**, which he co-owned with Paul Mack, a name already familiar to me from the Bay Area scene.

We met at a **Donny Hathaway** concert. Jim walked into the Oakland Theater and saw me and Paul working the ticket box together. Later, he told me, *"When Paul introduced me to Oakland,"* Jim once told me, *"he always talked about two promoters he respected the most, Lu Vason and Lewis Gray. He said y'all were the ones making it happen out here. The moment I saw Lu in the mix, handling business, I understood why Paul held him in such high regard."* - **Jim "Dr. Daddio" Walker**

That meeting sparked a lasting friendship and a professional alliance.

Together, we worked to expand our reach across six states, using Oakland and Denver as our base of operation points. The goal was clear, create a movement not just a moment.

Meanwhile, I kept strong ties with local venues, which every good promoter knows is essential. One of my go-to spots was a club in Chinatown called Dragon a Go-Go, a vibrant little place that became the home base for The Whispers, who I was managing at the time.

As the crowds grew, the club's owner, **Lu Chin**, realized we needed a bigger space. That led to the acquisition of Basin Street West, right on the Broadway strip in Oakland. Just like that, it became a new headquarters for our shows, further cementing our influence in the Bay Area's live music scene.

And the wins just kept stacking. One of my proudest moments was signing **Earth, Wind & Fire** to perform in Berkeley for their first-ever West Coast performance.

They were still finding their footing back then, but their power was undeniable. That show helped set the tone for a long line of firsts.

After Earth, Wind & Fire, I introduced **The Delfonics** to the West Coast. They were managed by Brenda Lum and produced by Stan Watson. When they went back to Philly, they couldn't stop talking about their California experience, and they made sure to drop my name in the right circles.

That buzz traveled fast.

Soon after, **Harold Melvin & the Blue Notes** made their California debut through one of my shows. When they returned East, they sang my praises to their manager, DeeDee Sharp, who also happened to be married to **Kenny Gamble** of the legendary **Gamble & Huff** songwriting and production duo. DeeDee caught the vision and got on board.

Before I knew it, I was bringing **The O'Jays** out West for the first time. Then came **Billy Paul**, riding high off his classic hit, *"Me and Mrs. Jones."* Those weren't just bookings, they were strategic moves. Calculated plays built on relationships, timing, and results.

I was also developing partnerships behind the scenes. At record conventions, I met **Jimmy Bishop**, who was managing **Barbara Mason**. We formed a working relationship to co-manage acts like **The Mad Lads**.

One moment I won't forget occurred while I was sitting in the beauty salon, listening to the radio, and I heard *"By the Time I Get to Phoenix"* playing. I got excited, thinking it was The Mad Lads' version, but it turns out it was Isaac Hayes' rendition from *"Hot Buttered Soul."*

That moment introduced me to **Stax Records**, and eventually, to **Jack Shields** out in Vallejo, California. That connection opened the door to working with **Con Funk Shun**, who would later become one of the major players in the funk and soul genres. The flow of talent didn't stop there.

I went on to manage **The Natural Four** for two years while they were signed to **Curtom Records**, Curtis Mayfield's label out of Chicago. Another full-circle moment. Managing artists who were now recording under the very man I'd once promoted, it was a sign of how far I'd come.

With everything clicking, national bookings, major artists, packed venues, I found myself asking, Alright, Lu...how do we take this to the next level? The stars had aligned, yes, but I wasn't content just basking in the glow. I wanted to expand the universe.

My recent success gave me leverage, real momentum, and that opened the door to broaden my portfolio beyond Black artists. That's when I started working with groups like **The Embers**, a white band well-known for their blend of beach music and R&B. Crossing that line into a more integrated roster was strategic.

Breaking barriers was just step one. What mattered most was showing up and showing out, like we belonged there, because we did. It was a move that led to a new collaboration with **Fantasy Records**, thanks to a connection with **Paul Rose**. Through him, I was able to step deeper inside the label's ecosystem. Before that, I'd already been managing **Rodger Collins**, best known for his hit *"She's Looking Good,"* which later got picked up and covered by **Wilson Pickett** and even **David Lee Roth**. That track had staying power, and so did Rodger.

Paul also managed a handful of up-and-coming acts, including a white band called **The Golliwogs**. They had a quirky look, fuzzy white hats and a raw sound, and I booked them to perform at my main club, which was my go-to venue for introducing fresh talent.

Now, I wasn't there that Monday night when they performed, but I sure heard about it. The club owner called me first thing the next morning, tight and furious. *"Lu,"* he said, *"if you ever book a group like that again, don't expect to use my club, or any club I'm tied to."*

I understood the climate. I understood the stakes. So I didn't push back. Sometimes in business, knowing when to nod is just as important as knowing when to fight.

Fast forward about a year later, I'm walking into my office, and I hear this tune coming from the radio. Something about it just felt like a hit. My wife Lillie looked at me and asked, *"Do you know who that is?"* I didn't. But I told her, whoever it is, they've got something. She smiled and said, *"That's the Golliwogs."* Except now, they weren't the Golliwogs anymore. They had reinvented themselves as **Creedence Clearwater Revival**. And the song? "Proud Mary." Yeah, that "Proud Mary." I stood there shaking my head, half laughing, half amazed. Timing is everything. And so is vision.

From there, I leaned further into developing diverse acts across the Bay Area. One long-standing relationship was with **Bobby Freeman**, known for his dance hit *"The Swim."* Bobby started out as a client, but before long, he felt like family, like a brother walking this road with me. We traveled across North America together, and I often joined him for his recurring appearances on Dick Clark's shows at Magic Mountain near Los Angeles. That phase of my career reminded me that greatness doesn't always show up dressed for the part. Sometimes it's in a fuzzy hat on a slow Monday night. Sometimes it's in a song you don't recognize, until it's too big to miss.

And that's the thing about expanding, you've got to see what's next, even when no one else does.

Listening to all the new records coming in, watching the charts, tracking rising names, gave me time to reflect. I thought about where I started...booking shows for acts nobody had heard of, and now some of those names were being recognized around the world. To go from unknown hustle to undeniable success, it was surreal.

I was part of a revolution in music. And I don't say that lightly. I watched it transform. I helped shape it. And even though I wasn't always front and center, I was in the room, and sometimes, I was the one opening the door.

But let me be clear, it wasn't all smooth.

Even after the wins, I had my fair share of disappointments. One that stands out was with The Whispers, a group I had been with from the ground up. I backed them in the early days, financially supported them, even covered their hotel bills when they were performing in the Bay and money was tight. I believed in them.

And I was proud when Walter and Wallace Scott, the twin brothers, returned to the group after finishing their military service. The timing was perfect, and momentum was building. But that's when the sudden change came.

Dick Griffey, a rising force in the industry, stepped in. He was working closely with **Don Cornelius** on moving *Soul Train* from Chicago to L.A., and he saw The Whispers as part of that bigger vision. He pitched the group on what he could offer, such as bigger deals, wider reach, industry connections. I had already gotten them their first spot on Soul Train, thanks to **Pam Brown**. That appearance gave them serious visibility. But they were hungry for more, and Griffey promised them the next level.

The group decided to vote on who would manage them going forward. It stung.

Because I was not only managing their shows, rather I had also been investing in their lives. But this is the business side of music, and sometimes, business decisions cut deep. They voted in Griffey.

He'd go on to form **Solar Records**, signing major acts like **Shalamar** and **Midnight Star**. It was a turning point for him, and a loss for me.

But even through the disappointment, we stayed cool. No bad blood. No bridges burned. Just a reminder that this industry moves fast, and loyalty doesn't always follow logic. It was a hard lesson. But one that every real player in this game eventually learns.

Because when you're building stars, you also have to build thicker skin. The music keeps playing. But sometimes, the lineup changes.

Even with the ups and downs, like losing The Whispers to Dick Griffey, I kept my head up and my hustle sharp. That chapter just confirmed what I already knew: timing, loyalty, and vision don't always line up, but when they do, they create magic. And speaking of vision, there was one person who shared that instinct with me early on, Landri Taylor.

Landri, one of my oldest and closest friends, was with me long before either of us fully knew where this path would lead. Back in our Berkeley Jazz Festival days, we were just two brothers with ambition, working stages and dreaming bigger every time the curtain dropped. We worked side by side, sometimes winning big, other times...learning the hard way. Landri puts it best:

"I took over as Chair of the Berkeley Jazz Festival in 1969 while I was a student at Berkeley and continued until 1973. Lu was instrumental in teaching me the business side of things. At 19–20 years old, I was well-versed in the arts and entertainment but lacked a grasp of the crucial business aspects. You can line up great talent, but without effective promotion to fill the seats, you won't sell tickets, and your concert could end disastrously."

"Lu and I worked on numerous concerts together, some wildly successful and others, not so much. One of our standout successes was a concert around 1971 or 1972. It was a masterful showcase of musical talent, notably marking the first live performance together featuring Donny Hathaway and Roberta Flack. That concert was a precursor to magic, paving the way for Atlantic Records to release Roberta Flack & Donny Hathaway in 1972. The album was a million-selling duet masterpiece that solidified their status as a magical musical duo." - **Landri Taylor**

Now, Landri's too humble to mention this, but I will. That show was a pivotal point. While Atlantic Records had both Donny and Roberta under contract, they hadn't been paired together before that night. That's the kind of intuitive matchmaking I've always prided myself on, seeing the synergy before the world catches on.

Opportunities kept coming. One of my proudest moments was bringing Earth, Wind & Fire to the Bay for the first time, thanks to my connection with Perry Jones, who worked for Warner Bros. back in the early '70s. But just like with The Whispers, not every play hits the way you want it to. Landri and I still laugh and cringe at one of our early misses:

"We once brought a group from Los Angeles to perform, but they were virtually unknown at the time, so despite our extensive marketing efforts across the Bay Area, we only sold 35 tickets. The venue seated over 3,000. It was disheartening, but just six months later, that same group released their first platinum album as Earth, Wind & Fire."

"We once brought a group from Los Angeles to perform, but they were virtually unknown at the time, so despite our extensive marketing efforts across the Bay Area, we only sold 35 tickets. The venue seated over 3,000. It was disheartening, but just six months later, that same group released their first platinum album as Earth, Wind & Fire." - **Landri Taylor**

And that's exactly what it was: a lesson. In this industry, the difference between legendary and overlooked sometimes comes down to one show, one song, one season. We had front-row seats to the rise of greatness, even if we didn't always catch the wave on its way up. But we were *in it*. And that meant something.

By 1973 and 1974, I was still working both sides of the business, styling and managing, booking and building. My crew was busy, and I was focused on making sure they stayed that way.

I was helping The Delights find new opportunities and connections, always looking ahead. One of the most strategic moves I made during that time was introducing them to **David Rubinson**, a heavyweight in the business, best known for producing legends like **Patti LaBelle** and **Herbie Hancock**. David ended up stepping in as road manager for The Delights, hitting the road with them on tours that also featured The Pointer Sisters and Oscar Brown Jr., while I continued to book shows for both The Delights and The Whispers.

It felt like everything was finally syncing. And I'll be honest, I was lucky.

Lucky to be surrounded by so many great people who believed in the vision, who hustled with integrity, who had just as much heart as they did talent.

One of those people was **Ray Taliaferro**, a bold, brilliant mind who helped organize a series of massive events across the country called **"Quakes"**, created to "shake things up." They were part celebration, part movement, driven by the vision of **Reverend Jesse Jackson Sr.** himself. Ray and I worked together on the "Black Quake" in San Francisco, hosted at the Civic Center, a powerful three-day festival featuring The Pointer Sisters, Barry White, and a full roster of talent. That event was a high point. The energy was wild, the crowd was electric, and the success was undeniable. It felt like something big was happening again.

But as is often the case in this industry, the highs eventually settle. Momentum is real, but so is gravity. The work got harder. The calls slowed down. And suddenly, the bookings for The Delights, who had been on fire for the first 18 months, started to taper off.

That's the part of management no one likes to talk about. It's not just about discovering talent, it's about keeping them relevant, keeping the gigs coming, keeping the brand alive, before we even had a word for "brand." Back then, we called it one thing: **"buttering the bread."** And when the bread started getting thin, I had to get creative.

As a result, I organized my first dance event at the Lemington Hotel, featuring The Delights and **Marvin Holmes**, a local favorite and funk staple. The goal wasn't glitz, it was survival. We needed to generate revenue, keep the wheels turning, and make sure everyone got paid.

That event marked a turning point. A moment where hustle met humility, where I had to balance the flash of concerts with the grind of keeping the lights on. All while still running my beauty salon, managing artists, booking shows, and answering phones from my office upstairs. The dream never died. But the hustle? It got heavier.

In the middle of all this movement, concerts, artists, venues, and late-night hustle, I had the good fortune of meeting someone who would become essential to my operations: **Neil Young**. I was introduced to Neil through **Bill Ehlert** of **Jolly Blue Giant Productions**, and from the very first handshake, the connection was there. We spoke the same language, get-it-done. Neil would go on to become my stage manager, and over the years, he was one of the reasons our shows ran like clockwork. *"The connection was instant,"* Neil says. He still laughs about our first day working together. *"Lu handed me this sheet of paper listing the duties of a stage manager, sound checks, backstage flow, understanding artist riders...I looked at him and said, If I'm here long enough, I might as well write the manual myself!"* - **Neil Young**

That's how Neil operated. He was thorough, adaptable, and always thinking ten steps ahead. He ended up bringing in a crew of talented theater students, many of whom would go on to careers in the industry. *"We gave them real experience,"* he says. *"And it paid off. It was a lucrative field, and we were building something that felt like family."*

And that's exactly how we ran our shows, with heart, hustle, and a sense of community. Neil was right there with me during some of the most memorable moments, including the early breakthrough of The Pointer Sisters, who were just finding their spotlight.

"Lu really went the extra mile for everyone," Neil recalls. *"He was a stand-up guy. No ego, just passion and professionalism."*

And of course, we had our fun. Let me tell you about a little prank I played on Neil once, I say with a grin.

*"Naw Lu let me tell it...We were doing a show with Jolly Blue Giant Productions, one Lu was co-producing. The headliners were **The Persuaders**, known for their hit 'It's a Thin Line Between Love and Hate.' I didn't know much about them at the time, and when I asked for their stage plot, someone handed me a sketch with marked positions... but no band setup. I asked where the band was, and Lu and Jolly just shrugged, saying, 'Oh, they didn't include that?' Like it was no big deal."*

"So here I am, scrambling. The artists show up, I try to explain the stage plan, and one of them just looks at me and says, 'You have nothing on the band? Here we go again!' I pulled my assistant, Ray Greenleaf, aside and asked him about the missing setup. He was just as clueless. I ended up prepping the stage with extra mics, hiding some behind curtains on wheeled risers, ready to adjust for a mystery band we might not see until showtime."

"Then I heard them warming up in the dressing room, smooth, tight, flawless harmonies. And that's when it hit me." They were an acapella group. There was no band. I turned and caught Lu and Jolly cracking up, they got me good. The Persuaders didn't need a sound check. Their voices filled the whole place."*- **Neil Young**

That was the magic of those days. We worked hard. We played hard. We laughed hard. And we made every show count. Neil was a great stage manager, and he was a great partner, someone who shared the load and brought order to the chaos. And in an industry where things could fall apart so fast, he kept everything and everyone on track.

As the curtain started to fall on one phase of my career, I found myself diving headfirst into a different kind of stage, one made of concrete, steel, and hope.

I had taken on the renovation of the Fox Oakland Theatre, a project that meant more to me than just bricks and seats. I was passionate about giving the Bay Area its own iconic venue, something like Harlem's Apollo. Oakland needed that. A cultural home for our sound, our style, our stories. The plans were ambitious, and we were making progress. Until everything came to a screeching halt.

In the middle of renovations, I got a call from the fire department, someone had either broken in or snuck into the building and completely sabotaged it, acid poured on the control panels, all the seats destroyed. It was heartbreaking. It was some bullshit!

We had a major show lined up. The energy was building. And just like that, it was gone. To this day, I add with a pause, I have my suspicions. That show was set to launch the same weekend the Paramount Theatre had a big event going on. You don't need a detective badge to raise an eyebrow or two. Still, I didn't let it break me. Because sometimes when one curtain falls, another stage calls.

Not long after that, I was sitting upstairs in my modest office above the salon. **Joyce Reynolds**, my loyal secretary, was nearby. The phone rang.

It was **Danny DeWitt**, a good friend, and unknowingly, the spark behind my next chapter. That call changed everything, I say now with a reflective laugh. "Was it phase three, four, or five of my life? Hell, who's counting anymore?"

What I didn't realize that day, in that little office above Telegraph Avenue, was that my biggest leap was still ahead of me. Because out in the distance, calling me with high altitude and even higher purpose, was a city I never expected to reshape my entire journey...**Denver, The Mile High City,** and the unexpected birthplace of a movement that would ride through history.

Chapter 7: FROM CALIFORNIA TO THE MILE HIGH CITY

First Gallop to Denver

You know how sometimes the most unexpected phone call can change your whole life? Well, that's exactly what happened one day while I was sitting in my office above the salon, right there on Telegraph Avenue. The phone rang. It was my good friend **Danny DeWitt**.

Now, Danny and I go way back. We used to play poker all the time, talking shop between hands, cracking jokes, keeping each other sharp. But this call wasn't about cards. Danny had something bigger in mind. *"My brother needs to talk to you,"* he said. *"He'll send a plane to come pick you up."* I sat there holding the phone like, "Wait...what?"

That's when he told me about **Eugene DeWitt (Gene)**, his brother. A commercial real estate developer and the owner of the 23rd Street East Club out in Denver. Danny figured that Gene and I would make a great team, and truth be told, he wasn't wrong.

Gene had heard about me, heard I was managing The Natural Four, and he wanted to bring them to Denver for a show. When we got on the phone, Gene didn't waste any time. *"I understand you've got a lot of power,"* he told me. *"But you don't have no juice."*

Now that was a line. I laughed and said, Well, what kind of juice you talking about? *"I'll send my plane to come get you,"* he replied, real casual, like it was a taxicab. That stopped me in my tracks. He had my attention. A Black man with a private plane? In the early '70s? I turned to my secretary, Joyce Reynolds, and said, Is this guy for real?

Joyce, always calm and steady, just looked at me and said, *"You don't have anything to lose, Lu. If nothing else, this sounds like a relationship to have."* She was right.

So I packed a bag, made my way to the airport, and there it was, Gene's plane, waiting for me on the tarmac like something out of a movie. I climbed aboard, wheels up, and just like that, I was headed to Denver.

I didn't know it yet, but that flight would mark a major turning point in my life. What started as a one-off trip turned into a regular rotation, Oakland to Denver and back again, until eventually, Denver became home. What began as a music deal blossomed into a deep friendship and business bond with Gene, one of the sharpest and most loyal men I've ever had the pleasure of working with.

That trip turned out to be more than just another gig, it marked the beginning of an entirely new chapter. Looking back, it's wild to think how some of life's biggest shifts can start with something as simple as a card game and a phone call.

After that first trip to Denver, it didn't take long before Gene and I were in sync. Business partners, brothers in the grind, and visionaries from two different worlds who just happened to see eye to eye.

I remember checking out the place for the first time and thinking, okay, this could work. After that visit, I started commuting regularly between the Bay Area and Denver, working closely with Gene and another local businessman, **Jim Rhoth**. I handled the talent bookings for Club Cabaret and The Warehouse, and by the mid-1970s, those spots were buzzing.

I was stepping into something new, but it felt familiar. And the way we clicked was natural. Even Joyce, my trusted right hand, saw it from day one.

"Lu really got his start with Gene at the 23rd Street East club, which he co-owned with our friend Jim Rhoth. But soon, that space was too small for their ambitions, and they expanded, opening another club named The Shapes, later renamed The Soundtrack for its musical vibe. They launched it on Lu's birthday, April 6, 1972, showcasing acts like the Five Stairsteps and Jesse James." - **Joyce Reynolds**

That launch on my birthday? People thought it was just a grand opening. Nah, what we did that night? That was a cultural blueprint in motion.

"I remember the moment Lu chose to go all-in. That was my most defining moment with Lu. There he was, partnering with Gene, a Black man who not only had significant financial resources but even owned his own plane back in the '70s. Gene's setup was impressive, he had a beautiful office in the Office Shores complex in Denver." - **Joyce Reynolds**

She wasn't just impressed with Gene, she admired the chemistry between us. The way we moved. The way we respected each other's lanes.

"Lu always had a knack for building solid business relationships with progressive Black men," she explains. Even if I didn't say it out loud, Joyce saw it as one of my defining qualities. I knew how to connect with people who were going somewhere. And she was right on.

"It's rare, you know, for many Black men to have close friendships with other Black men in business or to socialize in those circles. But Lu wasn't just any guy; he was exceptionally intelligent. Being around him and Gene felt like being in the presence of super brains. Gene, in particular, was ahead of his time, and his achievements were a testament to his advanced thinking." - **Joyce Reynolds**

Gene and I came from different backgrounds, me from entertainment, him from real estate and development, but we spoke the same language when it came to **vision, execution, and excellence.**

"Lu might have started in entertainment, where it's a different grind from real estate, but he was no less innovative or driven than Gene. And perhaps the most powerful part of our partnership? Thanks to Lu, Gene exploded deeper into the promotions business." "He always maintained beautiful offices and the pomp and circumstance that went with it, complete with all the trappings of success. Watching them work together, you could see the respect they had for each other, it was a partnership of equals, each bringing their own strengths to the table." - **Joyce Reynolds**

She said it perfectly. Me and Gene didn't just hustle side by side, we lifted each other higher every step of the way.

Opportunity brought me to Denver, but it was the people who made me stay. Gene DeWitt? He was the anchor. A businessman, sure, but more than that, he was a builder, a dreamer with both feet on the ground.

We hit it off because we saw the world through a similar lens: not for what it was, but for what it could become. We spoke the same language when it came to vision. We didn't see limits, we saw blueprints.

"Back then, Denver wasn't exactly on the main drag," Gene explains. *"It wasn't a regular stop like L.A., Chicago, or New York. It was a bit off the beaten path, cattywampus, as they say in the deep South, meaning askew or disarrayed. It wasn't on everyone's radar, which is what I aimed to change. And change it, we did." -* **Gene DeWitt**
.
Gene saw potential everywhere, in property, in people, in possibilities. He wasn't trying to make Denver the next New York. He was working to make Denver its own kind of capital, one with soul, class, and community.

"The city had all the right elements to become a cultural and entertainment hub. It was just about pulling the right strings and setting the stage," Gene reflects.

It all came about because one day during one of those big-picture conversations, Gene's brother, Danny, threw my name into the mix.

"My brother knew of Lu's success with entertainment in California. He suggested that Lu could really shake things up here," Gene says. So Danny made the call. And just like that, things started to move. *"I told him to get Lu on the phone. After a brief talk, I decided to fly him out to see our venue in person,"* Gene recalls. We didn't dance around it. Gene got straight to the point.

"I asked Lu, 'When can you come?' He was ready, so I told him, 'Pack your bags; my plane will be there in a couple of hours.' And just like that, we flew him in." - **Gene DeWitt.**

That's how Gene operated, decisive, bold, no time wasted. And I respected that. Gene wasn't just investing in me, he was inviting me to help reshape a city. To bring music, energy, and movement to a place most promoters had overlooked. And over time, that foundation would become the launchpad for something bigger than we had initially imagined.

"Lu brought a fresh energy that was contagious; his involvement was a catalyst for change, transforming Denver into a destination for major acts and cultural events. It all started with that first phone call and a flight." - **Gene DeWitt.**

That momentum carried forward when **Linda Motley** entered the picture. She quickly became a friend and pivotal force in my professional journey, the kind of partner I would look for time and time again. She had set the mold.

Linda had a strong grip on the entertainment business, bringing a sharp mind and bold personality that matched perfectly with my vision.

Together, we jumped into concert bookings, talent management, and even opened a record store. From our very first collaboration in promotions, Linda's creative edge and strategic thinking helped take every venture to the next level.

Starting this new chapter, I found myself drawn more and more to **Denver**, even though, at first, I couldn't quite figure out why. It gave me a release to come to Denver because I didn't know anybody, Denver felt like a hick town compared to the vibrant, urban life I was accustomed to in California. I kept wondering, why am I coming back to Denver?

At the time, it felt like I was trading rhythm for quiet. But looking back, I realized that my move mirrored the journeys of so many African Americans during the Great Migration, heading westward to carve out new beginnings, to build futures from scratch, in the so-called Wild West.

It was here that my bond with Linda deepened, and her sister **Karen Motley** remembers it well:

"Once Lu moved to Denver, he and Linda quickly developed a close bond. Linda had been working with Barry Fey, a renowned rock concert promoter known for introducing major acts like Jim Morrison & The Doors and Jimi Hendrix to the U.S. audience. Her extensive experience in the promotion world made her an invaluable asset to Lu." - **Karen Motley**

That experience meant everything. Barry Fey's influence loomed large, shaping much of the national rock scene, and Linda had been right there in the mix. With that background and her sharp mind for promotion, she was the perfect partner for what I was building next.

As Linda and I began promoting our own shows, we brought in a wide range of talent, blending styles and audiences in ways Denver hadn't seen before. And it wasn't just business. What we had felt like family. That trust, that closeness, laid the groundwork for some of the most important work I would ever do.

We didn't stop there. We also opened a record store, seeing it as a strategic piece of our entertainment blueprint. We were not just focused on selling music, it was more about creating a community hub. We hosted artist signings, built buzz around performances, and gave fans a chance to connect up close with the music they loved.

That mix of strategy, soul, and hustle became our signature. Together, we weren't just running promotions, we were building a cultural movement. And Denver, once that so-called "hick town," was quickly turning into the backdrop of something historic.

When Gene invited me back to Denver to bring in **Harold Melvin & the Blue Notes**, I found myself once again asking the same question that had been echoing in my mind for a while. Again, why do I keep shuttling back and forth to Denver? But the real question is why was I asking? I knew what I was doing.

It was a question that lingered, even as the bookings kept growing, the relationships kept deepening, and the opportunities became harder to ignore. Eventually, I had my answer.

I made the decision to go all in. I handed the keys to my salon, Lu Vason's Hair-o-scope, over to **Bea Davis**, one of the most trusted people in my life, and officially made Denver my home base.

Gene watched that transition up close. He saw me go from guest to resident, from curious to committed.

"Denver was a fresh landscape for Lu in the '70s, and what many don't realize is that it was quite the vibrant hub, It boasted a nightlife more active than California's at that time. We had a whole strip of businesses along Leetsdale Blvd. in Glendale, CO, including another club of ours called The Warehouse."

"That strip was known as the 'Million Dollar Mile', and back then, it was buzzing, nightclubs, restaurants, and energy you could feel in your bones. On a good Friday or Saturday night, you could see upwards of 10,000 people out and about," Gene recalls. *"You'd expect this in San Francisco or L.A., but Denver's bustling scene was a hidden gem."* - **Gene DeWitt.**

And he was right. I thought that I was stepping away from the action when I left the Bay Area. Turns out, I was walking straight into the next big wave.

By the time I officially touched down in Denver, it was clear, this wasn't just a detour anymore. It was destiny. Everything I had built in California, salon, stage, structure, I now had the chance to recreate in the Mile High City, but with even greater potential. I wasn't starting over. I was expanding the blueprint.

With Gene's business savvy, Linda's promotional sharpness, and a growing network of creative partners, I began turning Denver into a new kind of entertainment hub. It was the same formula I had applied in the Bay. Relationships, rhythm, and reinvention. But the market was different. The people were different. And the opportunities? They were huge, but so were the lessons to come. Denver gave me room to stretch, to grow into something more than just a promoter or a stylist.

It challenged me to think bigger with more expansion, move smarter, and to take risks I had not dared before.

And speaking of risks…Just when I thought I had my footing, I found myself at the center of a bet. One that involved a legendary group, a major leap of faith, and the kind of payoff you can't plan, you can only believe in.

That story? Well, that's the next chapter.

Chapter 8: The P-FUNK BET

> *"I made the bet on behalf of our company that we could put black acts in football stadiums and that we could do well with it. I said to Lu, 'now that I've opened up my mouth and made this bet, now we've got to figure what the hell we're going to do to pull this off.'"* - Gene DeWitt

Sometimes, the music business feels less like a plan and more like a poker table, and you don't always know the hand, but you can feel when the stakes are high.

Gene remembers it clearly, the day **L&E Productions** was born. *"I had teamed up with Barry Fey, a well-known promoter deep in the music scene. One afternoon, Barry called me, clearly distressed. He was several hundred thousand dollars down and struggling to manage a tour with a major Black act. He needed help, and fast."* That call would flip the script, not just for Barry, but for Gene and me, too.

Let me pick up the story right where it left off. It was late 1977, I remember, and I had just started working more closely with Barry. I was at our office on Parker Road, knee-deep in planning shows, when Gene called. He sounded like it was urgent. *"You got a second to meet?"* he asked. Of course, I said yes. When Gene said "meet," you met. We linked up shortly after, and Gene hit me with a question that caught me off guard, but in a good way.

"You ever heard of Parliament-Funkadelic?" I looked at him like he'd just asked me if I knew how to breathe. "Yeah!" I said, eyebrows raised, grin already creeping in. But Gene didn't stop there. *"Well, Barry's got 52 dates booked for them...and he's already lost money on 25."* That grin? It froze. "Whoa," I said, leaning back.

Back at the office, Gene and I sat down and went over the details. Barry was out on the road with P-Funk, right in the middle of the 'Mothership Connection' era, a tour backed by one of the biggest albums in Black music at the time.

Crowds were packing in. The funk was undeniable.

So, how was it bleeding money? We scratched our heads, I recall. It didn't make sense. Barry had the artists, the hype, the demand. But somehow, the machine wasn't working. There was no social media platforms to push the tour to save it. Right then, we knew what had to happen.

It became clear, I say now. Gene and I would take over the scheduling, the promotion, the management, the whole operation from the ground up. Barry had the contract, sure. But it was obvious he needed our expertise if this thing was going to survive, let alone thrive.

We weren't just stepping in. We were placing a bet on ourselves, on the power of funk, and on the belief that two Black men with a vision could take control of something everyone else assumed was already spinning out of control.

And just like that, the **P-Funk Bet was on.**

Once we stepped in, Gene and I knew we had to flip the entire strategy. This wasn't just about plugging holes in a leaky tour, it was about setting a new standard for how Black music was promoted, managed, and respected on a national level.

"We needed a fresh approach to revitalize the tour, to tap into the energy and fervor that Parliament-Funkadelic naturally inspired in their fans," Gene said. And he was right. This was more than business. It was cultural architecture, building something that would last. So we hopped on a flight to California, heading straight into a high-stakes meeting with **Barry Fey** and the group's management team, **Ron Strasner** and **Charlie Basobeni**.

"It was the perfect setting to showcase the blend of our skills. While I focused on the numbers, Lu had an unparalleled grasp of the artistic angle. Our combined strengths formed a powerful partnership." - **Gene DeWitt.**

When we arrived, there was much skepticism in the room, a mix of curiosity and caution. I could feel it. But I also knew P-Funk's power, their fanbase, their stage presence. They called us for a reason. I spoke their language. And Gene? He was surgical with the math.

We listened to Barry lay out his challenges, venue costs, overhead, dwindling returns, and then we hit them with what probably sounded like madness. "What if we jammed 27 shows into 30 days?" I asked. The room froze. *"Are you crazy? We can't do that!"* they shouted. They were stunned. But Gene didn't flinch. *"What the hell do you mean you can't do that?"* he fired back. *"Can't you sing 45 minutes...27 times...over 29 nights?"*

It was blunt. It was bold. And it was exactly what the moment required. *"The industry hadn't seen such an aggressive scheduling strategy in ages,"* Gene later reflected. *"There was a fear of the unknown. But the more we explained the vision, the more they saw the sense in it."*

My role was to bridge the logic with the art. I helped them see that this wasn't just doable, it was profitable. That this wasn't about exhausting the artists, it was about reigniting the audience. And slowly, we turned disbelief into buy-in.

We locked it in. **27 shows. 30 days.** And when it hit? It hit hard. 25 of those 27 dates were sold-out. Packed. Funk-fueled. Electric. What started as a financial crisis became a full-on revival tour, and it changed everything, not just for Barry, but for us too.

It wasn't easy, I say now with a grin, but we took Parliament-Funkadelic on those next 27 dates and made it a resounding success. That moment cemented something powerful. Gene and I saved the tour.

We made history.

And from that moment came something even bigger: The birth of the Funk Festival, and a blueprint that would forever reshape how we promoted Black music. With the tour schedule locked in, we knew the real work was just beginning. Getting butts in seats wasn't luck, it was the strategy. And I knew exactly where to start.

I went in and secured advertising with Black radio stations across all the markets. That was something Barry had missed. He hadn't tapped into the heart of the community, where the real promotional power lived. If you wanted to move tickets for a Black act, you had to go where the people were listening.

I even took it a step further. To boost the lineup, I added **Rose Royce** to the bill. They were hot at the time, right up there with **Bootsy Collins**, who had branched out from Parliament-Funkadelic and was holding his own as a major draw. With that addition, we didn't just have a show, we had a full-on experience.

And when it came to grassroots marketing, I knew the secret weapon. We had a 'Street Guy' named **Billy Barnes,** I say with pride. He was crucial because knowing how to reach Black folks and where to reach them, made all the difference. Billy would roll into each city a week or two before the concert, plastering flyers, handing out posters, getting the word out where it mattered most, barbershops, clubs, pool halls, churches, and community centers. You can't buy that kind of visibility with a billboard. It worked like magic.

The result? Nearly every show sold out. And the capstone? Gene remembers it like it was yesterday. *"That night marked the last of our sold-out shows. Easter Sunday in Memphis, Tennessee. It affirmed our success and dramatically broadened Lu's reach into the talent pool."*

That moment meant more than just taking the win; it was about changing the way folks looked at Black entertainment. We showed 'em it could be packaged right, pushed right, and still rise to the top. We set a new bar, plain and simple.

Funny how some of the biggest ideas start off as jokes over drinks. The idea for the Funk Festival was born in a hotel suite, just some light-hearted back-and-forth with a few of us in the game: **Lewis Gray**, **Marvin Webster**, and **Alex Cooley**. We were tossing around thoughts, talking shop, when someone said, *"Why don't we do a Funk Festival in some football stadiums?"*

At first, it felt like one of those late-night what-ifs. But the more we talked, the more it started to sound like a real plan. *"We just need more acts,"* someone said, and just like that, we were off to the races.

However, not everybody was convinced. Especially Barry Fey, who had doubts from the jump. He couldn't see Black acts filling up a football stadium. What do you mean you can't put Black acts in football stadiums? I pushed back. Why not? You've got plenty of Black kids who want to see those acts.

That conversation got heated, then competitive, and before I knew it, we had a bet on our hands. Had we not just saved Fey's butt? Still, now there I was, pacing, thinking, "Damn. I've made the bet... now what the hell are we going to do to pull this off?" Gene looked at me and said, *"Alright, Lu, who are the top Black acts in the country right now?"*

I froze for a second. Then I rattled them off:

- **Parliament-Funkadelic**
- **The Isley Brothers**
- **Rufus and Chaka Khan**
- **Rose Royce**
- **The Brothers Johnson**
- **Bootsy's Rubber Band**

Gene smiled and said, *"That's the show."* Even with all that talent, I wasn't sure we could make it happen. But I had claimed we could and so we had to. The logistics, the money, the egos**,** it was a tall order. But Gene had faith. And when Gene believed something was possible, you started to believe it too.

We mapped out a 10-city tour, and that's when the real challenges began. The first stop was Kansas City. Except there was a problem, no money in the box office. **Lewis Gray**, who was supposed to be handling the local promotion, had vanished, took all the cash and ghosted.

Fortunately, Gene didn't hesitate. He got on a plane and flew straight to Kansas City to figure it out. And Gray's disappearance with the cash wasn't the last curveball. When we got to Los Angeles, we ran into a major issue with the Mothership stage rig for Parliament-Funkadelic. The crew refused to hoist it up, worried it might fall. What did we do? We hired a crane.

Another big hit to the budget, but we weren't about to let fear or red tape stop the show. We felt the resistance. There were a lot of folks who didn't believe we could pull this off, they just swore that Black promoters couldn't handle something that big, that complex, this historic. But we proved them wrong.

We promised the artists they'd get paid if they showed up in L.A. We kept that promise. That moment sealed our reputation. From then on, people knew we handled business.

Nah, we didn't pack out every single seat in the Coliseum, but don't get it twisted. The people came out. Thousands deep. Loud, proud, unified and standing together. It was never just about a full house, it was about making a statement. Showing that Black music belonged on that kind of stage, with that kind of presence, under that kind of spotlight. The Funk Festival was bigger than just a show; it was a whole movement. And trust me, the odds were stacked high, but we made it happen.

Looking back on that stretch of my life, the tours, the concerts, the nonstop grind, I can still feel the weight of how fast it all moved. Everything was happening at once. It was all converging at the same time and we couldn't miss a beat. We were building something massive, managing egos, juggling logistics, watching the money, protecting the vision, all while trying to protect ourselves from getting burned out in the process. It was a hell of a time...but it was a lot.

I remember one night after a show, back in the hotel room. Tired as you know what. Linda, looked at Gene and said,*"We're going back to the mountains, huh?"* Without skipping a beat, Gene answered, *"We're going back to the mountains."*

It was a quiet moment, but it said everything. We needed to get away. Step back. Breathe. And that's exactly what we did. We retreated to the mountains, leaving behind the bright lights and the buzzing phones, for a minute, at least. But it was not a simple break to rest, get back up and go to the next round . It was Gene's exit.

From that point forward, Gene stepped away from the entertainment world to never step back in. And with Barry Fey still operating out of Denver, I shifted into a tighter working relationship with Barry from that point on.

"Look, I wasn't trying to be the biggest Black promoter, even though we might've been at the time, I saw an opportunity, and I went for it. But dealing with folks like Lewis Gray, people we tried to help who ended up betraying our trust, just made me realize...it wasn't worth the stress for the exposure I was chasing." - **Gene DeWitt**

Then he looked me square in the eyes, gave me a half-smile, and said: *"Okay, buddy, you got this. I'm outta here. They got the last dollar out of me in this business."* And just like that, he was done.
You have to admire a man who knows what's good for him and what's not. That moment marked the end of an era. The Funk Festival had been a win, no doubt. The cost was real.

Behind the crowds and curtain calls, I was carrying more than I realized. I had built the machine. But now the machine was starting to consume me. I was saying yes to everything. Moving fast, working harder, chasing the next show, the next opportunity, until I could barely hear myself think. Somewhere in all the noise, I started to lose my rhythm. Not in the music. But in myself.

Chapter 9: GETTING UP AND BACK ON THE HORSE

> **"I thought I was down to my last nickel, not just my last dime...literally," - Lu Vason**

If you've ever lived in the Midwest, then you know a thing or two about tornadoes. They don't always come with thunder.

Sometimes, it's that eerie silence that gets you first. Then the winds start to shift. The sky goes gray, the air gets thick, and the sirens sound, but by the time you realize it's real, it's already on top of you.

That's exactly what life felt like for me in the mid and late 1970s, like a Category 5 tornado touched down right in the middle of everything I thought I had under control. Now Denver ain't exactly Tornado Alley, but for me, it was the epicenter of a personal storm I never saw coming.

By 1972, my marriage to Lillie had ended. Truth is, and I'm not proud of this, I had already started another relationship while we were still married. Her name was Kashaun, and while that relationship brought its own kind of light, it also added more weight to a life that was already getting heavy.

Then in 1974, my mother passed away, and that hit me like nothing else ever had. I was devastated. Numb. You think you're ready for that kind of loss, but you're not. That loss leaves holes you don't even know how to fill.

I married Kashaun, making it my third marriage, and took on the role of father to her daughter, Shelly. But that marriage didn't last long either.

I wasn't showing up the way I should have. I was too busy trying to outrun my personal life by burying myself in my professional one.

Sometimes we hide behind the hustle. Work becomes the excuse. The stage becomes the escape. And while I was out there promoting shows, shaking hands, booking acts, making moves, I was neglecting the one stage that mattered most: home.

I didn't take care of my marriages the way I should've. I didn't show up for my kids the way a father's supposed to. And that's something I've carried with me ever since, a quiet guilt, a permanent ache.

The entertainment life? Man, it was beautiful. It was electric. The energy. The women. The spotlight. The rush of sold-out nights and standing ovations. But that world doesn't come without a cost.

It gives and it takes. Sometimes it gives you applause…and sometimes it takes everything that matters behind the curtain. The tornado warnings were there. I just wasn't listening. And when it hit, it didn't just knock down buildings…it tore right through my foundation.

By the time the dust settled, my relationships were in ruins, my spirit was drained, and the truth was staring me dead in the face: I had lost control.

I think about Frankie Lymon sometimes. Here was a kid who had the world wrapped around his finger. Talent, fame, and women, and in the end, his relationships with women mirrored his unraveling. He didn't marry two women at the same time by design, it was confusion, avoidance, and emotion all tangled together. And while I wasn't legally married to two women at once, I know what it feels like to have your life, your loyalties, and your love all twisted together until you can't tell where one ends and the other begins.

I was in love with ambition. In love with escape. And in doing so, I left some good people, people who loved me, standing in the wind.

That storm? It didn't destroy me. But it sure knocked me down with a force I was not ready for.

Life has a way of humbling you. It hits different when it's trying to wake you up. And I needed that wake-up call, because before I could build anything new, I had to learn how to get up, dust off, and climb back on the horse.

L&E Productions officially disbanded, marking the end of an era, and Gene DeWitt's full exit from the entertainment business. Gene chose to leave a winner still standing. He was out. And I? I was at the bottom.

The year before had nearly broken me. I had taken a heavy hit producing a show that featured **Brass Construction, The Sylvers, and Johnny Taylor**. The numbers didn't add up. The crowd didn't show up. And the bills? They were overdue. That loss cleaned me out.

To add fuel to the fire, my third marriage ended, and to make matters worse, I got into a car accident that left me stranded and stunned. The car wasn't running. My pockets were empty. My pride was bruised.

Everything I'd built felt like it had collapsed.

There I was, me, Lu Vason, sleeping on survival mode. I kept my food in a Styrofoam cooler like I was tailgating my own downfall. Top Ramen and canned tuna became my daily menu. You don't need seasoning when you're broke, you just need something to fill the hole.

I remember a friend's girlfriend showing up with a small refrigerator out of pity or compassion. It didn't matter, you would've thought she brought me a new Cadillac. I was grateful, but I was also ashamed. That's how far things had fallen.

During my darkest hour, **Linda Motley**, who had always been more than just a business partner, more like family, looked at me one day and said, *"Put the car in the shop. You'll find a way to get it out, or they'll sell it."*

She was talking about my Fiat convertible. Man, that car used to turn heads. It was sleek, flashy, driven up from California by my third wife when times were good. It used to symbolize success. Now it was just another thing I couldn't afford to fix. So, I listened to Linda. I took it to the shop, knowing full well I didn't have the money to get it out. Not long after, I got a call: *"If you don't come get it, we're going to sell it."*

Desperate, I swallowed my pride and applied for a job at United Airlines at the old Stapleton Airport. When they offered me $3.25 an hour, I laughed just to keep from cussing.

$3.25? I had made that in minutes back when I was running shows. Now they wanted to give it to me for a whole hour? I walked out.

Kashaun, who was somewhat still in my life at that time, she was furious. *"Go back to the post office,"* she said. But I just couldn't do it. I couldn't go back. Not like that. Even with my pride in pieces, I still had enough left to say no. But saying no didn't fix the mess I was in and that was the last straw for Kashaun.

I was running on fumes, financially, emotionally, spiritually. And for the first time in a long time...I didn't know what came next.

While I was fighting to stay afloat in Denver, trying to hold on to my name, my pride, and my future, there was someone else caught in the storm, my son, Corey.

Corey Vason remembers those years with a clarity that I didn't have at the time.

"Back in 1977 or 1978, Dad was going through some really tough times during his third marriage in Colorado," Corey shares. *"Even though he was struggling, he turned down a job at the airport. He told me once that he was down to his last 16 cents."*

It was rough. Not just for me, but for him too. Because while I was out trying to build something that would last, I wasn't there. Not as a father. Not the way I should've been.

"My dad and I weren't close at the time, I was a young boy living in California, being raised by my mom. I think I was 15 or 16, and I started resenting him, because he wasn't there for me. He wouldn't help me. He didn't show up."

Those are hard words to hear, but he's not wrong. And the truth is, a lot of fathers, especially in the hustle, miss the moments that matter most.

"I wasn't talking to him for a while, I think a couple years went by without us even seeing or speaking to each other. He wasn't there for my high school graduation. The pain and resentment just kept building."

And that's real. When you're a kid, it's hard to understand why a parent isn't around. You don't see the battles they're fighting. You just feel the absence. And absence hurts. But sometimes life gives you a moment to rewrite the story, even if just a little.

"I remember one day I was working at a shoe store in Richmond. I looked up... and my dad was standing right in front of me. There was no warning. No buildup. Just presence. I couldn't believe it. And immediately, all the anguish, all the bitterness, all that stuff just went away. We embraced. We hugged. And we just lived in that moment." - **Corey Vason**

That moment? That was the reset.

"We went to dinner later that night in Oakland, and he shared things I never knew, about why he and my mom got divorced, why things didn't work with Kashaun. Stuff I always thought was all his fault...but I realized it wasn't all on him." - **Corey Vason**

That night, truth made space for healing. And it reminded me of something I'd forgotten in all the noise: Success doesn't mean anything if you leave your people behind.

Corey shared heart with a mix of frustration and admiration. Because that's how complicated fathers can be. It's hard to explain to a child, especially a son, how a man can be strong enough to survive, but not strong enough to show up I've carried that guilt with me. I didn't know how to be a father in those years. And by the time I looked up, the damage was already done.

What I didn't realize back then was that you can't raise your legacy if you've abandoned your roots. The shows, the lights, the business deals, they were never supposed to come before the people who shared my name.

Corey's pain? It wasn't just his. It's universal, the ache of every child who needed their father and got silence instead.
And for every father reading this, let me say something from experience: If you're too busy to see your kids, you're already too lost. I learned that the hard way. And though I couldn't undo what had been done…I knew it was time to start facing the music, not just the one I promoted, but the one I had to live with.

After hitting bottom, it wasn't the industry that saved me. It was the people who still believed in me when I didn't believe in myself. Friends from California, **Cleo Blanton, Vera Harvey, and Bobby Freeman**, they saw what was happening from afar. They heard it in my voice, felt it in my silence. And when I couldn't even scrape together the money to get back home, they bought my plane tickets themselves. That's real friendship.

I landed in California flat broke. I didn't even have enough money to call **Joyce Reynolds** for a pickup. I searched my pockets and came up with a single dime.

The phone booth at the airport? Ten cents. Exactly. That one call led me back to Joyce, and back to something I didn't even know I was looking for. I stayed with her for about a week, trying to catch my breath, but Joyce could see the struggle all over me.

"Once Lu arrived, I saw he was a mess," she says plainly. "He was depressed and confused. You could tell he didn't know which way was up."

It started with nothing more than curiosity. I was browsing Joyce's shelf, restless, and picked up a book on Buddhism. I wasn't looking for religion, I was just looking for a reason to keep going. But those words reached me. **Joyce and Bea**, two women who were always in my corner, saw the shift. They didn't just encourage me, they stepped into that space with me, helped me climb out of my own fog.

"We ended up going to a temple," Joyce remembers. *"But more than that, we had to help Lu change his mindset. Motivate him to start thinking positively. To stop spiraling and start climbing."* She told me flat out: *"Life is good. You just forgot how to live it."* And she was right.

Watching Chuck Mangione on TV, calmly conducting a full orchestra with grace and clarity, I saw something I hadn't felt in a long time: control. The way he moved, the way the music responded…it reminded me that life still had rhythm. I just had to find mine again.

Though that moment didn't fix everything. It gave me one thing I desperately needed: **Hope.**

After I returned from California, something in me had shifted. My time with Joyce and Bea had relit the flame I thought was gone. They reminded me that I still had something left to give, and more importantly, something left to live for.

When I got back to Denver, I had a conversation with **Linda Motley** that I'll never forget. We were talking about Buddhism, something I had just started exploring, and she listened patiently like she always did. Then, in that calm, thoughtful way of hers, she said: *"You've tried everything… why don't you try God?"*

That was Linda. She didn't preach. She'd just pose a question so clear, so direct, that you couldn't ignore it. In one of the darkest stretches of my life, she was my lifeline. We spent a lot of time together.

She saw me, **really saw me**, when I was unraveling. And somehow, without ever making me feel judged, she offered love, comfort, perspective, and spiritual grounding that went deeper than just advice. Even when she didn't know it, her words cut right to the heart. They had a way of shifting my way of seeing things, rearranging my thinking.

It was Linda's suggestion that led me to begin exploring the *Science of Mind* teachings more seriously. I started by attending lectures, just to grasp the basics, and eventually began studying Ernest Holmes' book, "The Science of Mind."

No, I never became a practitioner, though I thought about it. Told myself I was too busy. Maybe I was. Maybe I was scared of the commitment. But I did become something else: a recruiter. I started inviting people to join me. I wanted them to feel the same spark that I was starting to feel again.

One of the first people I brought was an old childhood friend, **Helen Jackson**. We'd grown up together, me, her, her sisters, and **Herbert Mims**. I didn't have anyone else to go with that Sunday, so I reached out and said, "Come with me to Founders Church."

I didn't expect anything more than company. But what happened next? Helen embraced it fully. She dove into the teachings, became a practitioner, and found real purpose in that community.

Watching her thrive, and knowing I had helped plant that seed, it gave me a deep sense of peace. Even if it was brief. Even while I was still searching.

The *Science of Mind* didn't fix everything. But it gave me a language for hope and a framework for healing. And sometimes, that's the most powerful kind of faith, the kind you grow into one decision at a time. It taught me that faith ain't always loud. Sometimes it's just showing up, when you don't feel ready, when the answers aren't clear, when all you've got is belief that there's more ahead than behind.

Eventually, with a little humility and a lot of pride swallowed, I went to Barry Fey and asked him for a loan to get my car out of the shop. He came through, and that moment quietly solidified our working relationship moving forward. He saw I was serious, even if I was at my lowest. And I was grateful.

With no real job prospects on the horizon, and refusing to take a $3.25/hour gig at the airport, I went back to what I knew best: doing hair. I picked up some hours at Rudy Barnes' Beauty Salon, a small spot tucked inside a house with two-pane glass windows. Nothing fancy, but it was steady.

I was styling Peggy Wortham's hair one afternoon when the phone rang. It was **Rose Royce**, calling to invite me on tour. I didn't hesitate. Because I wasn't tied to a clock or a company or a desk, I said yes on the spot. I was on the road with them just before Thanksgiving that year, and spent the holiday with the band in Pittsburgh.

That kind of opportunity? It never would've happened if I'd taken that job at the airport, because it's a different mindset and a different vibration. See, it was sheer will, and what some might have called arrogance, that kept me moving forward.

Even broke, even bruised, even beat down, I never let go of the belief that I could still win.

And little by little, the doors began to crack open again.
By 1982, I launched Jazz Lives at the Quality Inn Hotel on Colorado Blvd. It was there I met a young sales manager named Elbra Wedgeworth. I watched her blossom, from hotel staff to Denver City Council President, helping to bring the 2008 Democratic National Convention to the city.

It was beautiful to see that kind of rise, especially knowing we both started out grinding in small rooms with big dreams.

Elbra helped me secure the space for my jazz concerts from 1979 to 1983, before we eventually outgrew it. Those nights laid the foundation for my next big move, The Casino Cabaret in Five Points.

There, the energy shifted again.

We hosted artists like **Ramsey Lewis, George Sharon, Bobby "Blue" Bland, Esther Phillips, and Z.Z. Hill**. The music was alive. The rooms were packed. And I was slowly finding my rhythm again.
Over the years, I've learned that people come into your life for a reason. Some stay for a season. Some shape your future. All of them leave a mark.

At the time, I couldn't see what was coming, but I felt it.

The wind was shifting, and my career was about to take a dramatic turn.

Chapter 10: THE GREAT RODEO EPIPHANY

> *"When Lu told me he wanted to do a rodeo, my initial reaction was, "Lu, you need to get the information from George Hayes, because he can help you." George had been around horses all of his life in Guthrie, Oklahoma. We have a farm back there, that's where I'm from. George has a brother, Robert Hayes, they now run those farms in Oklahoma. Lu just persevered, moved forward and made it happen." - Herbert Mims*

After the high of the Funk Festival, things started to shift again. Gene, my trusted partner through so many victories, decided to step away from the entertainment game for good. And just like that, I was on my own again, back to navigating the industry solo.

But something was changing inside me too. Not just business. Something deeper.

I've always had this habit of reading everything in the newspaper, not just the headlines, but the classifieds, the community events, the ads tucked in the corners. I believe if you pay attention, life drops clues in the margins. And one day, one of those clues caught my eye.

It was an ad, nothing flashy, but it had these images of cowboys, Native Americans, and stagecoaches, like something straight out of a childhood daydream. And that's exactly what it sparked in me: memory.

Back when I was a kid, like a lot of little boys, I was fascinated by cowboys and Indians. The freedom, the wildness, the stories. That ad pulled something up from way down in my spirit. I casually mentioned wanting to check it out.

Didn't even think twice about it.

But the next morning, bright and early, **Linda Motley** called me up, 8:00 AM sharp, and said *"We're going to Cheyenne Frontier Days."*

That was Linda. She didn't waste time. We got the crew together, piled in, and hit the road toward Cheyenne, Wyoming. What I walked into that day wasn't just an event, it was a whole different world.

Cheyenne Frontier Days was like stepping back into another era. Ten days of full-on Old West energy: square dancing, western cook-offs, carnival lights, country music stages, and designated spaces like "Frontier Town" and "Indian Village." But the heart of it all? The rodeo.

We managed to hook up with a gentleman who saw we were curious, and maybe a little out of place, and he took us under his wing. Gave us a behind-the-scenes tour, breaking down how the rodeo really worked. That's when I started seeing the details. The lanky, lean cowboys who handled the bareback riding...The stockier, more solid men who thrived in steer wrestling, bulldogging. And the bulls? Man, 2,000 pounds of pure attitude and muscle.

It was all raw power, rhythm, and precision, just like a great concert. Only this time, the stage was dirt, and the headliners had ropes, spurs, and heartbeats that matched the thunder of the crowd.

And something about it all started stirring in me, like maybe this wasn't just a road trip. Maybe this was something more. I had gone to Cheyenne that day on business, to talk with **Charlie Pride**, the country music legend, about putting together a concert in Denver. That was the plan.

But as the day unfolded, my attention started drifting, not from boredom, but curiosity. The rodeo itself had pulled me in. The energy. The tradition. The grit of it all. It was a far cry from the world of lights and stages I knew so well. And yet...it felt familiar.

It felt like a show. Just a different kind. And I couldn't shake the question forming in my mind. Where are the Black cowboys?

We'd been sitting in the stands, me, Linda, and her sons, just soaking in the spectacle. At one point, one of her boys had a seizure. We rushed to get help. Thankfully, he was okay and even came back to finish watching the rodeo with us. But after that scare passed, my mind locked back on that one question.

All around me were cowboys, tall ones, short ones, riders, ropers, and wranglers. But not a single one of them was Black. That didn't sit right with me.

This observation sparked a conversation between Tom, Linda and me. Having successfully organized concerts before, my mind started painting the vision. Among the roar of the crowd, I leaned in and whispered to Tom first and then to Linda, and just said it, low and direct, so no one else would hear: driven by a sudden spark of inspiration, "Man, you know, we can do this." Foster, caught off guard, gave me a sideways look, confused. *"Do what?"*

I looked back out at the arena, eyes scanning the dirt, the bulls, the grandstands...and the opportunity. We could put on one of these rodeos ourselves.

Now, that wasn't something people like me, Black concert promoters, were supposed to say. It wasn't something people expected. But the vision was there. Clear. Loud. Alive.

Tom and Linda just sat in silence for a moment. I could tell they were trying to process it. So I said it again, this time with a visionary's clarity and more weight behind it.

Produce a rodeo, but we'll make it all Black, black cowboys and black cowgirls. That moment of realization planted the seed for what would eventually become a significant endeavor: organizing a black rodeo. This idea not only tapped into a niche that was evidently missing at traditional events but also connected deeply with my cultural roots and childhood interests. To my friends, I knew this idea would seem as wild and unpredictable as the bucking broncos in the arena.

The more I sat there and watched this exciting event, the more detailed the vision became. I could see fathers and sons, fathers and daughters, entire families, mothers with their children all in the bleachers. Grandparents, teenagers, young adults, seriously, people of all ages would come to the rodeo and love it! And once I saw it, I mean, everything-the venue, the horses, the cattle, the bulls, the cowboys, the cowgirls, the procession of dignitaries, the vibrant parades, and the solemnity of the Black National Anthem sung by celebrities who stood in solidarity with my cause. I saw the competitions, the awards, the joy, and the community, all coming together in a grand event that was as much a reunion as it was a revelation. I saw the awards! I saw it all and I knew that my vision was a reality.

That moment didn't just change the day. It changed my life. I knew we had just stumbled onto something revolutionary.

After we got back to Denver, I couldn't shake the idea. The vision was still burning hot in my mind, but now, I needed direction. I needed proof that the story I wanted to tell was real. That's when Linda said, *"Well, I know this guy who's got the Black American West Museum. His name is Paul Stewart."*

About a week later, Linda, her sister Karen, and I paid Paul a visit. Now **Paul Stewart**, **founder of the Black American West Museum,** back in 1971, was more than just a historian. He was a keeper of legacy. And that day, he handed me a piece of history I'd never heard before.

He introduced me to a name that would change everything for me: **Bill Pickett.** I was surprised I hadn't come across him before, not with all the reading I'd done, not with my love of history. But Paul began to fill in the gaps.

Bill Pickett wasn't just another cowboy. He was the pioneering cowboy. The man who invented bulldogging, known back then by that very term, now known as steer wrestling. I was hooked. I started digging, researching, and flipping through archives. And what I found blew my mind. Bulldogging is the only rodeo event that can be definitively traced back to one man, a single originator. One Black man. Bill Pickett.

As Paul continued sharing Bill's story with us that day, me, Linda, and Karen sitting there, taking it all in. I knew I had found my anchor. I wasn't just going to organize a Black rodeo...I was going to name it after Bill Pickett.

That decision was intentional. I could've taken the easy route, calling it "The Black Rodeo" or something generic. But that wouldn't have meant anything. That wouldn't have taught anybody anything. It wouldn't have honored Pickett's legacy or educated others about his significant contributions to the Western frontier.

Naming it after Bill Pickett? That was about reclaiming legacy. It was about honoring the man who started it all and educating every person who walked through those gates.

Once I made the decision to name the rodeo after Bill Pickett, the mission became clear. I wanted to enlighten our community, especially our young people, about who he was and what he stood for. Bill Pickett wasn't just a name in a forgotten history book. He was a pioneer, a Black man who carved out a place in the rugged world of rodeo, a space few even knew we had been a part of.

I remember one afternoon, sitting in the kitchen with my cousin Charlene Hayes. She was staying with me in Denver at the time, and we were watching planes fly low over the old Stapleton Airport.

I turned to her and said, clear as day, I'm gonna put on a rodeo. She looked at me sideways at first, but then said something that turned the whole thing up a notch. *"I know somebody who could help. A friend of mine's a stock contractor."*

That was the piece I needed. But Charlene didn't give up the contact right away. Took me a whole month of asking, nudging, waiting. Finally, she handed over the number. His name was Elmer Anderson, and he was based out of Oklahoma.

When I called him, he didn't waste words. *"Yeah, I can come up there. You got a place?"* I told him I had a few ideas. He said, *"Fly me up there, and we'll figure out what we need to do."* So that's what I did.

Elmer flew into Denver, and I took him straight out to look at the Adams County Fairgrounds with one of my assistant Jeannie Potts. We walked the grounds, and Elmer gave a little nod like he'd seen something. *"Yeah,"* he said**.** *"This would be a great place for a rodeo."*

That's when things started to shift from vision to blueprint. With Elmer's expertise on board, I started learning everything I could. How sponsors worked. What kind of events cowboys competed in. What each discipline required. I dove headfirst into a world I knew nothing about. I wasn't intimidated at all. I was energized.

Then Elmer invited me to a rodeo down in Okmulgee, Oklahoma, to get some real exposure. And let me tell you…it was a different world down there.

Most folks didn't know who I was, and I could tell some of them didn't know what to make of me. Maybe they thought I was just another slick city guy trying to ride in on someone else's culture. But one person stood out, his name was **Robert Dugas.** He greeted me like I belonged there. Introduced me to folks. Made me feel like maybe… just maybe…I had a shot at building something real.

Even though I still had a long road ahead, that experience confirmed one thing: The Bill Pickett Invitational Rodeo wasn't just an idea anymore. It was in motion.

As the dream started picking up steam, word began to spread, and that's when **Cleo Hearn** reached out. Now, I didn't know it at the time, but I had already seen Cleo in action. He had actually competed at the Cheyenne Frontier Days, the very same event that had lit the fire in me. Turns out, I had arrived just after he'd finished performing. Funny how things come full circle.

When Cleo got wind of what I was trying to build, he didn't hesitate. He offered his support and opened-up his network, giving me access to the broader cowboy community, names and contacts I never could've found on my own. That kind of help was priceless.

Meanwhile, M&D's Restaurant became my unofficial rodeo headquarters. If you were looking for me, that's where I'd be, seated in my regular booth, piecing together this dream over plates of catfish nuggets and sweet potato pie.

Mack and Daisy Shead, the owners, had deep Texas roots and a long legacy in barbecue that stretched back to the 1940s. The food was the kind that made you sit back and close your eyes with the first bite. Fried green tomatoes, homemade hot links, ribs, and peach cobbler that tasted like somebody's grandmother still made it by hand. And on Gospel Sundays? Whew. The place felt like church and family reunion rolled into one.

It was there that I had a conversation that changed everything. Elsie, who worked at M&D's and also pulled shifts over at the Renaissance Hotel (formerly the Doubletree), leaned over and said: *"There's a Black bull riding champion staying at the hotel. You should meet him."*

She didn't have to say anything else. I got up, followed her lead, and soon found myself knocking on the door of none other than **Charlie Sampson**. At that point, Charlie had just made history. The first Black cowboy to win a World Championship in Bull Riding with the Professional Rodeo Cowboy Association (PRCA).

In a sport dominated by white cowboys, Charlie broke through the barrier and never looked back. We sat down and had one of the most real, honest conversations I've ever had. He didn't sugarcoat anything. We talked about the organizational challenges in Black rodeos, the reputation they had, especially when it came to starting late, disorganized events, no sense of time.

Charlie looked me square in the eye and said something simple, but powerful: *"Make sure they start on time."* That advice stuck.

For over 30 years now, that's been a core rule of the Bill Pickett Invitational Rodeo: We start on time. No excuses. No delays. Just respect for the audience, the cowboys, and the legacy. Launching an all-Black rodeo wasn't just some side hustle or vanity project.

This was a full-scale mission, a cultural reset disguised as a live event. And like anything worth doing, it came with real work.

This wasn't just about putting on a show. It was a massive undertaking, demanding meticulous planning, strategic foresight, and a hands-on understanding of every moving piece. And let me be clear: money was only one part of the puzzle.

I started by crafting a full "run of show" plan. A detailed roadmap that outlined every beat of the production. From the sequence of rodeo events to transitions between competitions, to who was managing what behind the scenes, every detail had to be locked in. It wasn't just about finding a venue or booking talent. I had to source the right livestock, coordinate transportation, ensure animal care, and rent the cattle and steers along with their handlers who'd stay on-site throughout the show. That was just the groundwork. Then came the real hook: prize money.

If I wanted top-tier talent, I had to make sure the cowboys felt it was worth their while. Rodeo athletes, especially the Black cowboys I was trying to spotlight, already had enough stacked against them. I knew even a small purse could be the difference between "maybe" and "I'm in." And even though the price tag was steep, I wasn't shaken.

I have been producing events my whole life. I understood how to stretch a dollar and deliver something unforgettable. Financially, it was a beast, but not one I couldn't tame.

To get this thing off the ground, we were looking at a projected cost of anywhere between $160,000 and $188,500. That's not pocket change. But I also understood the game wasn't just about costs, it was about building revenue streams and growing an audience. Ticket sales, sponsorships, vendor fees, merchandise, every channel had to be mapped and maximized. But the real challenge? Marketing.

How do you build buzz around an all-Black rodeo when most people didn't even know Black cowboys existed? The rodeo world wasn't exactly brimming with diversity, and this kind of event was unheard of in mainstream circles.

Hence, I went all in with a visibility strategy. My belief was simple: if you want a community to embrace something new, you've got to surround them with it. Repetition matters. Let's talk numbers for a minute. Most rodeos break even at around 60% to 70% capacity. That's your threshold. But it varies, especially if you're launching in a new city versus returning to an established market. Normally, you're going to lose money if you're building a new market, I would tell folks. That's just the reality. Therefore, I built my approach around patience.

My rule, go into a market at least three times before making a call. You can't judge it off one show, people need to be educated, introduced to the culture, the sport, the history.

The first rodeo in a new city might just be planting seeds. The second one starts to sprout. And by the third, if you've done it right, you start to see the crowd come alive. This wasn't just about ticket sales. It was about shifting culture.

What I was really building was an experience, deep commitment to cultural education, a determination to showcase the talents and history of Black cowboys and cowgirls to a broader audience, a celebration of Black heritage in the West, a reclamation of our place in cowboy history. That meant being smart with numbers, but also staying true to the mission.

Because this wasn't just about bulls and broncs. It was about letting people, our people, see themselves in a spotlight that had been kept from them for far too long. And I was committed to making sure they never got left out again.

Now, if I was going to name this rodeo after Bill Pickett, I knew I couldn't just throw his name on a flyer and call it a day. That name meant something. It carried history. Legacy. Responsibility. Accordingly, I did what I knew was right, I sought permission from the Pickett family.

Bill had passed in 1932, but his descendants were still around, proud of his name, but cautious about how it was used. And they had every right to be.

The first person I reached out to was **Willie Wilson** down in Oklahoma City, one of Bill's great-great-grandsons. When I told him what I was building, he didn't hesitate. *"You've got my support,"* he said. That endorsement meant the world to me.

Next, I connected with **Frank Phillips**, another direct descendant living in Silver Spring, Maryland. Frank didn't just support it, but he helped me formalize it. He drafted the agreement that gave me exclusive rights to use the Bill Pickett name for the rodeo. That paperwork didn't just protect the brand, it protected the legacy. It gave this rodeo a foundation rooted in honor, family, and permission.

Frank and I grew close after that. He became more than a partner, he became a friend, and we stayed in touch until his passing.

Now that process, it took years. Years of conversations. Letters. Follow-ups.

But in 1983, I finally had the family's full blessing. That was the moment it became real. This wasn't just a rodeo anymore. This was the Bill Pickett Invitational Rodeo. The first and only one of its kind, carrying the name of the man who changed rodeo forever. And honoring that name, preserving that legacy, has been one of the most fulfilling parts of my entire career.

When people hear "Bill Pickett" now, they don't just think about the past. They come out to see the present. They see our cowboys and cowgirls. And they understand that we've always been here.

By 1984, after seven long years of dreaming, planning, pushing, and praying, we were finally ready to launch the very first Bill Pickett Invitational Rodeo.

The rodeo was set for September 8th and 9th, 1984 at the **Adams County Fairgrounds** in Colorado, a venue Elmer Anderson had long ago stamped with his approval. I had been working nonstop to secure sponsors, make phone calls, sign deals, doing the kind of work you don't always see from the stands. I had secured Coors Brewing Company as a sponsor and I was elated, but what I didn't know was that this rodeo, the one I had spent years bringing to life, was about to be caught in the middle of something bigger. Something far beyond the arena. Here's that story.

It starts with one woman who helped open those doors for me, **Mattie Springfield**. She was the first person in Denver to truly welcome me in, not just as a businessman, but as a brother. She introduced me to the heart of the Black community in Denver, and through her, I met **Rae Taylor**, who would become a key ally and friend in those early days.

That connection led me to **Moses Brewer**. Now Moses was selling home water purification systems at the time, and when he first came to pitch me, I brushed him off. "Man, I drink Perrier."

But something about him stuck. Maybe it was his roots in **Alabama**, just like mine. Maybe it was the fact that he believed in what I was building before he fully understood it. Whatever it was, that sales pitch turned into a friendship that's lasted decades.

Moses would later say: *"At that time, Lu was very direct in his approach, very much to the point."* And he wasn't wrong. I wasn't trying to impress anybody.
I was just trying to get this rodeo off the ground. And I wasn't going to let anyone, or anything, stop it.

Moses was the first person to really hear me say the words out loud, **"This is MY rodeo."** Not just a show. Not just a flyer. Not just another event on the calendar. Mine. Ours. A legacy in motion.

But just as we were preparing to open those gates, Denver was about to be rocked by a controversy that would test everything we had built, and forge bonds that would carry this rodeo into history.

"A few months after trying to sell him that water, I got a job at Coors. Meanwhile Lu had met Mack Davis, one of the first blacks to be in the marketing department at Coors and he headed up our special marketing. When I came to Coors, my job was as a Coors Brewing Representative. Lu and Mack Davis did a program called "Jazz on the Rocks," up at Red Rocks (an outdoor concert stadium carved out of red rock foundations up in the Rocky Mountains). The program was sponsored by Herman Josephs, one of our brands. That was one of the ways Coors was trying to make headway into the black community." - **Moses Brewer**

After Moses got settled in at Coors, things started to connect. I was already in talks with **Mack Davis**, one of the first Black men to hold a key spot in their marketing department. Mack was sharp, progressive, and he saw what I was trying to build.

Together, we put together a show called "Jazz on the Rocks" up at Red Rocks Amphitheatre, a project we believed could begin bridging the gap between corporate brands and the Black community. It was working. The momentum felt real. We were close to locking things in for the rodeo.

And then... everything changed again.

Just as we were gearing up for our biggest moment, **Bill Coors**, an executive at the company, made a comment in a public seminar that would set off a firestorm across Denver and beyond. Racially charged. Tone-deaf. And impossible to ignore.

Everything we'd built, the trust, the partnerships, the progress, was suddenly on the line.

As reported by the Rocky Mountain News: On February 23, 1984, at a seminar held by the Minority Business Development Center in Denver, Bill Coors, discussing if it was unfair that black ancestors were dragged to America in chains against their will, Bill Coors stated:..."*Your ancestors were dragged here in chains against their will...I would urge those of you who feel that way to go back to where your ancestors came from, and you will find out that probably the greatest favor that anybody ever did you was to drag your ancestors over here in chains, and I mean it.*" Mr. Coors added in the speech his position about issues in Africa. He said: "*They lack the intellectual capacity to succeed, and it's taking them down the tubes. You take a country like Rhodesia (now Zimbabwe), where the economy was absolutely booming under white management. Now, black management is in Zimbabwe, and the economy is a disaster, in spite of the fact that there is probably ten times the motivation on the part of the citizens of that country to make it succeed. Lack of intellectual capacity, that has got to be there.*"

Mr. Coors suggested that Black ancestors dragged to America "in chains" somehow owed a debt of gratitude for their forced migration. Bill Coors apologized the next day, saying that he was misquoted, but the damage had been done – they started eating his ass up. His comments ignited a firestorm, leading to a nationwide boycott of Coors products.

In the middle of all this controversy, Coors scrambled to save face, launching a community outreach campaign aimed at mending its image, and part of that effort included support of our rodeo.

But the fallout was real.

Mack Davis, the same brother who helped bring "Jazz on the Rocks" to life and had stood beside me as we built the foundation of this rodeo, resigned on principle. He wasn't going to represent a company so deeply tied to such offensive rhetoric. That's when **Ivan Burwell** stepped in. And let me tell you, Ivan was solid. His brand manager, at one point, even had the nerve to ask him if Black cowboys actually existed. Can you believe that?

But Ivan didn't flinch. He stood tall, stayed committed, and continued to back our event when others might've folded. That kind of loyalty? That kind of courage? I never forgot it.

Moses reminisces, *"Things exploded within Coors. Having one of Coors leaders saying some disparaging remarks about Africa and African Americans, it caused a hullabaloo. Being an African American with the organization, I was on the forefront as Coors tried to overcome Bill's remarks. I attended lots of meetings with the community. Coors ended up having outreach programs. Through these programs, I was provided the opportunity to work with Lu's on his rodeo."* Coors supported the rodeo through sponsorships. This led to the creation of the "Coors Heritage Series" calendar. The calendar depicted those individuals that made significant contributions that were from the West. We profiled Bill Pickett, Aunt Clara Brown, Jim Beckwourth, William Alexander Leidesdorff, and several other cowboys and black Western figures.

The Bill Pickett Invitational Rodeo debuted in September instead of August to an enthusiastic crowd of about 2,500 at the Adams County Fairgrounds, featuring numerous Black cowboys and cowgirls.

Carolyn Carter, a Cowgirl, One of 3 Barrel Racing Sisters expressed her delight, *"Lu had thrown a party for the cowboys and cowgirls after the rodeo. Up to that point, there had not been any black organization that had organized a rodeo. We were like, "Yeah, somebody's finally thinking about the Black Cowboys and Cowgirls." Now he's giving us a party and introducing us to all of the sponsors. It was great, I said, "Wow! This is different!"*

After pulling off the first Black rodeo in Denver, **Ivan Burwell** came to me with an idea. "*Lu, let's take this thing to Washington, D.C.*" At first, I was hesitant. The concept of a traveling rodeo, especially one focused on Black cowboys, was ambitious. Sure, there were long-standing Black rodeos in places like Boley and Okmulgee, Oklahoma, but those events were local traditions. They didn't move. They didn't tour. What we were building? It was different. It was national.

Everybody loved the idea, from the fans to the cowboys and cowgirls themselves. Still, I wasn't sure if expanding was the right move, especially with the Coors controversy still simmering. So, I reached out to a trusted mentor in Denver, someone with ties to Belva Davis and a good read on business and politics. I laid it out for him: Man, what do you think? You think I should take that money?" He didn't hesitate. "*Yeah,*" he told me. "*Make 'em pay double. But don't hurt yourself.*"

With that, we pulled the trigger on D.C., and man, it landed. The energy, the crowd, the response, the show hit different. You could feel it in the crowd, in the applause, in the way people walked out standing taller. Unmatched. That's when it hit me, we weren't just entertaining. We were educating, honoring, reclaiming a part of history that deserved the spotlight. We weren't just producing rodeos. We were telling stories. We were reclaiming legacy.

Riding that momentum, Coors suggested another market: Jackson, Mississippi. That recommendation wasn't random. Coors had close ties to **Charles Evers**, the brother of civil rights icon **Medgar Evers**. Charles was a well-connected political figure in his own right, a Republican with serious influence. He had a direct line to power, literally, with a red phone on his desk. At the time, he was organizing a music festival with **The O'Jays**, and he made it clear: "We need a rodeo, too."

So off we went to Mississippi, and just like D.C., it was another major success. City by city, we kept building. Now, my rodeo became the first nationally touring Black rodeo in U.S. history.

At every stop, we didn't just entertain, we educated. We told the stories of historical Black figures of the West. We honored the unsung heroes, the original cowboys whose names had been left out of the textbooks.

Coors stayed involved, too, not just for the visibility, but as part of a broader commitment to repair the damage left behind by Bill Coors' remarks.

That commitment included a $325 million investment in Black communities, a deal that came out of a historic agreement with Jesse Jackson Sr., Operation PUSH, and the NAACP. For me, it wasn't just about the money. It was about having the resources to push this movement forward, expand the mission, and bring the legacy of Black cowboys to every corner of the country. And that's exactly what we did.

The rodeo's success and Coors' backing helped establish it as the first national touring Black rodeo. **Corey Vason**, reflecting on the impact, noted, *"I remember Dad's first show in Denver and his first rodeo in the Oakland, California area. It was something to see. The fans were really excited because they had never seen anything like this. I think it was highly significant in bringing that culture to all Black people, not just those in the South." For Dad to see this – to have this vision, to promote it throughout the country for people of color – it was highly significant. Being established especially for Black cowboys, it became another sport where a Black man could aspire to do well in, outside football, basketball, and baseball. It was significant in that not a lot of black people knew about it, at least in the West Coast. Plus, the fact that he has done it for over 30 years now is so remarkable."*

The partnership with Coors elevated the rodeo to new heights, opening doors to major cities like Washington D.C. and Jackson, Mississippi, expanding both its reach and its cultural impact.

At every stop, we honored historical Black pioneers of the West, turning each rodeo into more than just a show, it became a celebration and a history lesson rolled into one.

For the Washington D.C. event, we added star power to the lineup. Coors brought in big names, including **Anthony Elmore**, a world champion kickboxer; **Cheryl Glass**, the first Black female race car driver and a national sprint car champion; and the smooth vocals of **Jeffrey Osborne**, whose performance of the national anthem at a Lakers game had made him a household name. But we did hit a snag.

When I asked Jeffrey to sing the Black National Anthem, he told me, flat out, he didn't know it. I was stunned. I pulled Moses aside and said, "If he can't sing the Black National Anthem, I don't need him here." The room went quiet. Folks couldn't believe it. After all, **Jeffrey Osborne** was the reason Coors had signed him on. He brought prestige, visibility, and yet, he didn't know the anthem that meant something to us.

That's when my assistant, **Jeannie Potts**, stepped in like a champ. She scribbled the lyrics to "Lift Every Voice and Sing" right onto Jeffrey's hand. And when it came time to perform, he stood tall, opened his mouth, and sang it, reading straight from his palm.

That moment sparked an idea. I decided to introduce reenactments into the rodeo program. Live portrayals of real Black historical figures from the Old West. What started as a simple addition evolved into something far bigger. An immersive educational experience that connected our audience to a past they were never taught in school.

Happy Haynes, a former Denver City Councilwoman, remarked, *"When you went to the rodeo, Lu would bring history to life through the characters, Clara Brown, Nat Love, Bill Pickett, and more. He didn't go as far as having someone bite a steer's lip like Bill Pickett did, but he always made sure the story was told. Lu used his entertainment background brilliantly, he knew how to blend showmanship with education. His rodeos weren't just events; they were experiences where you learned something without even realizing you'd just sat through one of 'Professor Lu's' lessons on the history of the West."*

I'll admit, after a while, I got tired of producing those segments. But the audience, they never did. They craved it. They came back for it. They brought their kids and their cousins. They wanted to know more. They wanted the truth. And we gave it to them.

What started as a spark of curiosity turned into something far bigger than I ever imagined. This wasn't just about bulls, broncs, or boots on dirt, it was about reclaiming space, rewriting narratives, and giving our people a front-row seat to a history they've always been a part of.

Each city we visited, every hand we shook, and every crowd that rose to its feet reminded me that we weren't just building a show, we were building something that mattered.

We turned stories into showcases. We turned rodeo grounds into classrooms. And we turned disbelief into pride.

This wasn't just about me. It was about us. And the journey was only just beginning.

Chapter 11: FOLKLORE OF THE WEST IN BLACK

"Lu is the Visionary Cowboy; that's how he should be remembered. Because, he always looked forward by always connecting us to our past." - Landri Taylor

When I set out to create a Black rodeo, one of the very first places I visited was the Black American West Museum, right in the heart of Denver's Five Points neighborhood. Tucked inside the historic Justina Ford house on 31st and California, that place wasn't just a museum, it was a time machine.

It was built by a man with a mission, **Paul Stewart**, who spent his life preserving the stories America tried to forget.

See, I was raised on the myth most of us were: that Black folks didn't exist in the Old West. That we weren't riding, roping, or building anything out here.

Paul blew that lie wide open. In his museum, I didn't just see artifacts. I saw lives, Black sheriffs, settlers, ranchers, stagecoach drivers, and yes, cowboys. Real people who had shaped the frontier just like anybody else. And it didn't take long for me to fall head over boots in love with it all.

These stories aren't just history," I'd say with a grin. They're inspiration. They're alive. And they deserve to be shouted from the rooftops, or better yet, from the middle of a rodeo arena!

So saddle up. Because this chapter? This one's a classroom in boots and spurs.

Let's start with a woman whose strength rivals any cowboy who ever mounted a bronc, **Clara Brown**. Now, she wasn't in the arena lassoing steers or breaking wild colts, but make no mistake, Clara Brown was a pioneer in every sense of the word.

Born into slavery in 1800 in Virginia, her life began in chains and heartbreak.

She was sold off at auction, separated from her husband and children, and forced to endure the unimaginable. But when freedom finally found her, Clara didn't just survive, she soared. She packed up and headed west, right into the heart of the Colorado Gold Rush. And that's where her legend really begins…

Around 1859, she ventured west and settled in Central City, Colorado. There, Clara didn't just survive; she thrived. She started a laundry business, leveraging her skills as a midwife, cook, and nurse to cement her place in the community.

They called her the "Angel of the Rockies," not just for her businesses, but for her immense heart. With the wealth she accumulated, Clara poured it back into the community, aiding in the construction of churches and schools, and helping other African Americans settle and find work in the area.

Imagine the guts and grit of that woman, I would tell anyone who'd listen at the rodeo. Clara Brown wasn't just living in the West; she was building it, making sure it was a place where others could find a new start, just like she did.

Her legacy was deep, marking her as the first African American woman to join the Colorado Pioneers' Association and earning her a rightful place in the Colorado Women's Hall of Fame. In her story, we see not just resilience, but a boundless generosity that helped shape the Western frontier.

Hearing stories like Clara Brown's lit something in me. I knew I couldn't keep these histories locked up in a museum or hidden in dusty archives.

They needed sunlight. They needed applause. They needed to ride right into the spotlight, just like our cowboys do.

I fell in love with these stories, I've said more times than I can count. And I couldn't wait to share them with the world, from center stage, inside a rodeo arena.

Consequently, when I created the Bill Pickett Invitational Rodeo, it wasn't just about bulls and broncs, it was about building a living museum on horseback. It was about honoring the Black men and women who helped shape the West but were written out of the script. These weren't side characters. They were central. Every reenactment. Every name we called out. Every piece of history we brought forward, was our way of taking back the narrative, of giving credit where it had always been due.

This rodeo became more than a cultural event. It became a movement. A reclamation. A celebration of truth wrapped in tradition. And the stories didn't stop with Clara.

Next up? Let me introduce you to a man whose life was so full of adventure, it reads like a dime-store Western novel, but every word of it's true: **James "Jim" Beckwourth**.

Born into slavery in Virginia in 1798, Beckwourth was the son of a white plantation owner and an African American slave woman. His father eventually emancipated him, setting the stage for an extraordinary life of adventure and exploration.

Beckwourth moved westward during his youth, where his daring spirit led him to become a renowned mountain man, fur trapper, and explorer. His intimate association with several Native American tribes, especially the Crow Nation with whom he lived and rose to the status of a chief, marked a significant chapter in his life. Known for his heroism in battle, Beckwourth was embraced by the Crow and earned the nickname "Bloody Arm."

Perhaps one of his most enduring legacies is the discovery of the Beckwourth Pass through the Sierra Nevada during the California Gold Rush.

This pass became an important route for settlers moving west, alleviating some of the dangers of more treacherous paths and solidifying his place in the records of Western expansion.

In 1856, his adventures were chronicled in "The Life and Adventures of James P. Beckwourth," penned by T.D. Bonner. While some aspects of Beckwourth's life as recounted in his autobiography are debated for their embellishment, the book remains a key account of his extraordinary exploits and his unique perspective on frontier life.

Beckwourth's final years were spent continuing his work as a scout and rancher until his mysterious death in 1866 at a Crow village. His legacy, however, remains strong. The town of Beckwourth, California, the Beckwourth Trail, and numerous historical markers continue to honor his contributions. His story is not just one of adventure but also a testament to the complex interactions and mutual respect between African Americans and Native American tribes during a formative period in American history.

And just when you think the West couldn't possibly hold another hidden giant, along comes William Leidesdorff, a man whose influence helped lay the financial foundation for what would eventually become the state of California.

William Leidesdorff, born in 1810 in St. Croix, Danish West Indies to a Danish sugar planter and an African mother, became one of the most influential and wealthy businessmen in pre-gold rush California. After working as a merchant ship captain in New Orleans, he arrived in San Francisco (then called Yerba Buena) in 1841, becoming one of the first African American settlers in California under Mexican rule.

Leidesdorff quickly established himself as a prominent businessman, building San Francisco's first hotel, its first commercial shipping warehouse, and launching the first steamboat to operate on San Francisco Bay and the Sacramento River.

He became a Mexican citizen in 1844 and received a massive 35,000-acre land grant along the American River. As a member of the San Francisco city council and city treasurer, he helped establish the first public school in California.

His business empire expanded to include real estate, shipping, and agriculture. He served as U.S. Vice Consul to Mexico in the region, making him the first African American diplomat. Leidesdorff's land grant proved enormously valuable when gold was discovered on his property in 1848. However, he never saw the full fruits of this discovery, dying suddenly in May 1848 at age 38, just months before the California Gold Rush began. When his estate was settled in 1856, it was valued at over $1.5 million (equivalent to tens of millions today).

Leidesdorff's legacy as a pioneering Black businessman and diplomat in pre-statehood California represents a unique chapter in African American history. Despite his mixed-race heritage being known, he successfully navigated the complex racial and political landscape of Mexican California, becoming one of the most powerful men in early San Francisco.

Today, Leidesdorff Street in San Francisco's Financial District bears his name, commemorating his significant contributions to the city's development.

From the gold-rushed streets of early California to the unforgiving business landscape of the Colorado frontier, we now meet **Barney Lancelot Ford**, a man who didn't just survive slavery, he built a legacy of leadership, entrepreneurship, and civil rights that still echoes through the Rockies today.

His journey expresses everything we honor in this rodeo: grit, vision, and the power to turn hardship into history.

Born into slavery in Virginia in 1822, Ford's early life on a South Carolina plantation was marked by secret lessons in reading and writing, skills that would later underpin his pursuits for freedom and equality.

At the age of 17, seizing his destiny, Ford escaped to freedom via the Underground Railroad, eventually settling in Chicago. There, his commitment to the abolitionist cause grew as he aided other fugitive slaves.

The 1860's Gold Rush drew Ford to Colorado, where he transitioned from seeking gold to establishing a legacy of business success and civil advocacy. In Denver and beyond, he opened a series of businesses, including barbershops, restaurants, and notably, the Inter-Ocean Hotel in 1873, one of the finest in the region at the time. His entrepreneurial spirit was matched by his resolve to fight for civil rights, playing a pivotal role in pushing for Colorado's statehood that included suffrage for all its citizens.

Despite the societal barriers of his time, Ford became known as the "Black Baron of Colorado," not only for his business acumen but also for his relentless advocacy for the African American community.

His efforts were instrumental in defeating the initial statehood bid that would have denied voting rights to Black citizens. Ford's life and work underscored a dual commitment to economic independence and equal rights, earning him a place as one of Colorado's first Black millionaires and a lasting respect in the community.

While Barney Ford carved his legacy in the heart of Denver's business and political scene, **Isaiah Dorman's** chapter unfolded on the rugged battlefields of the Great Plains. His name may not appear in textbooks, but his sacrifice is etched into one of the most infamous confrontations in American military history, the Battle of Little Bighorn.

Born in 1832 in Pennsylvania, Dorman was of both African and Native American descent. A rare identity that gave him not only a cultural bridge between two worlds, but the ability to serve as a skilled interpreter for the U.S. Army during the Indian Wars. It was that unique skill set that placed him under General George Custer's command during one of the most disastrous defeats in U.S. history.

Dorman was the only Black man known to fight and die in that battle, a sobering reminder that the reach of African American contributions stretched far deeper into the Western frontier than most people realize.

His story is a complex one, marked by duty, divided loyalties, and deep courage. And like so many others, it deserves more than a footnote. It deserves a seat at the table, and a place in the arena.

In his personal life, Dorman's marriage to a Hunkpapa Lakota woman further cemented his ties to the Native American people, highlighting his deep integration into the community he served. Isaiah Dorman's story is not just one of personal bravery but also of the broader narrative of African American and Native American relations in the West. It reminds us of the diverse and intricate histories that shaped this loud period in American history.

After learning about lives like Isaiah Dorman's, I'm always left reflecting on the incredible resilience it took just to survive, let alone to lead, to serve, or to stand out in a world that tried to erase them. Each of these pioneers rewrote the narrative by simply living boldly, pushing back against the boundaries history tried to set for them. Their courage wasn't always loud, but it echoed, and it left a mark.

Now let's talk about a woman whose grit could rival any gunslinger's and whose legacy still rides strong in Western stories. **Mary Fields,** better known as **Stagecoach Mary,** was born into slavery in Tennessee around 1832, and went on to become a legend in the wild terrain of Montana.

After gaining her freedom following the Civil War, Mary ventured West, where she broke ground in ways few could have imagined. In Cascade, Montana, she became the first African American woman and only the second woman in the U.S. to serve as a mail carrier for the United States Postal Service.

Mary's role was not just a job; it was a testament to her indomitable spirit. She managed a star route, delivering mail across the harsh terrain of Montana by stagecoach, armed with both a rifle and a revolver to protect her charges from the dangers that lurked on these remote passages.

Stagecoach Mary was known for her tough exterior, necessary for the challenges she faced, but those who knew her also saw her generous heart. She was beloved in her community for her kindness, offering help where it was needed, often blurring the lines of her rugged persona with acts of profound generosity.

Mary Fields, born into slavery around 1832 in Tennessee, became a legendary figure in the American West known for her fierce independence and unbeatable spirit. After being freed following the Civil War, she worked for a convent in Toledo, Ohio before moving to Montana Territory in 1885 to help establish St. Peter's Mission near Cascade. Despite her short temper and unorthodox behavior, including carrying a pistol and drinking in saloons, the nuns appreciated her hard work and dedication.

In 1895, at the age of 63, Fields secured a contract with the U.S. Postal Service to become the second woman and first African American woman to work as a "Star Route" mail carrier. She earned her nickname "Stagecoach Mary" for her unfailing reliability in delivering mail regardless of weather conditions, using a stagecoach or wagon in summer and snowshoes or skis in winter.

She never missed a day of work and was known for her strength. She could knock out any man out with one punch and handle horses as well as any male driver.

The people of Cascade held Fields in such high regard that she was the only woman allowed to drink in the local saloons, and the town even closed its schools to celebrate her birthday. Beyond her mail carrier duties, she ran a successful laundry business and was known for her kindness to children, often giving them candies and flowers from her garden.

When she wasn't working, she could often be found smoking her characteristic black cigars and wearing men's clothes for practicality.

Mary Fields continued working well into her seventies, retiring from mail delivery but remaining active in the community until her death in 1914. She was buried in Cascade, Montana, and her funeral was one of the largest the town had ever seen. Her legacy as a pioneering Black woman who defied racial and gender conventions of her time continues to inspire, and she represents the often-overlooked diversity of the American frontier experience.

Where Mary Fields defied expectations with grit and a loaded shotgun, **Bose Ikard** made his mark in quieter, but no less heroic ways. A trusted trail driver and the real-life inspiration behind characters in Western novels, Ikard rode alongside legends and proved that loyalty, skill, and integrity had no color.

Let me tell you about the man who helped shape the frontier from the back of a horse and earned the respect of every cowboy who rode with him.

Bose Ikard was born into slavery in Mississippi in 1843 and raised in Texas, where he later became one of the most trusted trail drivers for the legendary cattle rancher Charles Goodnight. After emancipation, Bose learned the fine art of cattle handling and horsemanship, skills that would not only define his career but carve his place in Western history. His reputation for absolute honesty and his natural way with cattle made him indispensable on those dangerous cattle drives of the 1860s and 1870s.

His most important role came through his work on the Goodnight-Loving Trail, where he served as a scout, tracker, and Charles Goodnight's right-hand man. Bose wasn't just a hired hand, Goodnight trusted him with money, business dealings, and his life. At a time when trust between Black and white men was rare, especially in the wake of the Civil War, Goodnight once said he "trusted Bose farther than any living man."

Beyond his strength with cattle, Ikard had the instincts of a master tracker and deep knowledge of Native American lands and customs.

He helped guide herds from Texas to New Mexico and Colorado, surviving attacks, outlaws, and rough terrain. His skill helped lay the foundation for routes that would become legendary in cowboy lore.

Later in life, Bose settled in Weatherford, Texas, and died in 1929. Goodnight paid for his gravestone, calling him a loyal friend and a brave man. He even inspired a character in *Lonesome Dove*.

Now, if Bose was the quiet, steady hand of the West, Isom Dart was the shadow riding just outside the law. Let me tell you about a man whose story reads like a Western novel with the pages still smoking.

Isom Dart, born Ned Huddleston in Arkansas in 1849, transformed from an enslaved person into a skilled horseman and rancher in the American West. After emancipation, he worked as a ranch hand in Texas, where he developed exceptional skills in horse breaking and cattle handling. He changed his name to Isom Dart after allegedly being involved in cattle rustling operations along the Texas-Mexico border.

Moving to Brown's Hole (now Brown's Park) in northwestern Colorado in the 1870s, Dart established himself as a respected rancher and horse trainer. Despite his past, he built a legitimate ranching operation and was known for his extraordinary abilities with horses.

He gained particular recognition for his skill in capturing and training wild horses, a highly valued talent in the frontier West.

Dart's life became entangled in the brutal range wars of the 1890s. Though he had reformed from his earlier days of rustling, his past made him a target during the unstable conflicts between cattle barons and smaller ranchers.

The tension peaked when notorious range detective Tom Horn was reportedly hired by large cattle companies to eliminate suspected rustlers in the region.

On October 3, 1900, Dart was killed near his cabin in Brown's Hole, allegedly shot by Tom Horn while tending to his horses. His death marked the end of an era in the Brown's Hole region and exemplified the violent transitions occurring in the American West as open range culture clashed with emerging corporate ranching interests. Despite the controversial aspects of his life, Dart's story represents the complex reality of African American cowboys in the post-Civil War West, where skill and ability could sometimes transcend racial barriers, even as danger and prejudice remained constant threats.

While Isom Dart's life rode the line between outlaw and legend, **Nat Love** brought his own brand of boldness to the West. A sharp shooter, a fearless rider, and a storyteller who made sure his legacy wouldn't be forgotten. Let me introduce you to the man folks called **"Deadwood Dick."**

Nat Love, was not just another cowboy; he was a legend whose life story was as dramatic and vibrant as the Wild West itself. Born into slavery in June 1854 in Davidson County, Tennessee, Nat's early life on Robert Love's plantation was steeped in adversity. Yet, under the guidance of his father, he learned to read and write, a rare and invaluable skill that would serve him well beyond the confines of the plantation.

After emancipation, life opened up for Nat. It was like the world just unfolded before him," I'd say when sharing his story. Freed by the Civil War's conclusion in 1865, Nat's innate resilience and quest for adventure led him west to the very heart of cowboy country. With $50 in his pocket and a determination as vast as the plains, he ventured into Dodge City, Kansas, where fate had it that he'd meet the crew of the Texas Duval Ranch.

Here's where Nat's legend truly begins. Tasked with breaking a horse known as Good Eye, infamous for its wild spirit. Nat's success not only secured him a job but marked the start of his reputation as a formidable cowboy. "Riding 'Good Eye' was the toughest ride I ever had...but I rode him," Nat wrote in his autobiography. This victory was a turning point, and soon he was known for his unmatched skills in roping, shooting, and riding.

His adventures took him through numerous cattle drives across the rugged terrain of the Old West, where he not only honed his skills but also became a respected leader among cowboys.

In 1876, the same year he adopted the moniker "Deadwood Dick," Nat participated in a Fourth of July cowboy contest in Deadwood, Dakota Territory. Competing in events like roping, saddling, and shooting, Nat showcased his exceptional prowess and walked away with the $200 prize, forever cementing his nickname and legendary status.

Nat Love was a man of deep complexity. Fluent in Spanish and respected as a cattle buyer and brand reader, he navigated diverse cultures and challenges with ease. "Nat was more than just a cowboy; he was a symbol of what you could become no matter where you started from," I often reflect. His later years as a Pullman porter allowed him to travel and share his tales, inspiring countless others. In 1907, he published his autobiography, "*Life and Adventures of Nat Love*," offering a firsthand account of his extraordinary experiences.

> **"Mounted on my favorite horse, my...lariat near my hand, and my trusty guns in my belt...I felt I could defy the world."-**
> **Nat Love, 1907**

As I explored deeper into the rich history of Black cowboys, those around me began to notice a shift not just in my focus but also in my style. Gone were the days of tailored suits and polished shoes from my modeling era. I was now wearing jeans, cowboy boots, and my signature piece: a "man bag" shaped like saddlebags straddled over my right shoulder. For those who knew me, this transformation was striking.

I had always prided myself on being a sharp dresser, a nod to my days on the runway, but this was no mere fashion statement. This change was my way of stepping into the role of marketing my burgeoning passion for the rodeo.

Some folks took me more seriously with this new look, while others, less familiar with my background, simply saw me as an urban guy playing "Cowboy", and sure, the actual cowboys and cowgirls got a good chuckle out of it. But for me, it was more than just adopting a new fashion. It was a strategic move to cement my commitment to bringing the history and culture of Black cowboys to the forefront through my rodeo vision. The snickers and sideways glances didn't bother me. If anything, they fueled my resolve even more.

In embracing this style, I was embodying the urban Black cowboy. Though I had never lived the cowboy life firsthand, my knowledge coming from books, films, and rodeos I'd attended, I had always admired the cool, rugged appeal of cowboy culture. My new style captured the essence of what it meant to be a cowboy and represented everything I believed an authentic Western design should be, especially one that honored the legacy of Black cowboys in America.

Over time, this look became synonymous with me, complementing what was quickly becoming the most important endeavor of my career. I was no longer just Lu the fashion-forward entrepreneur; I was Lu the urban cowboy, spearheading a movement to celebrate the unsung heroes of the American West through the Bill Pickett Invitational Rodeo. This wasn't just a change of clothes; it was a transformation of identity, one that intertwined my personal legacy with the cultural heritage I was so passionate about preserving and promoting.

Now, speaking of trailblazers, let me tell you about a woman who didn't just ride with the best of them…she trained wild horses, spoke multiple languages, and ranched like she was born in the saddle. Her name was Johanna July.

Johanna July was a remarkable Black Seminole woman who gained fame as a skilled horse trainer and wrangler along the Texas-Mexico border. Born in 1860 near Brackettville, Texas, she learned horsemanship from her mother and became known for her unique method of breaking wild mustangs by swimming them in the Rio Grande River, exhausting the horses while protecting herself from injury.

As a member of the Black Seminole community (descendants of escaped slaves who lived among the Seminole tribe), July straddled multiple cultural worlds. She spoke Spanish, English, and Seminole, working as both a wrangler and occasional guide. Her expertise in horse breaking was so renowned that wealthy ranchers specifically sought her services to tame their most difficult horses.

July's horse-breaking technique was distinctive: she would drive wild horses into deep water where they had to swim, making them more manageable while reducing the risk of being thrown or kicked. This method demonstrated both her innovation and deep understanding of horse behavior. She typically worked along the Rio Grande between Eagle Pass and Del Rio, Texas.

Her life story was documented by the Federal Writers' Project in the 1930s, preserving a rare first-hand account of a Black female horse trainer from the frontier era. Through her marriage to a Seminole scout working for the U.S. Army at Fort Clark, her story provides insight into the complex relationships between Black Seminoles, the U.S. military, and frontier life. Her legacy represents the often-overlooked contributions of Black women to frontier ranching culture.

Johanna July's story proves that the frontier didn't belong to men alone. She held her own with grit, grace, and grit again. But if you're looking for someone whose life reads like a lawman's legend, look no further than **Bass Reeves**.

Deputy U.S. Marshal. Sharp shooter. Tracker. And one of the baddest men to ever wear a badge in the American West, Black, bold, and absolutely fearless.

Let me introduce you to the real-life figure who likely inspired the Lone Ranger himself.

Bass Reeves was one of the most legendary lawmen of the American frontier, serving as the first Black deputy U.S. marshal west of the Mississippi River.

Born into slavery in Arkansas in 1838, he escaped to Indian Territory (now Oklahoma) during the Civil War and lived among Native American tribes, learning their languages and tracking skills that would later prove invaluable in his law enforcement career.

In 1875, Judge Isaac C. Parker appointed Reeves as a deputy U.S. marshal, launching a remarkable 32-year career in which he arrested over 3,000 criminals and killed 14 outlaws in self-defense. Standing 6'2" and known for his exceptional marksmanship and detective skills, Reeves often worked in disguise to catch criminals, displaying both cunning and unwavering integrity. He was known to never kill an outlaw unless absolutely necessary and could reportedly read the warrants to arrested suspects from memory, despite being illiterate.

Reeves's most challenging case came when he had to arrest his own son for murder, demonstrating his uncompromising commitment to justice.

He patrolled 75,000 square miles of territory, including the notoriously lawless Indian Territory, bringing order to a region where many other lawmen feared to venture. His territory included present-day Arkansas and Oklahoma, and he became known for his fair treatment of both Native Americans and settlers.

After Oklahoma achieved statehood in 1907, Reeves joined the Muskogee Police Department, serving until his death in 1910. His legacy as a frontier lawman has inspired numerous books, documentaries, and is believed by many historians to have been an inspiration for the character of the Lone Ranger.

Recent years have seen growing recognition of his contributions, including a bronze statue in Fort Smith, Arkansas, and his induction into the Texas Trail of Fame. Some historians argue that Reeves was not only one of the greatest frontier lawmen but also one of the most significant law enforcement officers in American history.

The untold stories of African American cowboys and cowgirls represent a rich tapestry of courage, resilience, and pioneering spirit that helped shape the American West. From Bass Reeves' unwavering commitment to justice, to Mary Fields' indomitable determination delivering mail, to William Leidesdorff's entrepreneurial legacy in early California, to Isom Dart's expertise with wild horses, to Bose Ikard's trusted partnership with Charles Goodnight, and Johanna July's innovative horse-breaking techniques - these remarkable individuals defied racial barriers and left an indelible mark on frontier history.

Now ladies and gentlemen, hold onto your hats because I'm about to introduce you to a man who didn't just ride into rodeo history - he revolutionized it with nothing but his bare teeth and raw courage! Meet my personal hero, the legendary **Bill Pickett,** the most fearless cowboy to ever set foot in an arena.

Picture this: It's the early 1900s, and a crowd watches in awe as a daring Black cowboy chases down a wild steer at full gallop. In a move that would make modern daredevils think twice, he leaps from his horse like a panther, grabs the steer by the horns, and - here's the kicker - clamps down on the animal's upper lip with his teeth! This wasn't just showmanship; this was Bill Pickett inventing "bulldogging," a technique that would transform rodeo forever.

Ladies and gentlemen, saddle up for the most electrifying story in rodeo history - the legendary Bill Pickett! Let me take you back to Texas, 1870, where a young man born to former slaves would revolutionize the sport of rodeo forever and blaze a trail for generations to come.

Picture this: 5'7", 145-pound dynamo who looked at how cattle dogs controlled bulls and thought, "Now that's interesting!" While other cowboys played it safe, Pickett created the most daring technique ever seen in the arena - "bulldogging."

This wasn't your ordinary steer wrestling. No sir! Pickett would leap from his galloping horse at full speed, grab a thousand-pound steer by the horns, and - hold onto your hats, folks - clamp down on the animal's upper lip with his teeth!

This death-defying move earned him the nicknames "The Dusky Demon" and "Bull-Dogging King."

Starting at small county fairs, Pickett's fame exploded when he joined the Miller Brothers' 101 Ranch Wild West Show in 1905. Imagine the audacity - a Black cowboy in the segregated era, performing alongside legends like Buffalo Bill Cody and Will Rogers! He took his show international, dazzling crowds from England to South America. When Hollywood came calling, Pickett became one of the first Black cowboys to star in motion pictures, featuring in "The Bull-Dogger" and "The Crimson Skull."

But this wasn't just showmanship - this was a revolution. Despite having to sometimes perform as a "Mexican" or "Indian" due to racial segregation, Pickett's influence was unstoppable. His bulldogging technique evolved into modern steer wrestling, now a standard event in every major rodeo competition. Through sheer grit and determination, he rode through barriers of racism to become the first African American inducted into the National Rodeo Hall of Fame in 1971.

Tragically, Pickett's story ended in 1932 after a fatal kick from a horse at the 101 Ranch. But his legacy? That's still bucking strong! The Bill Pickett Invitational Rodeo, founded in 1984, continues to celebrate Black cowboys and cowgirls, ensuring his pioneering spirit lives on in every arena.

This, my friends, is why Bill Pickett isn't just another cowboy story - he's a testament to the power of innovation, courage, and determination. He didn't just ride in the rodeo; he transformed it, creating a legacy that continues to inspire cowboys and cowgirls of all backgrounds to this very day.

When we talk about legends of the American West, remember the man who dared to do what had never been done before - the one, the only, Bill Pickett!

And with that ladies and gentlemen, I'd like to "Welcome you to the Bill Pickett Invitational Rodeo."

Chapter 12: BILL PICKETT RODEO: IN FULL STRIDE

"There were cowboys who said: 'He's trying to do a tour? That won't last a year.' I still think about those same people. I don't have to say I told you so, they see it., I don't ever have to mention it. There are many of my cowboys and cowgirls walking around with 30-year jackets, buckles and stuff. It hits them right in their face. BAM!! - Lu Vason

Over the years, the Bill Pickett Invitational Rodeo has thundered across 32 cities in 12 states, holding the title as the only national touring Black rodeo in the country. From that very first show in Denver in 1984, we knew we had something special. The crowds were electric, the energy was real, and our early partner, Coors, stood firmly behind us.

That momentum carried us quickly to new cities. Washington D.C. and Jackson, Mississippi were standout stops, packed houses, enthusiastic sponsors, and communities that showed up hungry for a celebration of Black cowboy culture they could finally call their own.

After seeing what we could build, I went to **Ivan Burwell**, my key man at Coors, and laid out the vision. A multi-city rodeo series that could take this movement even further. Ivan didn't blink. He green-lit the expansion, and just like that, we were headed into major markets like Atlanta, Houston, and Oakland.

But not every city welcomed us with open arms.

When we rolled into Oakland, a local riding club leader tried to muscle in and take over, wanting to control the brand we had worked so hard to build. I stood my ground. **"This is MY rodeo,"** I told him, plain and simple. We skipped Oakland that year. But we didn't miss a beat. Instead, we pushed forward on to Los Angeles, keeping the tour alive, the mission intact, and the spirit of the Bill Pickett Rodeo in full stride.

1985 saw us back in Atlanta, and by 1986, we were lassoing stars in Los Angeles. Hollywood turned out in full force, led by Glynn Turman and his road buddy, actor-director Reginald T. Dorsey, who became such fixtures that we dubbed them our rodeo spokesmen. By 1987, we circled back to Oakland, this time bringing in big names like Woody Strode, the actor and former UCLA football standout, proving that our rodeo, despite the hurdles, was a force to be reckoned with in the arena and beyond.

"I had done some motion pictures where I played a cowboy and Lu knew this about me. Also, in the quest of trying to fulfill my dream at that time, I owned some Arabian horses. Lu had a deal where he would call on celebrities to ride in the Grand Parade. I had a chance to ride in the parade to the cheers of thousands of people who had turned out for the rodeo."

"That was my introduction to the Bill Pickett Invitational Rodeo and to Lu Vason. In further talking and getting to know Lu over the years, I understood what it took and the sacrifices he had made to make this happen, to how important he felt it was to get this knowledge across the country as a salute to the Black Cowboys and Cowgirls of Color."

"Lu was on a mission. Although never losing that smile, he was on a very serious mission to make this a nationally known event and had asked me to help make this event recognized. That was an undertaking that I truly appreciated."- **Glynn Turman**

During this vibrant chapter, **Liz Young** galloped into the scene as our first Atlanta coordinator. Liz was a linchpin in the community, her rolodex brimming with contacts at companies keen on tapping into cultural events. These were the decision-makers eager to sponsor events that resonated culturally and boosted their product sales.

Inspired by this new energy, we started attending other rodeos, soaking up a myriad of fresh ideas. I remember countless brainstorming sessions at **Judy Barnes'** kitchen table, where creativity flowed as freely as coffee.

We envisioned an arena rimmed with vendors, the air sweet with the aroma of freshly baked pies and cakes. We dreamed up a variety of contests that would not only entertain but also deeply engage our audience in the festive spirit of the rodeo.

"When Lu initiated the rodeo, he was green about the specifics of rodeo management. He was versed in event promotion but lacked rodeo-specific knowledge. Thus, he collaborated with experts from the rodeo world, who, conversely, were unfamiliar with the nuances of promotion. Yet, Lu's passion for African American culture and his dedication to community support were unwavering."

"Lu was determined to elevate the Black Cowboy and Cowgirl, recognizing them as true athletes. He strived to equip them with the same accolades as PRCA rodeos, offering trucks, belt buckles, and saddles."

"Lu's aim was for Black cowboys and cowgirls to feel valued for their contributions to the community. He had the good fortune to connect with notable figures like Charlie Sampson, the first Black world champion bull rider, and Fred Whitfield, who started at the Bill Pickett Rodeo before becoming a World Champion in the PRCA. There was also Lee Akin, who, unfortunately, was injured years back in Mesquite. Lu has consistently worked not just to promote the Black community but to foster a sense of family among them." - **Reneee Penick, Lu's Secretary**

As the rodeo ventured into new cities, I enlisted local coordinators to manage each event. In Los Angeles, Lynn Dillard led the charge with her assistants, **Margo Wade and June Dennis**.

After years of dedication, Lynn transitioned to television, producing shows like "Comic View" on BET. Margo and June initially took the helm together, but when June left to get married, Margo stepped up as the sole coordinator. She has been doing a stellar job ever since.

In Beaumont, Texas, my first two coordinators struggled to meet expectations. That's when **Acynthia Villery**, a rodeo enthusiast, came into the picture. She quickly rose from a local coordinator to becoming the rodeo secretary, proving herself an invaluable addition to our team.

"I hail from a long line of rodeo enthusiasts. My grandfather, alongside my uncle, founded one of the earliest Black rodeo associations in southeast Texas and Louisiana. Rodeos are in my blood; I was practically raised at them. My family was deeply involved, handling everything from concessions to event coordination."

"My uncle was a rodeo coordinator, and I often say I grew up in rodeos from the time I was in my mother's womb. I'm well-versed in what we call 'backyard rodeos,' where events are held in someone's personal arena. Interestingly, my daughter's father owned one such arena in Cheek, Texas, near where much of my family was raised."

"Back in 1982, Lu brought a concert featuring Rose Royce to Beaumont. I attended as a spectator without ever meeting him, not realizing our paths would eventually intersect." - **Acynthia Villery**

At the inaugural Bill Pickett Rodeo in Denver, I noticed a young lady who wasn't scheduled to compete. Curious, I asked about her and learned she hadn't entered. Determined to see her ride, I covered her entry fees. That decision paid off, she rode brilliantly and has been a staple of the rodeo ever since. **Carolyn Carter** is her name, and she's only ever missed one event due to an unavoidable nursing school commitment.

In 1985, I crossed paths with a young cowboy named **Jesse Guillory**. He started as my assistant but quickly proved his mettle. After just a few rodeos, I promoted him to General Manager, overseeing all operations. This move ruffled some feathers among the older cowboys who felt overlooked due to their experience. However, I chose Jesse because, despite his youth and lesser experience, he showed a knack for leadership, but the truth was I didn't know them.

"When Lu joined us, our scope expanded beyond borders; we went global, we turned into a commercial entity, a tangible product. We became part of a narrative that isn't found in textbooks but started gaining recognition in the media. While we were in Detroit, Michigan, suddenly news anchors were approaching us, eager to cover stories about the Black Cowboy. It was our chance to educate the world about legends like Bill Pickett and Nat Love. Additionally, we initiated what we call 'Rodeo for Kidz' Sake,' targeting young kids from the inner cities who dreamt of being cowboys. They got to experience and participate in the rodeo firsthand. It was no longer just something they saw on TV, embodied by the likes of John Wayne or Clint Eastwood. Now, it was real, up close, and featured faces that looked like theirs." - **Jesse "Slugger" Guillory**

"One of the things that inspired Lu to get involved in the rodeo was remembering when we were in the South and we were always going to see the western movies and characters like Roy Rogers, Gene Autry, the Lone Ranger, Lash LaRue, the Cisco Kid, Range Rider, Jack Mahoney and others. He was inspired by all of that. The only thing was, none of them looked like "us." - **Moses Brewer**

Today, Bill Pickett's legacy has grown significantly, now widely acknowledged by Black folks and even mentioned at rodeos organized by White folks.

"Bill Pickett was a character largely absent from our educational narratives, especially when compared to his White counterparts, and there weren't any films about him either. That really struck a chord with me. Growing up, my screens were filled with the likes of Roy Rogers, Gene Autry, the Lone Ranger, and Tom Mix. Yet, nobody ever mentioned Bill Pickett. These White cowboys became my heroes.

"I remember being a nine-year-old at a rodeo in Madison Square Garden, right in my hometown of New York City, thinking, 'I want to be a cowboy.' But all the cowboys I admired were White, which made my friends laugh at my dreams. Despite their laughter, I was serious about it."

*"Then, years later, along comes this man with a whole troupe of Black rodeo cowboys into town. I was instantly captivated and rushed to the event at the Los Angeles Equestrian Center. What I witnessed was a magnificent display of Cowboys of Color, and at the heart of it all was a man with a beaming smile, someone I would grow to know and love, named Lu Vason." -***Glynn Turman**

Our inaugural Atlanta rodeo was a hit; it drew an impressive crowd, including celebrities. Howard Rollins graced the event, fresh from his role in the Western TV series "Wildside," where he starred alongside William Smith, J. Eddie Peck, and Meg Ryan. Unfortunately, the show aired on ABC for just one season, likely overshadowed by its prime-time competitor, "The Cosby Show."

Two years later, the film "Silverado" was released, featuring Danny Glover. I had connections with Danny's wife, a talented performer and singer, which brought both **Danny Glover** and **Howard Rollins** to our Atlanta event. Singer **Jeffrey Osborne** was another celebrity who supported us by attending our rodeos right from the start. Over the next three decades, we expanded our reach to more than 31 cities across 12 states, including Washington D.C., covering California, Texas, Georgia, Colorado, Oklahoma, Arizona, New Mexico, South Carolina, Missouri, Wisconsin, Illinois, and Michigan.

In California alone, we held rodeos in Oakland, Los Angeles, Sacramento, and San Diego. The concept of Black cowboys was novel and exciting there, attracting large, enthusiastic crowds. These events remain among our most successful, reflecting the strong, continued interest in our unique rodeo experience.

"I always assumed everyone was familiar with Black Cowboys. It wasn't until I began traveling with Lu and visiting places like Detroit that I realized many people were unaware of our existence. Many kids and adults there had never even seen a horse, let alone ridden one. This lack of awareness ignited my passion for education, for sharing why our history and presence are significant."

"People often dismissed what we did, labeling it as 'country' or 'dirty.' I made it my mission to educate them, to explain that if it weren't for our forefathers, who were trail riders, cattle handlers, and skilled rodeo participants, and some of whom were linked to the Underground Railroad, the very jobs they hold might not exist.

"I am wholeheartedly committed to supporting Lu's vision of maintaining an all-Black rodeo. We are professionals in every sense, some of us are dedicated rodeo professionals, while others balance different careers. Our passion is to preserve what has now become dominated by other races. We do exist, we do make a difference, we do matter." - **Acynthia Villery**

The rodeos have attracted a host of celebrities including **Angela Bassett, Denzel Washington,** and **Sinbad**, along with **Dawnn Lewis** from "A Different World," **Obba Babatunde**, and **Kiki Shepard** from "Showtime at the Apollo," all of whom became regulars. Actress **Pam Grier**, a true cowgirl at heart, also graced our events and has become one of our esteemed female spokespersons.

"I recall when Cicely Tyson visited, she expressed disappointment that her seats weren't closer to the action. We scrambled to accommodate her with better seating. Above all, the rodeo was a magnet for celebrities. But more importantly, if there's one takeaway from these events, it's that they served as a profound lesson in our own heritage." - **Pat Duncan, Photographer and Ticket Manager**

I chose Houston as a rodeo location primarily because a significant number of the cowboys hailed from there. I wanted to host something closer to their homes to minimize their travel. Additionally, Houston had a large Black population, roughly 600,000 at the time, yet surprisingly, many locals were unaware that real cowboys existed right in their midst, even in a state famous for rodeo culture like Texas. This revelation was quite a shock to both the Houston and Beaumont markets.

In Beaumont, I was joined by actors Reginald T. Dorsey and Willie Pugh, who is famously known as Harpo from *The Color Purple*. Our relationship evolved beyond mere business; we became close friends.

When we initially launched the rodeo tour, there were skeptics in Texas and a few in Oklahoma who doubted its longevity, claiming it wouldn't last a year. Now, I often think about those same doubters. I don't need to say, "I told you so." They can see it for themselves every time they notice our cowboys proudly wearing their 30-year jackets and buckles. It's a clear testament to our success that's undeniable. BAM!!

"Lu elevated everything to new heights. The prize money, the awards, it all skyrocketed under his leadership. He saw the gaps, recognized the needs, and filled them."

"Lu took the rodeo beyond the backyard events. Many cowboys who started with him were used to competing in small, local rodeos, maybe just 100 miles from home. Lu turned his vision into a reality, creating a full-scale traveling rodeo that not only entertained but educated people nationwide. Thanks to him, many of us, myself included, traveled to cities and states we might never have seen otherwise." - **Acynthia Villery**

The cowboys quickly recognized the value in what we were doing because they were earning significant prize money. While there were other black rodeos in Texas, none matched the prize payouts I offered then and continue to offer today.

Thirty years ago, I was truly pushing the envelope, setting new standards for black rodeos without any doubt.
"Lu is the kind of person who teaches you how to fish rather than just handing you one. It's typical to see him at the rodeo surrounded by 15 to 20 people, all vying for a moment with him. His legacy should be recognized for bringing together a diverse group of people from various places and all walks of life." - **Lee Gilliam, Hair Salon Owner where Lu worked in Oakland and Friend**

Cowboys are a unique bunch; some express gratitude, while others seem indifferent. For many, their involvement is just part of their circumstances, which they may or may not view as an opportunity. Some cowboys relish the chance to travel from coast to coast, from the Pacific to the Atlantic, experiencing sights they would never have encountered otherwise. However, others are less observant, simply traveling from one place to the next without seizing the chance to explore.

That's just the cowboy way, the way of the Wild West.

"Getting to know the cowboys and learning about their lives gave me a whole new level of respect for what they do. Being a coordinator exposes you to a lot, but nothing compares to seeing the kinship among the Black Cowboys and Cowgirls. It's like a family, no matter who's competing against whom."
"Every cowboy and cowgirl in our events is ready to risk their life for another if things go sideways in the arena. And let's face it, things can go wrong anytime, no matter how much you practice or how skilled you are. You can't predict everything, those animals ultimately call the shots, and all you can hope for is that your training is enough to make it in and out safely."

"And when I say safely, I mean it, because there's not a single event, from Barrel Racing to Bull Riding, that doesn't carry the risk of severe injury or even death. Everything happens so fast, all under the pressure of time. This has deepened my respect not just for what they achieve in the arena, but also for the dedication and effort they put into preparing for it." - - ***Jeff Douvel, Oakland Bill Pickett Invitational Rodeo Coordinator***

Many of our cowboys have graduated to mainstream rodeos. Take Lee Akin, for instance, who joined the Professional Bull Riders circuit (PBR) before his severe injury in 2007. Our rodeo dates often align closely with those of mainstream events. We have a bulldogger who consistently clocks in at 3.1 seconds, and he's even hit 3.0 once.

He's got the talent for mainstream rodeos, where scores like that are rare and highly prized. Sometimes, it seems the bulls are more famous than the cowboys themselves. While many of our cowboys prefer to stick close to their home regions, our rodeo offers them opportunities to travel and compete across the nation.

"The Bill Pickett rodeos have been instrumental in grooming cowboys to compete successfully in mainstream rodeos. Notable individuals like Fred Whitfield, Clarence LeBlanc, Myrtis Dightman, Gary Richards, Craig Jackson, and Neil Holmes have all gone on to compete in the PBR and PRCA circuits."

"Some of these guys started with us, fueled by a deep passion, and just look at where they are now. They've been able to walk through doors that were likely closed before. I remember talking to Gary Richards about the '80s, and he shared stories of times when he had to enter through the 'back gate' or rush to compete and then head straight home. But at the Bill Pickett Invitational rodeos, our cowboys are the stars when they arrive in a town; they're the main attraction. They're not only athletes but fierce competitors. While they compete against each other, they also support one another." - **Acynthia Villery**

"One of the key innovations Lu brought to the rodeo scene was the 'rodeo for kids' program. He's always emphasized the educational aspect, aiming to teach kids that Black individuals were historical figures in cowboy culture. Growing up, my heroes were 'Matt Dillon' and the cowboys from 'Rawhide' on TV. I had never heard of Bill Pickett until I met Lu. It was through him that I discovered the significant roles Black people played in the Wild Wild West." - **Michael A. Hancock, Lu's Friend and Promoting Partner**

"I'm particularly impressed with Lu and his dedication to the rodeos because he's focused on creating a legacy for the Black Cowboy. He remained true to that mission, distinguishing himself from other rodeo organizers. Lu doesn't just run rodeos; he invests his time and energy into supporting his cowboys and cowgirls, not for profit, but genuinely to support them. That's really commendable, as not many think in such selfless terms.

"Lu also leverages the rodeo for educational purposes, notably with a special day dedicated to children before the rodeo starts. Being in Denver, right in the heart of the West, brings its own significance. When I became a minority director here, people often wondered if there were any Black people in Denver. While there weren't many, I've always maintained that Denver has been a positive place for Black individuals. It's also been an excellent location for Lu to host his events, be it in entertainment or the rodeo." - **Nelson Ball**

Initially, our rodeo didn't attract many non-Black attendees because it was labeled as an all-Black event. At first, this led to a misunderstanding, people assumed it was only for Black spectators.

It took several years for the broader community to understand that our rodeo was open to everyone; it was just that the cowboys and cowgirls competing were Black.

"Our rodeo primarily drew Black attendees from the local community, but the White visitors who came were die-hard rodeo fans who simply loved the sport. Convincing the broader masses to attend was a challenge, but once they experienced it, they were hooked. Lu transformed the rodeo into a high-level entertainment spectacle, featuring contemporary music, from jazz to R&B, and appearances by celebrities, movie stars, TV personalities, and political figures. It felt like a grand show, reminiscent of the excitement at a Ringling Brothers Circus, but in all the best ways.

"Moreover, despite the large crowds, we never faced any security issues. I remember when I first joined Lu, I warned him about the potential need for increased security due to the large number of attendees expected. He was always so calm about it, assuring me with a simple, 'We don't need extra security; what are you talking about, little girl?' and would just point out a few robust guys at the gates.

"I took on the responsibility of ensuring that celebrities and dignitaries had security in the green room. Throughout all the years, whether I was working or just attending as a spectator, I never witnessed a single problem at his rodeos. Even in Detroit, where I managed the rodeo for a few years, the atmosphere was always peaceful, even if it seemed like every attendee from the Crips to the Bloods was there, but they came with their families, grandmothers and children in tow. It was a testament to the effective, yet understated security measures Lu had in place. The peace and order at these events were truly phenomenal." - **Lynn Dillard Wright, Bill Pickett Invitational Rodeo Coordinator**

"I was part of the Rough Rider organization, a Western cowboy group in Maryland. When the rodeo first came to our area, I was absolutely astonished by all the activity and surprised that many locals were unaware of it."

"That sparked my interest in participating in the BPIR rodeo, and once I started riding, I was eager to get more involved. Meeting Lu, Valeria, and their family, I asked how I could contribute. As a local politician, Lu mentioned they needed assistance with securing grand marshals."

"I leveraged my connections well. I managed to get the county executive and the sheriff to serve as Grand Marshals in different years. That's how I really got entrenched in the rodeo community. Since then, I've had the honor of being the Grand Marshal myself four or five times."

"I also noticed a gap in hospitality for the cowboys after the events. They had no centralized place to gather for a meal. I proposed to Lu that I could organize lunches for them. He was thrilled with the idea. Consequently, when the city's budget planning rolled around, I made sure funds were allocated for these rodeo luncheons. We began hosting a midday gathering every Friday during the rodeo, right after the Rodeo for Kidz Sake."

"Lu then tasked me with another important role, engaging the youth. I started visiting schools with other cowboys, speaking to students at elementary, middle, and high schools about the rodeo and inviting them to attend. Over the past five or six years, we've introduced over 2,500 kids to the rodeo through special matinee performances."- **Eddie Martin, Washington D.C./Maryland Rodeo Assistant, Supporter**

TAMING THE WILD CHALLENGES

Now, don't misunderstand it, hosting the rodeo wasn't without its fair share of hurdles, objections, and stumbling blocks, especially those tied to our cultural expressions.

In 1985, when I brought the rodeo to Houston, I always thought, if I didn't display the African flag (three broad stripes in red, black, and green), then who would? At many black community events, while the Black National Anthem was sung, the flag was often absent. So, I began showcasing the flag, and folks were puzzled, asking, "*What the heck is he up to? What's that?*"

My biggest challenge came when a member of the esteemed Heritage Society, which included Coors, our main sponsor, called in Moses Brewer and Ivan Burwell. He insisted I couldn't display the African flag at our rodeos. He recounted an incident where the rodeo announcer asked everyone to stand, and they played what he referred to as a "black African song." Unbeknownst to him, it was the Black National Anthem, and the flag represented our heritage.

This sparked a major controversy, and Coors pressured me not to use the flag. That was the moment I had to assert, "This is MY rodeo!"

Frustrated, I reached out to Arie Taylor, the Black state representative at the time, exclaiming, "Can you believe they don't want me to raise the black flag?" While Arie supported me privately, she declined to discuss it with Coors. Nevertheless, I went ahead with it.

It wasn't really the sponsors who opposed; it was more about the initial staff at the National Western Rodeo during our first MLK Rodeo. They resisted the flag display, but as new staff came in, they were more receptive to everything. Nearly two decades later, everything has smoothed out, and the initial resistance from the naysayers has subsided, largely due to the success of the rodeos.

However, this stance did lead to some tense moments. Some people firmly believed that only the American flag should be displayed. The controversy around the flags became a focal point, especially after an unfortunate incident involving Judy Barnes, one of my top assistants.

"There was a discussion about the red, black, and green flag. Lu had this magnificent, large African flag. Unfortunately, I wasn't prepared to ride that day; I didn't have a horse ready, nor was I dressed for riding." *"But then Lu approached me with a surprise, it was the flag. We managed to find a horse; though not a top bucking bronco, he was gentle enough, and I figured I could handle him since I grew up around horses. However, I didn't have the flag with me just then. As I entered the arena, the horse seemed to remember his bucking days."*

"The wind was gusting, snapping at the horse's rear, so we made a swift circuit around the arena. The cowboys were cheering, hats flying through the air. I was just relieved I didn't fall off on those first sharp turns; the crowd was ecstatic." *"As I passed the gate, some cowboys shouted 'Jump!' and in disbelief, I just went for it. I landed, only to realize later I had broken two bones."*

"At the time, I didn't realize I was injured. As I regained my senses, they were dusting me off. By then, dignitaries like the governor, the mayor, and State Representative Arie Taylor were poised on well-behaved horses, ready to be introduced to the crowd. It dawned on me that I had to get up, though I was unaware of my fractures. That's when I truly understood what adrenaline could do. I remounted the same horse and led the procession. As we entered and 'The Star-Spangled Banner' began, following 'Lift Every Voice and Sing', the pain hit me full force. It was then I realized the severity of my condition and knew I needed medical attention." - **Judy Barnes**

You need a horse that isn't spooked by a flag snapping in the wind when you're riding fast. Unfortunately, the horse Judy was on got startled and threw her off, which led to her getting injured. That incident happened before we had a Grand Entry Coordinator. Carolyn stepped into that role and has been our reliable coordinator since then.

The situation with the flag turned into a somewhat amusing story later on. I recall Ivan and Moses giving me a hard time about the African flag. Yet, a couple of years later, I noticed a Coors promotional lapel pin featuring two flags: the American flag and the African flag. I thought to myself, well, some folks just need a little longer to catch on.

There was this incident in Oakland when animal rights activists showed up and disrupted our operations; they had their picket signs and were blocking our patrons. I confronted one of the protesters and removed him from the property. I felt justified in doing so because I was paying for that property; it was my responsibility, covered by my insurance and rent.

However, the next day, the Hayward Recreation Department got in touch and told me I couldn't remove the animal rights protesters. I argued that it was my right since I was paying for the use of the property unless they wanted to take on that responsibility.

Later, when we held The Rodeo For Kidz Sake in LA, the animal-rights activists showed up again. I challenged them, asking if they cared more about these animals than about the Black kids benefiting from the event, which didn't sit right with me. During this event, a woman and her small group tried to picket, and my wife, Valeria, stepped in and managed the situation more calmly than I would have.

Another incident occurred in Virginia Beach. Around 1 or 2 in the morning, my colleague Slugger and I received a call saying that all the animals had been let loose. The animal rights activists had released all the bulls onto the streets, posing a danger to motorists and causing issues for the stock contractor. This reckless act completely erased any respect I might have had for the animal-rights groups. These were the few times I recall being truly angered.

The rodeo brought a variety of experiences. On a separate note, there was an accident involving Ngoma and Karimu, who later became our primary t-shirt vendors for the rodeos.

"We were en route to the rodeo in Atlanta when our car rolled over three times near Grambling, Louisiana, eventually landing upright. The entire family was in the van at the time, which made the incident extremely distressing. The whole front windshield was shattered. Our baby was in the front with my husband, one of our daughters was in the middle seat, and our son was in the back. It was nothing short of a miracle that we all survived. It truly was."

"Given our commitment to Lu, we could have easily decided to turn back and head home. Instead, we rented two cars and continued our journey to Atlanta. These are the kinds of efforts that often go unnoticed when you're striving to keep things running smoothly." - **Ngoma and Karimu McNeal, T-Shirt Vendors for Bill Pickett Rodeos**

Another incident that really angered me occurred when one of my vendors, whom I had approved to sell popcorn, was confronted by a concessionaire at the Denver Coliseum.

He insisted she couldn't sell popcorn. This confrontation really brought out the fighter in me. The concessionaire attempted to seize her popcorn, claiming she was not allowed to sell it. I countered, "She can sell the popcorn; I'm renting this place." Supporting my vendors was crucial because they relied on these events to make a living, and at that time, there were no Coliseum rules prohibiting the sale of merchandise. However, the following year, the Coliseum and I entered into a contract that explicitly stated they controlled the concessions, which really upset me as it felt like the venues were manipulating the rules to get what they wanted.

On another note, I played a significant role in helping Bea Harris launch the Urban Spectrum, a monthly newspaper focused on people of color. I introduced her to my bank, Citywide Bank, to secure some funding she and her partner needed to start the publication. This indirectly led to another frustrating episode that challenged the cultural integrity of the rodeo. A local Black cowboy who was dating a white woman was approached by her questioning why she couldn't participate in the rodeo. I explained that it was an all-Black event and non-Blacks were not allowed to compete. Unhappy with this, she contacted a friend who ended up writing about her complaint in Bea Harris' newspaper. I was deeply upset, not only because of the complaint but also because the story was published without fully understanding the context or considering my significant support in the newspaper's launch. This misunderstanding troubled me greatly for a long time but never damaged our friendship.

SPREADING OUR SPURS

In 1994, Frank Phillips, a grandson of Bill Pickett, successfully pushed for the issuance of a commemorative Bill Pickett Stamp. However, an error occurred when the US Postal Service accidentally used a photo of Ben Pickett, Bill's brother, instead. I collaborated closely with Frank to rectify this mistake.

By 2006, I made the bold move to host my rodeo finals in Las Vegas, a location traditionally dominated by the PRCA for their finals. Alongside the finals, I organized a celebrity golf tournament, which brought a western flair to the greens, certainly not your usual sight in Vegas!

Around the same time, Bob Willis and I initiated a project to honor three pioneering African American golf figures with a fundraiser. We celebrated Charles Sifford, the first black golfer with a PGA player's card; Pete Brown, the first to win a PGA tournament; and Renee Powell, one of the first black women on the LPGA tour, with an event titled "Legends Before Tiger."

Creativity always spurred my ventures, leading me to launch Soul Strollin', a magazine catering to black tourists in Denver and social clubs hosting events. The magazine enjoyed four years of popularity before rodeo responsibilities took precedence. Initially, my plan was to expand Soul Strollin' to San Francisco and Atlanta. However, despite laying the groundwork in these cities, another party launched a similar magazine in Atlanta named Black Heritage. To this day, the concept hasn't been replicated in other cities.

Lynn Dillard Wright laughs as she thinks about Lu, *"When you saw Lu, man, he was the real deal, head to toe. The boots, the hat, the full cowboy get-up. And not just for show, he was a stickler about being authentic. He used to clown me all the time about my so-called 'Hollywood Cowboy' look. I'd come in there trying to look the part, but Lu wasn't having it. He actually had a couple of the real cowboys take me to a Lee Jeans or Wrangler store so I could get some proper boots and a real cowboy hat. Because according to Lu, if I didn't, I was just out here perpetrating."*

"He said, 'If you're going into radio stations or talking to clothing stores to try to get sponsorships, you gotta look like you're part of the rodeo.' And he was right. I had to represent. But I'm not gonna lie, I felt like a fish outta water the whole time. I didn't grow up around horses or livestock. I didn't come off no ranch or farm, I came straight outta Hollywood."

Over the years, we tossed around a bunch of ideas beyond the rodeo. Back when I was just getting the rodeo off the ground, I was also exploring the idea of launching a roller derby. I even had some concepts around track and field events. Like I said before, I've always had a creative mind.

One idea that really stuck with me was doing a track meet at the Denver Coliseum. I got inspired after seeing a meet held right in the heart of downtown Denver. There was this elevated track built so folks could watch from all around. It was a striking visual. I even had conversations with the Chamber of Commerce about bringing that idea to life, but for one reason or another, it never got off the ground.

Around that same time, Coors ended their direct sponsorship of the rodeo after supporting us for seven years. That was tied to the covenant created following Bill Coors' controversial remarks. When that agreement expired, so did their sponsorship. But I wasn't about to let that slow us down, I ended up connecting with various Coors distributors across different markets to keep the rodeo rolling.

"I think the last time I worked with Lu was back in '75, Natalie Cole show in Sacramento. That was a good one."
"When I later heard he was doing a rodeo, I thought, "Man, that's wild, but that's Lu." I was genuinely glad he found something new to grab onto. Whether or not he was tall in the saddle or even all that into horses didn't matter, what mattered was, he found a whole new lane and just went full speed into it."

"See, Lu had that rare gift. He could take a concept, doesn't matter what it was, and figure out how to make it a show. And once he had the vision, he knew how to build it out exactly the way he wanted. He brought in his family, teamed up with some top-tier cowboys, and made it all come together. That's just who he was. He knew how to put a thing on its feet and keep it moving." - **Neil Young, Stage Manager**

By that time, I had really started to polish up who I was. I used to have some pretty rough edges. Growing up in the projects gave me a whole lot of street in me. I was sharp, tough, and quick to go toe-to-toe if needed. I always had that fire, and truth be told, it didn't take much to set me off. I was what folks now call a hothead.

But then I met Ivan, Moses, and Valeria, who would later become my wife, and my man Bob Willis. It wasn't that any of them came from some big corporate background or wore suits and ties all day. No, it was just *how* they carried themselves. They kind of took some of the bite out of me. They helped pull me up by my bootstraps and gave me a model of how to move through the world with more finesse.

Valeria, especially, she worked on me the most. But I was also paying attention to how Ivan, Moses, and Bob handled situations. Ivan, in particular, had this way about him, and Bob was smooth as silk. Watching them, I started picking up on some of those traits, adapting, evolving.

Now don't get it twisted, a leopard don't change its spots completely. Every now and then, that wolf or bear in me still comes out. But thanks to those four, I learned how to keep that side of me in check and lead with a more polished version of myself.

Looking back, I realize just how truly blessed I was to be surrounded by some incredible people. The success of the Bill Pickett Invitational Rodeo wasn't just about me, it was the result of a village, a team of committed, passionate, and talented folks who believed in the vision as much as I did.

Every step of the way, I had people who brought their gifts to the table. People who didn't just show up to do a job, but showed up with heart. Whether it was the ones who handled the logistics, the sponsors and community leaders who opened doors, or the cowboys and cowgirls who brought the arena to life, it all mattered.

Every hand, every mind, every voice was part of building something that had never been done before.

I've always said I had a creative mind, but that mind needed a crew to bring the ideas to life. My team gave the rodeo its legs. They brought the polish, the organization, the professionalism, and they pushed me, too. They helped shape me into a better leader, a better man.

We created more than a rodeo, we created a movement, a family, and a legacy. And that would've never been possible without the people who stood beside me. I'm forever grateful.

Chapter 13: VALERIA AND THE SECRET WEDDING

"Before long, whatever it was that I got into, Valeria was right there. If I was digging horse manure, she would be right beside me digging horse manure. So she really became my soulmate." - Lu Vason

When I embarked on the journey of the Bill Pickett Invitational Rodeos with Coors as our main sponsor, the responsibility heavily rested on Ivan Burwell, the Coors marketing director. Ivan was a close associate of my good friend Moses, both of whom played pivotal roles as special marketing directors, steering Coors' multi-million dollar initiatives aimed at engaging the black and Hispanic communities.

Back in 1985, Moses was called to Atlanta to expand their market efforts and he invited me along. It was during this trip that I met Liz Young, who would become my first Atlanta rodeo coordinator. Our return trip to Denver was memorable. As we waited at the Atlanta airport, Moses spotted a young lady sitting in the corner. Captivated, he nudged me and exclaimed, "Whoa! Who is she? And she's heading to Denver too? I've never seen her before." Her presence marked another beginning in the series of events that would shape our rodeo endeavors.

"It was January 7th, 1984, my birthday, a date marked not just by celebrations but also by touching memories, as I had just lost my mother, who was my best friend on December 28th. I was in South Carolina for Christmas, my mother passed, causing me to stay to prepare for my mother's funeral, address personal, and to take care of everything since I was the oldest."

"The journey back to Denver, where I was living at the time, was not straightforward. From Columbia, South Carolina, I had to connect through Atlanta, no direct flights could spare me the additional leg of travel. There I was at the Atlanta airport, a hub of bustling activity, where fate was quietly setting the stage for a remarkable introduction."

"I was sitting in the airport in Atlanta, waiting for the plane to Denver when I noticed these two brothers: Moses and Lu. I didn't know who they were at the time. They sat down and then it was time to board the plane. The plane was one of those big DC 10 planes, but I think there were only 12 people flying on the entire plane. I found a row, let the arms up and got me some pillows and blankets. I was going to get comfortable and get some rest." - **Valeria**

When we boarded the plane, I settled in to do what I always do on flights: sleep. The plane was pretty empty with fewer than 20 passengers, so there was an abundance of empty seats. Moses and I chose seats on one side of the aisle, while the young lady, Valeria, sat across from us. But it wasn't long before Moses moved over to her side to strike up a conversation. He learned her name was Valeria and soon, he was introducing us.

"Have you met my friend here?" he asked her, nodding in my direction. "His name is Lu Vason." Valeria looked puzzled and with a curious smile, she asked, *"What's a Lu Vason?"*

"After we took off, Moses came over and struck up a conversation with me. We chatted about various topics, and then he asked if I knew Lu Vason. When I admitted I didn't, he seemed almost offended, exclaiming, "What do you mean you don't know Lu Vason?" I repeated, "I don't know Lu Vason." At the time, Lu was asleep, which I later learned is his usual routine during flights. Moses introduced us briefly. We talked for a bit, and then Lu went back to sleep." **Valeria**

I talked about my work, and she described hers. I learned that Valeria had recently returned from Columbia, South Carolina, where, sadly, her mother had passed away just three days after Christmas. Once we arrived in Denver, I asked for her number and later called her to offer my condolences for her mother's passing.

"When we arrived in Denver, Lu handed me his business card. At that moment, the guy I was seeing approached us. He knew Moses, so they struck up a brief conversation. After grabbing my bag, we left the airport. On the drive home, my friend started questioning how I knew Moses and Lu. He got upset over my responses and ended up dumping my bags on the side of my driveway instead of bringing them inside. That was the last straw for that relationship." - **Valeria**

"Valeria's boyfriend was at the Denver airport when we arrived, and he didn't look too happy about things. Then, just a few days later, Lu and Valeria showed up together at my place. I lived on Xanadu Street, which is just a block behind where Lu's house and office were on Billings Street in Montbello." - **Moses**

"About two days later, Lu called and invited me to a tennis tournament featuring Chris Evert and Martina Navratilova. He asked me to meet him at his house, but when I arrived, he wasn't there; instead, another guy was. This guy told me, "Lu had to run to the bank real quick, but he'll be right back. You can go in and sit down and wait for him."

"I was a bit annoyed. How could he arrange to meet me and not be there? Despite my irritation, I went inside and sat down, not feeling particularly cheerful. Eventually, Lu returned and we headed to the tennis tournament. After the event, he took me to the Off Larimer Club, owned by his best friend, Gene DeWitt. There, Lu introduced me to some of his friends and others. I recall getting quite a few odd looks that evening, and when I say odd, I mean it."

Little did I realize that night marked the start of our relationship. Lu invited me to more events, and we started dating and spending more time together." – **Valeria**

We started talking more frequently and I began taking her out. Over time, these outings evolved into a relationship that lasted 16 years.

After all those years together, it was beyond her wildest dreams that I would surprise her with a wedding in the Caribbean, a wedding she knew nothing about. From that moment, the rest of our lives became history.

Marrying her came as a surprise to many who knew me well. It was no secret that I had been quite active in the dating scene, with women frequently coming and going from my office and home, making it seem like Grand Central Station. But it was Valeria who finally brought an end to that chapter of my life.

"As we began dating, I encountered quite a few challenges with other women. I recall one time, he wanted me to meet his business partner at the Hilton on Orchard in DTC. Back then, I didn't realize she was assessing me. I also remember his secretary at the time, September Browne. She bluntly told me, "Honey, you're not going to last a week." Valeria says, shaking her head.

THE COMPETITION

"Lu was quite the romancer back in the day. I remember telling Valeria she wouldn't last a week. I even said, "You're not going to make it for a month." I honestly didn't think she would, especially considering the woman Lu had been seeing before Valeria had a much darker complexion. Then along came Valeria, who is fair-skinned, and I thought, "Oh no, she won't last long at all."

"Lu was frugal when it came to his personal life, often saving his money for producing concerts or shows. He would eat Top Ramen noodles with tuna and soy sauce to get by. There were times his car wouldn't run, but he still managed to get where he needed to go and do what he needed to do."

"Despite the struggles, Lu always kept champagne in the fridge. Trust me on that. And the women would come over and bring their own glasses. When I worked at Lu's house in Montbello, I could look at the record player, see which record was on, and I'd know which woman had been there all night. And he knew that I knew." - **September Browne, Lu Former Assistant**

September always told me that she could tell exactly what women were there by what music I had on, Lu laughs. *"I found myself constantly having to screen his calls to manage the flow of different women Lu was seeing simultaneously; that alone was a challenge. I became quite adept at lying, because these women wanted to be close to me, knowing my proximity to Lu. They were always prodding for information about who he was seeing, what he was up to, and where he was going."*

"I just lied outright. But I made sure to tell them all the same story so I wouldn't trip up and forget my fabrications. At times, I even found myself playing the role of a matchmaker for him. We'd be at an event, and he'd spot someone attractive. "Who is that woman over there, the one with the long legs?" he'd ask. I didn't know, but he'd send me over to find out her name. And I'd think to myself, "Why am I doing this? What am I, a pimp?" September fondly remembers.

"I recall a night we were at a jazz club with a restaurant that Lu managed and Gene DeWitt owned. Lu climbed up a ladder to fix a light, and a friend of mine exclaimed, "God Dang! Who is that with those long fine legs?" I had to remind her every week, "Girl, leave him alone, he's taken, he has a girlfriend." Lu had a preference for "chocolate" girls; that was really his type. When he started seeing Valeria, though, everything changed. But before her, it was only chocolate girls for him. He didn't "do no snow," not even close. - **M. Rae Taylor, Lu's Friend**

I actually went back and forth between relationships; I dated a light-skinned woman, then a dark-skinned one.

"Lu was so smooth. He owned this long terry cloth blue robe that reached down to his ankles and even had a hood. He typically started his day late, around 10:30 or 11:00 a.m. By then, I would already be downstairs, handling calls. He'd casually ask, "What you doing?" and I'd playfully respond, "Why?"

After waking up, Lu would take his shower, splash on his cologne, Jazz by Yves Saint Laurent, slip into his robe, and then come downstairs. He'd spread out his papers everywhere, ideas, notes, newspaper clippings. It would all be scattered around. Then Lu would suggest, "It's time for you to go to lunch." I'd agree and head out. When I returned, sometimes there'd be a strange car in the driveway and unusual sounds coming from the bedroom. In those instances, I'd discreetly retreat and take a longer lunch break than usual. If he didn't have visitors, he'd question why I wasn't back just five minutes later. That was Lu for you." - **September Browne**

Rae continues, *"The women would practically bump into each other coming and going. Lu would greet them at the door in his robe, and I would think to myself, "Oh, Lord!" There he'd be, sitting all majestic in that fine robe, speaking slowly in that smooth voice of his, and the women would just melt. One would be driving off onto the freeway while another was just making her way there. Some of them would even take those champagne glasses, grabbing one for him as well. It was always like a party."*

I had to admit, it was a lot of fun. It got me in a lot of trouble, but you live and you learn. Again, Valeria was going to be the one to change ALL of that! It was time to get SERIOUS.

"When did things start getting serious for me? I can't really pinpoint it. To be honest, when we first started going out, it was all about having fun. I had mentioned to him that I was divorced and wasn't in the market for anything serious. He said the same thing." - **Valeria**

Initially, I was hesitant about getting married again since all my previous marriages had ended in failure. I was concerned that if I married Valeria, it might eventually fall apart too. The breakdowns of my past relationships were often due to a clash between my career choices and what my ex-wives expected from me. None of them were supportive of my promotional work; they all preferred that I settle for a conventional 9-to-5 job. However, Valeria was different; she had her own and she never once complained about my involvement in promotions, but I could tell the extra women would have to go.

"I've met all three of Lu's ex-wives. The mother of his son, Corey was a very sweet person but deeply religious. She maintained a very friendly and caring relationship with Lu, while she and I established a good relationship. His second ex-wive, Kashan, whose funeral we attended in December, seemed to always have a chip on her shoulder when I was around and it was clear she didn't care for me. The third wife, Lilly, I only met once, at Lu's stepfather's funeral. She came across as quite malevolent. I distinctly remember her calling me a bitch right there in the church. It seemed clear to me that her spirit was troubled, filled with jealousy, which is ironic because Lu always disliked jealousy." – **Valeria**

I often visited Valeria at her house in Highlands Ranch, a higher end community and predominantly white suburb of Denver. Her home was decorated with white paintings; there was nothing black in her decor. I used to joke that the blackest thing about Valeria was me. Lu laughed hysterically

"Lu would come over to my house and make a big deal about the decor to everyone, saying, "Oh, my God, her house is sterile! She's got white carpet, everything is perfectly arranged, she's got these sterile pictures on the wall. There is nothing black in her house." He always teased me about how my house looked. His place was the complete opposite, filled with black everything: black newspapers, black decor, stacks everywhere and so on... it initially drove me crazy, but I started organizing things and eventually got him to be more mindful." - **Valeria**

Before long, whatever I got into, Valeria was always right there with me. If I was digging horse manure, she would be right beside me digging horse manure. She really became my soul mate.

"At first, Lu's reputation with the ladies didn't bother me. But when I was at his house, people would just come marching in and out. I thought to myself, "Okay, this is interesting." Even people who worked for him seemed quite possessive. I observed all this for a few weeks, just quietly taking it all in.
Then one day, I decided that I wasn't going to compete with all of this chaos. So, I began to gradually put a stop to it. Being take-charge by nature, I started to assert control and set boundaries. I implemented some protocol, people needed to call before showing up. I didn't care who it was." – **Valeria**

One night, Valeria was staying at my house and Slugger was there too. I did something, I can't quite recall what, that really upset her. She got up at 3:00 in the morning, dressed, and drove back to her house in Highlands Ranch. She was pissed with me and took a couple of days off work to think things over, and during that time, she resolved, "*He is not going to drive me away.*" She returned, set me straight, and has been here and very direct with me ever since.

"When Lu met Valeria on that plane, she put an end to all his previous escapades. However, the women kept calling me since they knew we were friends. I found myself repeatedly telling them, "You have to leave him alone." Lu was like a little brother to me, and I always looked out for him." - **M. Rae Taylor**

Beyond her beauty, Valeria was intelligent and independent with a job of her own. I think that independence is what really won me over. She took an active interest in everything I was involved with, even if it was new to her. She knew nothing about the rodeo, but she'd come into the office and dive deep into the work with me.

Her business acumen was motivating and helped sustain me through these 30 years. Sometimes I could be like a loose cannon. I owe a lot to Bob Willis and Ivan Burwell for smoothing out my rough edges. They really helped tighten me up and I improved significantly. But I was quite edgy. If you ask what she saw in me, I might not have a clear answer. It might just be that old saying, "Opposites attract."

"I'm not sure if Lu verbally allowed me to take charge, but I went ahead and did it anyway. He was always involved in various activities, doing what he pleased. He might not have been aware of what was happening, but I can't say for certain. I assumed that since we were dating, anyone else from his past would just have to adjust. I decided, 'I'm sorry, I'm in the picture now, and if I was going to stay, this is how things are going to be.'" – **Valeria**

One of the young ladies I was seeing came over to the house, and somehow she and Valeria ended up having a confrontation upstairs. September was in her office, and I was in the conference room. We heard all this commotion. Valeria and this lady were really going at it.

Then I heard Valeria shout, *"If he had wanted you, he would've kept you!"* That pretty much ended that relationship. Valeria has often boasted about how she came in and cleared them all out. She said, *"Yeah, he's running around acting like he's got a harem."*

"I think Jeannie was assisting with the rodeo and traveling with Lu at the time. I can't recall exactly what transpired, but she stopped by the house/office and did something that really upset me. Lu and September were downstairs while upstairs, she and I had it out. I bluntly told her that "one monkey doesn't stop a show." I'm not sure what happened after that, but for me, that was the end of the conversation. Oh, it didn't turn physical. September hurried down to the office part of the house to inform Lu.

"I'm the type of person who will respect you as long as you respect me. I felt that I wasn't receiving the respect I deserved, so it was important for me to make it clear that I wasn't some young pushover. Eventually, Lu and I began living together; I'm trying to remember exactly how that came about. We had our disagreements because Lu was very protective at that time. By protective, I mean he seemed to avoid getting too close to anyone, keeping relationships light and fun. But I wasn't that type of woman. Things between us continued to evolve."

"I remember the first time I went to Lu's house, one of his ex-girlfriends had broken in while he was away on a trip. She had cut up all his pictures and art, and even poured motor oil all over his books. At the time, I didn't know all the details and didn't make any assumptions. But later, as we started dating, the ex-girlfriend would frequently call the house and threaten Lu."

I was staying at his house most of the time. One night, after Lu had been downstairs for a while, I went down to check and saw flames coming out of my car. His ex-girlfriends had tried to set both my and Lu's cars on fire by stuffing rolled newspapers into the gas tanks and lighting them. That's when I called the police, because someone could have been seriously hurt.

*"While we were talking to the officer, she happened to call the house. I simply let the police answer and speak with her. It was shortly after this that things started to calm down. I was thinking, what have I gotten myself into." -***Valeria**

THE SECRET WEDDING

I was in a relationship with Valeria for about two or three years, and during that time, it became clear to me that she was the one. Her support and understanding really stood out, convincing me that she was someone I could truly build a future with.

A partner isn't just someone who shows up when things are good, it's someone who sees your mess, hears your silence, and still believes in your vision. That's what Valeria did for me.

"I can't pinpoint exactly when my feelings for Lu began to develop. I've always had this personality trait, something my parents noticed early on: I'm not one to give up or back down easily. During that period in my life, it seemed like there were efforts to drive me away from Lu. What those people didn't realize is that I don't let anyone else control my decisions. That was the mindset I had at the time.

"As Lu and I spent more time together, having fun and hanging out, I started to really appreciate him. He was fiercely independent, held strong beliefs, and was passionate about his endeavors. These qualities drew me to him, but the one thing that concerned me was his money management."

"As our relationship progressed, I learned more about Lu's rodeos and his various entertainment projects. I was fascinated by how he managed his shows and the innovative ways he approached his work. Lu was always brainstorming, never resting; he was constantly reading something and then declaring, "I want to do that." Even when it seemed impossible, wondering, "Okay, you have no money, how are you going to pull this off?" We always found a way. His confidence and belief in his ability to achieve his goals were admirable, so I felt I had to help him."

"Moreover, some might not see Lu as a spiritual man, but I've witnessed that aspect of him. We've had deep conversations about religion, and while his beliefs might not align with conventional views, he definitely possesses a spiritual side that believes in a higher power looking out for him."

"Over time, Lu introduced me to his circle of friends, and I gradually became an accepted part of his life. I remember the first time he took me to Glenda and Odell Barry's home in Northglenn. We were leaving and I had gone to the car. I was sitting in the car, while Lu and Glenda stood talking on the porch, I overheard Glenda ask, "Should I remember her name?" That comment stuck with me, and importantly, I never mentioned to anyone that I had heard it." - **Valeria**

The four of us, Valeria, Odell, Glenda, and I, grew very close over the years. We made it a tradition to take trips together annually. In 2000, during one of these trips, Glenda turned to me and asked, "Okay, you two have been together long enough; when are you going to marry this woman?" I responded casually, I don't know. She then asked *"Why don't you plan it for our next trip?"* At that moment, I made up my mind to surprise Valeria with a wedding. She would know absolutely nothing about it, it would be a complete surprise.

"Over the years, as Lu and I grew closer, he also developed a strong bond with my wife. The four of us formed a close-knit group, and my wife even kept an eye on all of Lu's girlfriends, which naturally included Valeria. Glenda took a liking to Valeria, which only strengthened our collective relationship. One day, Lu approached my wife to gauge her thoughts on whether Valeria was the right one for him. My wife turned the question back on him, asking, "Do you think Valeria is the one?" Lu responded, "I think this is the one." - **Odell Berry, close friend of Lu.**

Originally, I had the idea to host our surprise wedding on an airplane, believing it was similar to a ship where the captain can officiate marriages. However, I soon discovered that weddings couldn't be conducted on an airplane. That revelation led me to switch our plans to St. Thomas in the Virgin Islands. We traveled to St. Thomas ostensibly for a vacation, but Valeria was under the impression that we were there for Odell and Glenda to renew their vows.

"In the vibrant swirl of daily life, it's the quiet moments and secret plans that often weave the most unforgettable tales. My story begins unsuspectingly, tied with laughter, good friends, and what I believed to be a simple favor for a dear friend. It was supposed to be a vacation that we would go on normally each year. This year we decided on being in St. Thomas with a small circle of our closest friends, Odell Barry, former player from the Denver Bronco, the first black mayor of Northglenn, Colorado, and his wonderful wife, Glenda. Bob Willis, and my friend Javonni.

"Little did I know, Lu and Lori Washington, had orchestrated a surprise that would beautifully disrupt my understanding of our trip. As the plot was unfolding, Glenda, with her usual charm, called to ask if I would help her renew her wedding vows with Odell. "It would mean so much to us if you could be my maid of honor and help me set everything up," Glenda says, her voice a blend of excitement and sincerity. Thrilled to be part of such a heartfelt moment, I eagerly agreed, immersing myself in the preparations without a second thought to anything different.

"As our plane touched down on the lush landscapes of St. Thomas, the warm Caribbean breeze carried a scent of adventure and blooming frangipanis trees. Our group was buzzing with anticipation. Each moment was meticulously planned, yet I was blissfully unaware of the larger script being written. The days leading up to the 'vow renewal' were filled with laughter, shared memories, and subtle diversions that kept me from suspecting the truth."

"So there we were, all in St. Thomas. It was Bob Willis and his wife Javonni, Odell and Glenda, along with Lu and myself. That morning, the guys had gone out shopping, so we decided to do some shopping too. Even though Javonni had already shopped for me in Denver, because I hadn't had the time, I was still on the lookout for a dress. She had selected a couple of dresses for me, and I brought two along on the trip. While we were shopping, I came across a green hand-painted outfit that seemed to match my eyes perfectly. I remember asking Glenda in the store if it would be appropriate to wear this outfit for their vow renewal ceremony, and she enthusiastically replied, "absolutely."

The night before the wedding, we managed to convince Valeria and Javonni to retire early to the hotel and prepare for bed. We had asked Javonni to say she wasn't feeling well. Valeria offered to stay with her and keep her company, which was perfect.

Once they were settled, we decided to have a spontaneous cocktail gathering, knowing that everyone that I invited had arrived.

While Valeria and Javonni stayed in the room, I headed up the hill to the restaurant to join Gene, Odell, Bob, and the rest of the crowd.

At the dinner table, through our many conversations and laughter, Gene suggested, *"Lu, I think you need to ask her."* I countered with, "No, I don't need to ask her." Then Mary, Gene's wife, chimed in, *"Lu, Lu, what if she says 'No,' you really need to ask her."*

So, I looked at the table, hoping for some support. I believed I had one ally, Robert, Valeria's brother, and possibly Glenda, who had previously questioned, "When are you going to marry this girl?" on our last vacation in Mexico.

I turned to Robert and asked, "Robert, what do you think?" He replied, *"Bro, I think you ought to ask her. My sister is crazy!"* Then Gene, always the joker, slammed his wallet on the table and wagered, *"Anybody want a piece of this? Because she's going to say 'No!'"*

I firmly responded, "Nope. The die has been cast." That ended the discussion for me. I felt isolated because it seemed I had no one on my side. After 16 years with Valeria, if I didn't know her well enough by then, I never would. I was determined but not scared.

MOMENT OF TRUTH

"We were getting dressed when a call came in from the front desk. I answered and they informed me, "There are some balloons that just arrived for Mr. Barry and they need to be blown up." I was baffled, thinking, Blown up? Odell must be out of his mind. I asked the hotel clerk if there was a local florist who could deliver some already inflated balloons. She confirmed there was and provided me with the number. I made the call, and we arranged for the balloons to be delivered."

"Glenda called about that same time, to let me know her sons, Jay and Damon, were not going to make it to give her away. She stated their plane got delayed out of Chicago. I panicked but stayed calmed. I said to her, I am sorry the boys will not make it but Lu can give you away. Don't worry, it will be alright."

"I told Lu about the boys and that he would need to walk Glenda down the aisle. He said, no problem like it was no big deal. Once we were dressed, it was time for Odell and Glenda's vow renewal. We gathered on a stunning patio overlooking the ocean, a truly breathtaking setting. Everything was in place. Lu escorted me out first, then returned to accompany Glenda. I was so happy for Glenda and Odell as they were about to renew their vows."

"We were on the rooftop of the Bluebeard Castle Hotel when the ceremony began. The minister asked, "Who gives this woman?" Just as he spoke those words, a gust of wind swept through and I heard a peculiar voice behind us declare, "I do." I thought to myself, That sounds like my brother. I blew it off because I know he doesn't fly and I was just imagining things." – **Valeria**

The wedding was held outdoors, and a strong gust of wind interrupted the proceedings, prompting Odell to ask, "Would you say it again?" The minister repeated, *"Who gives this woman?"* Robert answered, *"I do."* I saw Valeria pause and turned to look at Glenda, puzzled by the voice.

"I remember the minister repeating the question, "Who gives this woman to be wed?" Hearing the same voice again, I thought to myself, God, that sounds like my brother and I know what I heard. I was trying to convince myself that I wasn't crazy. I glanced at Glenda, she gave me a knowing smile. We both turned around, and to my surprise, it really was my brother." – **Valeria**

Valeria turned around to see her brother, Robert Hollis. It was a complete shock because he usually doesn't fly or leave South Carolina at all.

Overwhelmed by his unexpected presence, she began to cry. I gently reminded her that we needed to continue with the ceremony, as the minister had another wedding to officiate on a different island. Gathering her composure, Valeria turned back to face the minister, who resumed the ceremony. When it came to the vows he asked, "Do you take this man to be your lawful wedded husband?" she responded, "I'll think about it." Now, I was really worried, thinking maybe I should have listened to Gene, Robert, and Mary. I was sweating bullets.

"Seeing my brother was overwhelming enough, but as I looked down the aisle and saw all my friends from various places gathered together, I just broke down and started crying. It hit me all at once, "Oh my God! This is MY wedding!" I could hardly breathe but Lu supported me and said, "You don't have time to cry. We've got to get this over with. The minister has another wedding over on St. John's Island. We need to get this done." So the minister asked again, and I said MAYBE. He then said, "I'm going to ask again, and I need a Yes or No." I eventually said YES!" – **Valeria**

"Valeria turned around and was completely overwhelmed. Seeing all her friends gathered, she just broke down and didn't know how to react. Sharing that moment with Lu was an incredible experience; it deepened our friendship in ways that are indelible, whether he realizes it or not. It's something that has grown very dear to me. Along with my wife, it evolved into a family affair. We've forged a strong bond that, despite any ups and downs, will remain unbreakable." - **Odell Berry**

"So, our wedding finally took place after we had lived together for 16 years. Getting married didn't particularly concern me because our relationship was already solid, founded on love and respect. To me, a marriage certificate wasn't going to change anything. However, over time, as I had renewed my relationship with God and the church, I began to feel that simply living together didn't seem quite right anymore. So, for me, the timing of our wedding turned out to be perfect. When it happened, I truly felt that my God, who I believe always guides my life, orchestrated it all.

"After the ceremony, we had a reception where everyone went out to dinner. It was a joyful affair with everyone laughing and reminiscing about all the antics that took place to make this wedding happen."

"I now remember, one night, maybe six to eight weeks before the trip, or perhaps closer to two or three months, it's hard to remember exactly. Lori called me around eleven o'clock. She was crying, and I asked, "Lori, what's wrong?" She could barely get the words out at first, then said, "You're not going to believe this." I urged her to tell me, and she explained that the divorce she thought was finalized from her ex-husband wasn't. "If Tracy finds out, this is not going to be pretty," she said, the worry clear in her voice."

"I asked, "Do you have paperwork from the court that says your divorce is final?" She replied, "I thought I did, but I can't find it." Then she asked, "Do you have your divorce papers?" I said, "Yes." She asked if she could read them, just to compare. I told her, "Sure. I'll leave them out for you. You can come by the house tomorrow to look at them, but don't take them." She agreed."

"I didn't think anything of it at the time. But now, I realized they needed a copy of my divorce paperwork to apply for a marriage certificate in St. Thomas. I realized that I had been played by everyone."

"As I was listening, there were many conversations, including how they had tried to persuade Lu to reveal to me that the wedding was ours, not Odell's and Glenda's. They recounted how Lu had declared, "I'm not telling her, the die has been cast. I've lived with her for 16 years and I'm not telling her.""

"During all the activity, Glenda made a toast. After the toast, I walked over to her; she was wearing a green sun hat with a large brim. I lifted the hat and deliberately poured my glass of champagne over her head, saying, "I guess he did remember my name.""

"Glenda was utterly surprised because they never knew I had overheard her questioning Lu, "Should I remember her name?" It was a shocking moment for everyone, but then quickly everyone burst into laughter." – **Valeria**

Valeria poured a glass of champagne over Glenda's head because Glenda had doubted her staying power when they first met. In fact, no one thought Valeria would last. September had even told her she wouldn't last 30 days, noting how mild and meek Valeria seemed back then, sweet as pie. That memory goes back to the first time I took her to Glenda's house. As we were leaving, Valeria had already gotten into the car. Standing at the door, Glenda turned to me and asked, "Am I supposed to remember her name?" Unknown to us, Valeria overheard that comment, although we never realized she had.

"I believe Lu and Valeria have truly become one. They understand each other profoundly and seem to perfectly complement each other's actions. Ever since I've known them, I've witnessed their closeness grow even stronger. It's something that often happens in relationships; they've not only grown individually but also together as a couple.

"I can honestly say they act as one person. They anticipate each other's actions before they even happen, which is quite remarkable. You don't often see that level of connection in relationships these days, and they've been together for a very long time."

"It's truly inspiring to see a couple like them, especially because Lu isn't the easiest person to handle, and it takes someone with Valeria's character to manage someone like him. Valeria, with her heart of gold and no-nonsense attitude, is exactly the kind of partner Lu needs. She's the only one who can firmly say "no" to him and actually be listened to, which is crucial in their dynamic." - **Gisele McFarland**

"Lu was undoubtedly the creative genius behind all of his work, but he wasn't someone who focused on the details. It took Valeria, along with the coordinators and others on the team, to pull everything together and tie up all the loose ends." - **Leigh Hogan, Lu's accountant**

"That's just who I am, I'm not someone who sits back and waits for others to take care of me. I've always been the type to step in, contribute, and help wherever I can. In many ways, Lu and I were complete opposites. I'm pretty conservative when it comes to money; I'm frugal, thoughtful, and smart about how to invest. Lu, on the other hand, wasn't like that at all. If he had money, he'd spend it, he liked being the big guy. He surrounded himself with people who thought the same way, because that was the world he lived in.

"But over time, I came to understand that what Lu was trying to build was something no one else was really aiming for. To achieve that kind of vision, he had to take an unconventional route. That's when I started gradually stepping in, trying to help him manage the financial side of things, just making sure the basics were taken care of properly."

"I remember his phone would get cut off, and instead of avoiding that, he'd just run down and pay the extra to get it reconnected. I'd think, why not just pay it on time and avoid the fees? It was small things like that where I began to get more involved, just doing what I could to keep things on track." - **Valeria**

It never really mattered to Valeria what I was working on, she's always supported me. But now, I can tell I'm wearing her down. Between her full-time job and all of my projects, I've been running her ragged. Every time I come up with something new, she would say, *"You're not really going to do the project, I'm the one who ends up doing all the work."*

Take the Opera Jazz project with Angela Brown, for instance. Valeria was just patiently waiting, sitting on the sidelines, watching me lay the foundation. Then, when the time was right, she stepped in, and when she does, she takes over flawlessly. She's truly gifted at what she does.

Valeria is my soulmate, and you can't get any closer than that. She's been by my side through the highs and the lows, never wavering. She's always been there for me.

Love has a way of humbling you. I've stumbled through it, failed at it, and at times, let it slip through my fingers. I've hurt people, and I've been hurt. But every heartbreak carved a deeper understanding of what love should be, not just passion, but peace...not just chemistry, but commitment.
Through all of that, I found Valeria.

She came into my life when I was finally ready to build, not just chase. With her, it wasn't about trying to impress, it was about being seen. She didn't just support my vision; she grounded it. She knew when to push me, when to protect me, and when to remind me of who I really was.

Valeria... thank you for your love, your patience, your strength. You didn't just stand beside me, you helped hold me up. You were my peace, my partner, my home. I love you always.

Chapter 14: SERIOUS AS A HEART ATTACK

"I am lying in the hospital ... When I looked up and saw Slugger, he was crying; he doesn't usually cry about anything. When I saw him crying, then I got worried."- Lu Vason

In the early days of the Bill Pickett Invitational Rodeo, my vision and energy knew no bounds. The journey of my health through the years has been as volatile and unpredictable as the rodeos I so passionately produced. However, it was in these early days that I experienced my first major health scare, a moment that would be a prelude to a series of medical emergencies.

"It all began subtly at Judy Barnes' house, around the planning sessions for the very first rodeo. Gathered around Judy Barnes' kitchen table, ideas flowed like the Rio Grande, vendors selling pies, throwing contests around the arena, each concept more exciting than the last. I was just sitting at the table and fell out, and they had to rush me to the hospital. I vaguely remember anything about the incident, which was initially dismissed as minor. The doctors said it was because of the water in my ear? I didn't know what that meant.

Judy Barnes, who was Lu Vason's assistant at the time, shared a painful memory from 1980. "Lu had his first health issues at my place," she recounted. "We often worked late, usually at his house, but when it got late, he'd come over to mine because of my kids. That night, after some work, Lu stood up to stretch. He wandered into the living room to play with my baby, the very one he'd gifted chitterlings with when she was born."

She continued, "He was just lifting Yaz-min, who was only about three months old, and I thought nothing of it when he bent over. Suddenly, he collapsed, hitting the floor hard. Miraculously, he managed to position his left arm in such a way that my daughter fell safely to the side, avoiding injury from his fall."
"Lu was unconscious, and I rushed him to the hospital. Convincing him to see a doctor was always a battle, like pulling teeth," Judy added, reflecting on the severity of the situation.

This event marked the beginning of a pattern of health crises that seemed to shadow my high-paced lifestyle. My passion for the rodeo and relentless work ethic often brought me to the edge, physically and metaphorically. The subsequent decades brought more scares and close calls than most endure in a lifetime. Each incident, a stark reminder of mortality, shaped not just my life but also the fabric of the rodeo itself.

The intensity of my life did not slow down with time. By 1990, I started experiencing more alarming symptoms. "One day after one of the rodeos I just remember I was sitting behind my desk eating a peach...and started coughing. I figured the juice had just gone down the wrong pipe as I started coughing. It was one of those moments where everything seemed normal until it wasn't. Boozer was with me at the time, while Lynn Dillard, my Los Angeles coordinator and Valeria had taken off to explore the newly opened Cherry Creek Mall. There I was, trying to write a check for Pat Duncan, when the coughing took over. What seemed small to me at first turned out to be a real wake-up call. Folks around me saw it clear as day, even when I didn't.

"We were wrapping up some business, and Lu was about to pay me. He was at his desk, trying to write out my check. You know, if Lu got even a little tired, he'd start nodding off right there. So there he was, struggling to stay awake and write this check. I kept calling out to him, 'Lu, Lu?' Eventually, I just told him, 'We'll sort out the check later. I'll come back tomorrow.'" - **Pat Duncan**

Boozer came upstairs and noticed something was off with my face. It was drooping to the left. He yelled, *"Pop! Pop! What's wrong with you?"* Annoyed, I snapped back, "Nothing, get out of my face." But Boozer kept staring, concerned.
He immediately called Valeria and said, *"Mom, something's wrong with dad, you need to come immediately."* Soon after, Valeria and Lynn arrived. When Valeria saw me, she immediately declared, *"Oh, No! We're going to the hospital!"* I hadn't realized the left side of my face was sagging. I kept coughing, unable to understand why, not realizing it might have been because my throat was closing up.

I wasn't paying much attention at first. They said, I was having a stroke, and it led to a ten-day hospital stay, I painfully remember. I was lying in the hospital just after our rodeo when Slugger, who was also in town, came to see me. Seeing him in tears was a shock; he's not one to cry easily. That's when I started to worry.

Initially, at the hospital, they thought I had a stroke. After tons of tests, poking and prodding, it was determined to be a heart issue they couldn't pinpoint at the time. They sent me to a cardiologist and in 1991, they diagnosed me not with a heart attack but with Atrial Fibrillation, or A-Fib.

They insisted on a defibrillator, which I finally agreed to have done after Valeria's constant nagging. Did I say, constant nagging! The doctors told me the constant traveling and the sudden changes in altitude were taking a toll on my body. They said, "*Lu, you've got to stop flying for a while.*"

After being cleared to fly again, I remember once flying from San Diego to Denver; that was the first time I collapsed at the airport and busted my lip. Another time, traveling from Washington D.C. to Denver, I fell again, injuring my lip and nose.

Then, flying out of Atlanta, I collapsed and cracked my head. We figured out that the sudden changes in altitude were causing my blackouts. But these blackouts never really scared me. I'd wake up and feel normal again. I just had to remember to either drink lots of water or move slowly after landing. Boozer, being an EMT, always reminded me to walk around on the plane to keep my blood circulating.

Another incident happened when I was up in the mountains at Silverthorne, Colorado, where Odell and Glenda had a condo. Valeria, Odell, Glenda, and I were heading to the cabin. While they were walking ahead of me, I collapsed in the snow. They had to airlift me out because an ambulance would have taken too long. My blackouts seemed to happen when I moved from low to high altitudes, never the other way around.

The last major incident was during my third wife Kashaun's funeral. I blacked out as soon as I walked off the plane on the jetway in Denver.

Then there was a seemingly minor but painful incident at home. I was walking barefoot, stepped on a toothpick, and thought I had removed it all. It happened on Valentine's Day, and Valeria and I were heading out to visit a friend but ended up at the hospital instead.

The doctors assured me there was no toothpick left and gave me tetanus shots, but part of it was still in my foot. It wasn't visible on an X-ray because toothpicks are cellulose. It took until August to discover it was still there after my foot started turning black. I had been limping around, and by the time we landed in Washington D.C. for a rodeo, I couldn't walk. Valeria had to rush me to EmergenCare.

"Starting in August, Lu's foot began swelling pretty badly, and by September, right before we landed in Washington, D.C. for a rodeo, it had turned black and was so swollen he could barely walk. I rushed him to EmergenCare, and when the doctors cut his foot open, this thick, tar-like substance poured out. The smell was awful. The infection was severe. The doctors told me we needed to get him back to Denver immediately so his primary care team could assess the damage and decide what to do next."

"I got on the phone with the airline right away, and we were on the first flight out Monday morning. As soon as we landed in Denver, we went straight to the doctor's office. They took one look at his foot, picked up the phone, and called the hospital. They told me, "Take him straight there, do not pass go." So that's exactly what I did. They admitted him, started him on heavy antibiotics, and began the process of cleaning out the infection. It was intense. They had to clear the wound, treat the area, and begin a long healing journey. After that, it definitely slowed him down." – **Valeria**

Among the chaos of health scares, I found solace in a surprising element: water. I recall how Odell's birthday led to a transformative experience for me. Odell and Glenda invited Valeria and I to Martha's Vineyard, where we stayed at a quaint bed and breakfast, surrounded by the serene expanse of water.

I found myself simply sitting and watching the water, mesmerized. There was nothing else I could do but watch; it was incredibly soothing and played a crucial role in my recovery. That tranquil experience with the water helped bring me back to health.

From that point on, I developed a deep appreciation for waterfalls. After leaving Martha's Vineyard, we stopped in New York and I was captivated by the dancing waterfalls in front of the Hilton Hotel. Just observing the water's flow and where it was headed had a calming effect on me.

This newfound love even took me to Las Vegas, where I would spend hours just watching the waterfalls and fountains in front of the Bellagio Hotel. That's how I got hooked on waterfalls, they would relax me and shift my mindset entirely.

"One year Lu came in with an injured foot and he barely made it to the rodeo. It's incredible how smoothly things run even when he can't be there. Valeria keeps everything in top shape. His team, Sedgwick, General manager and everyone else around him, they all step up their game. They know exactly what needs to be done, no questions asked, they just get on with it." - **Eddie Martin**

By now, life has slowed down completely for me. Between the constant adjustments on my defibrillator and the constant medication for what has now been diagnosed as congested heart failure, life was changing even if I didn't want it to.

"Since Lu has been ill, I've seen people come from all corners of the United States just to see him. They stay for weekends or even a week, making a point to tell him personally how much he means to them. That's truly impressive to me. I know many families who don't even show up for each other's funerals. The effort these people make to be there for Lu really stands out." - **Les Franklin, Close friend, Director of Shaka Franklin Foundation**.

"Lu has had heart problems for a long time and has to avoid certain foods. But there we were, just the two of us in Milwaukee, everyone else had already left, and we were catching the last plane out. I visit Milwaukee often, so I suggested we eat out at a soul food place. Lu was all for it. He went all out and chose smothered pork chops and peach cobbler."

"Valeria warned me, 'I'm going to blame you when he gets sick.' And sure enough, he was down for about two days. I joked with him, 'Well, you'll never go back out to lunch with me anymore, at least not to that type of restaurant.' He just enjoyed himself, fully aware he wasn't supposed to. He said, 'ain't nobody around and you don't tell anybody.' That was about five or six years ago. And oh, he loves oysters." - **Nelson Ball, Lu's close friend.**

The toothpick incident was really the turning point. I never fully recovered from it. It made everything else worse, especially with me already dealing with congested heart failure and having to get multiple defibrillators implanted. The strain of it all, the blackouts, infections, hospital stays, started piling up. The doctors had to increase my medications, and over time, those medications began affecting my other organs, especially my kidneys. That's when traveling was no longer an option for me.

"As his health required more focused attention, those close to me rallied to provide support. At that point, I brought in Gisele to help care for him during the day while I was at work, because he needed constant attention."

"Of course, Lu still wanted to get up and do things, and his friends would come by and take him out. My niece, Tracy Nelson and Gisele would allow Lu to convince them to take him out to eat all the things he wasn't supposed to have, knowing full well that when I got home, none of that would fly. I didn't find out what they were doing until much later, when I gave Lu a stern warning that if he kept eating the wrong food, he was going to die sooner than later." – **Valeria**

"During this last health scare with Lu, I was on FMLA, Family Medical Leave. At that time, Lu was in the hospital. I went to see him, but they had moved him to cardiac intensive care and restricted his visitors to ensure he got the rest he needed. I decided I would call and check in instead."

"That's when I spoke to Valeria. I told her, 'Well, I'm not working right now, why don't you let me look after Lu? I love him and I don't mind helping out.' Every time Lu was in and out of the hospital, I always made sure he was okay. Back then, his condition didn't require constant care."

"Even when he wasn't ill, I would just come around and spend time with the family. I've been a part of their lives for a good 20 to 25 years," Gisele added, highlighting her long-standing relationship with Lu and his family." - **Gisele McFarland.**

There were still so many things I wanted to accomplish, but I had to significantly slow down. I focused more on relaxation to help rejuvenate my body. That's why I've scaled back on most of my productions, except for the rodeos.

My wife, along with people like Margo Wade and Acynthia Villery, have been instrumental in standing by Valeria and taking over some responsibilities to keep the rodeo going. It also bothered me to see the toll of my sickness was having on Valeria.

She never made me feel I was a bother and she did everything she could to make sure I got the best care and that I was taken care of when she wasn't around. No one knows better than me what I put her through, but she never wavered.

The lesson here is about love, the power of nature and its healing effects. Sometimes, in our relentless pursuit of goals and responsibilities, we overlook the simple elements around us that can offer profound healing and peace.

It's a reminder that sometimes, slowing down and embracing the calming aspects of our environment can be just as important as pushing forward in our endeavors and we should always take time for those that love us.

My journey with watching water taught me to appreciate the moments of tranquility and to incorporate them into my recovery and daily life.

There's a rhythm to life I've always felt, and maybe that's why jazz and water have meant so much to me. Both move how they want, unpredictable, soulful, never in a straight line. As I slowed down and faced illness, I found peace in that flow. Sitting by a waterfall, I didn't just hear the water, I heard Miles, I heard Coltrane. The way it moved reminded me that life, like jazz, is never really still.

Even in silence, there's a melody. Even in pain, there's a rhythm. In those quiet moments, just me, the water, and the music, I found something sacred. I found God. I found grace. I found myself.

Chapter 15: UNAPOLOGETIC BLACKNESS

"Lu taught me a lot of blackness. He educated me about black history. He always took me under his wing and told me stories about when dogs bit him, showed me his scars, talking to me about Bull Connors dogs and all that. This opened my eyes to the racism of the bigotry that a black man goes through. He reassured me that it was okay to be black and hold a black pride deep inside." - Lynn "Smokey" Hart

When you step into my home, you can't help but notice all of the black art and cultural items immediately surrounding you. Each corner brims with an eclectic mix of paintings, photographs, books, artifacts, figurines, handiwork, antiques, and relics. Every piece has a story, showcasing the depth and diversity of our heritage.

This collection isn't driven by a deliberate message I'm trying to send. Rather, it's more about my passion for collecting the unique and the meaningful. My collection of black art isn't just for show; it's a living, breathing celebration of our history.

I believe it's crucial for us to see and understand our history. These pieces aren't just decoration, they're a narrative of our past, inviting everyone who looks to see not just art, but stories, and to consider them not just as assets but as chapters of our collective memory.

Black art tells powerful stories. While some may see these items as mere decor or even as investments, I view them as narratives and lessons of history. Echoing the sentiments of Dr. Carter G. Woodson, the founder of what we now celebrate as Black History Month, I believe in the importance of remembering our past to secure our future. These artifacts are not just remnants of bygone days but reminders of the prejudice that once was, and still exists to some extent today.

Indeed, the landscape of racial understanding has shifted but not sufficiently transformed. The election of President Obama, while a monumental milestone, revealed deep-seated resentment and brought to light the ongoing challenges we face. His presidency, symbolizing progress for some, also underscored the reality that he was a leader for all Americans, not exclusively for Black communities.

Throughout my life, I've often been a pioneer, engaging in 'firsts' and pushing boundaries not yet explored by others in my community. While many white individuals were creating spaces and events for themselves, it seemed imperative to me that Black folks also carve out spaces for our voices and stories.
Is this all a reflection on my experiences of being a black man in America?

I remember those summers back in Alabama, when I was just a kid and then a teenager. Every weekend, my relatives and friends from the country would flood into downtown Montgomery. That place buzzed like a beehive on the weekends, especially around the Greyhound and train stations.
Back then, the signs "For Colored Only" and "For Whites Only" were just part of the landscape. As a youngster, you noticed them, sure, but you didn't really understand the weight they carried. It wasn't until I hit my teens that the reality of those signs, of what they really meant, began to dawn on me.

I'll never forget the summer of '53. I had come back to Montgomery from California. The city was charged with tension; there was a picketing protest going on. The Black community was fighting for the right to sit at the front of the bus. I was there, just observing, trying to take it all in, when suddenly, I found myself in the midst of chaos. Two police dogs, snarling and barking, lunged at me. The scars they left on my leg are a permanent reminder of that day. It was a pivotal moment, and little did I know that just two years later, Rosa Parks would refuse to give up her seat on a bus right here in Montgomery, sparking the Montgomery Bus Boycott and bringing Dr. Martin Luther King, Jr. to the forefront of the civil rights movement.

My understanding of race relations truly peaked later, when I was living in California. That's where I began to see the broader picture, where I started to understand my place in the struggle and in the world. But those days in Montgomery, they're etched in my memory, a reminder of where I came from and what it took to get here.

Back in the day, in the Bay Area, I was deep into managing entertainment artists and putting on concerts. Mary Ann Pollar was the dynamo bringing all these Rhythm & Blues and jazz artists to town, and we worked hand in glove. Then "Superfly" hit the screens and blew up big time, thanks to Curtis Mayfield's killer soundtrack. I had already promoted Curtis back when he was with the Impressions, right here in the Bay Area.

But then, when it came time to book Curtis post-"Superfly," suddenly, Bill Graham, a white promoter, had him locked down. Us Black promoters were left scratching our heads, wondering, "Since when did Bill deal with Black artists?" It didn't sit right with us. All the work we'd done to build these artists up in our neighborhoods, and now that they were hitting it big, here comes the "white boy" looking to cash in.

So, we got together, me, Mary Ann, Dick Griffey out of Los Angeles, and we faced off with Bill Graham. We laid it down clear: "You can't just swoop in on shows with Black artists without involving us." The agencies weren't helping either; they'd funnel successful Black artists to white promoters, bypassing us completely. We made some serious noise about that injustice.

Bill did bring Aretha Franklin to the Fillmore later, among other artists. That whole scene became a major flashpoint in the Bay Area, and Mary Ann was at the forefront, a true warrior. She was a "Sistah of the Sun," sporting a natural hairstyle way before it was mainstream, mingling with giants like Maya Angelou. Women like her didn't take nonsense from anyone and were trailblazers in every sense.

It reminds me of the time I managed Oscar Brown Jr. and the Pointer Sisters. Once, while Oscar and I were sharing a room, he threw a curveball at me, asking, "*What if I died, what would you do?*" I joked about getting him a movie deal. He pushed back, "*Do it now!*" But I knew the game, tributes flowed for the departed, not the living.

Oscar later sang "Ragtime" in a San Francisco stage production, a song by the great Black composer Scott Joplin. Tears streamed down his face every single night he performed. When I asked him about it, he revealed his pain over how Marvin Hamlisch had used Joplin's music in "The Sting" without giving Scott any credit, winning Oscars for music that wasn't rightfully his.

Like Oscar, I carry a deep resolve to shine a light on our Black heritage through my work, especially with the rodeo. It's not just about entertainment; it's about righting wrongs and telling our stories, making sure we honor where we came from and those who paved our way.

James Brown said it best, "I'm Black and I'm Proud." That's the charge we carry forward.

"I think what Lu will be most remembered for is giving us a blessing with the Black Cowboy. I believe the history of the Black Cowboy wouldn't have been told accurately without Lu. We wouldn't even get to see a black cowboy even now had it not been for Lu, not in the way that he puts on a show and how he showcases them." - **Carla Ladd, Owner of DenverBlackPages.com**

"Without the Bill Pickett Rodeo, an entire culture of cowboys would miss out on experiences like those I've had with our very own rodeo association. It's not perfect, but it certainly isn't the worst, it's a vital part of our heritage." - **Carolyn Carter, Lu Grand Entry Coordinator**

"Dad ingrained in me a profound sense of Black pride and empowerment from a very young age. He always had a clear vision of independence, from running a beauty salon to organizing concerts and managing the rodeo. His determination to forge his own path was evident in everything he did. He also emphasized the importance of Black pride in our personal lives. I remember him advising me in high school about the significance of dating a Black woman, stressing how crucial it is to cherish our Black sisters. That advice has deeply influenced my appreciation and respect for the women in our community, marking a significant point in my life." **- Corey Vason**

"Lu really deepened my understanding of Black culture. After serving four years in the Marine Corps, he introduced me to my first pig ear sandwich and educated me about Black history. He took me to the all-black Western Heritage Museum, where I learned about the Buffalo Soldiers and the civil rights movement. Lu also inspired me to advocate for honoring Dr. Martin Luther King Jr. in South Dakota, which at the time, was one of the last states to recognize the day as a federal or state holiday. This experience really opened my eyes to the racism and bigotry that Black people face."

"Lu reassured me that it was okay to embrace my Black identity proudly. Back then, I was a bit wild, drinking heavily and smoking a lot. Lu didn't just lecture me; instead, he encouraged me to find my own path, knowing I'd figure it out eventually. His approach wasn't about telling me what not to do, but allowing me to be my own man." **- Lynn "Smokey" Hart**

I also forged a strong connection with the Jewish community, which I believe was significantly influenced by my time stationed in Dachau, Germany, about 15 years after World War II. The horrors that occurred there were still vivid in the collective memory. Seeing the death ditches, gas showers, and ovens firsthand was profoundly disturbing. The atrocities were unimaginable, people were killed in horrific ways, and there were even lampshades made from the skin of prisoners, a chilling detail that stuck with me.

The atmosphere at Dachau was haunting. Even years after the war, if you walked outside the base surrounded by trees late at night, you could hear eerie sounds, whispers and murmurs that made guard duty intensely unnerving. Nobody wanted to be out there; it felt like the trees themselves were speaking.

This profound experience deepened my appreciation for the struggles and resilience of the Jewish people. Later, when I worked with Barry Fey at the Rainbow Music Hall and got involved in concert promotions, I collaborated with two Jewish kids, Rob and Mark. They further educated me about their history and cultural ties, enriching my understanding and respect for their community.

ONE ART PIECE AT A TIME

I've always had an eye for the arts, a knack I picked up during one of my first gigs after the military, working at the post office. There, I sold postcards featuring works by artists like Van Gogh and Monet, which helped me understand their techniques. This sparked a deeper interest in art, and I soon began exploring the works of Black artists, learning about their unique mediums like charcoal and paint.

My passion for collecting began somewhat unexpectedly. While doing hair, a young artist who worked with pen and ink introduced me to the world of real art created by Black artists. My third wife, Kashan, and I then ventured into collecting antiques and unique items, like old oak refrigerators and sewing machines from Alabama, which we would restore to their former glory.

Our collection expanded to include peculiar pieces, such as an old tobacco can labeled 'Nigger Hair' that we found in a New Orleans antique shop. We thought it was unique and started collecting more items that represented Black heritage, like old magazine covers featuring Black artwork and cereal boxes with Black figures, rare at the time. We believed these items were not only investments but also important cultural artifacts.

As our collection grew, we faced criticism for some of the items we chose to preserve. People questioned why we collected such things and suggested we should destroy them. Instead, their reactions only fueled our desire to collect more. We joined a society of collectors dedicated to preserving Black artifacts, which was founded by a lady in Berkeley. She was instrumental in helping us value and understand the significance of our collection.

As my interest deepened, I transitioned from collecting general artifacts to more modern Black art. I began with originals but soon moved to limited editions and serigraphs due to the high cost of originals. My collection became quite extensive, featuring works by artists like Charles Bibbs and John Toms, as well as Denver local Darrell Anderson.

I even commissioned artworks for my shows, keeping my focus on promoting unknown Black artists and sharing their talents with a broader audience. For instance, for a function with Norwest Bank, we celebrated Black golfers, the legends before Tiger Woods. Darrell Anderson created a painting for the event, and we sold prints while keeping the original, which is now in my basement. Through collecting and promoting, I've had the pleasure of meeting incredible artists and sharing their works, contributing to the recognition and appreciation of Black culture and history.

"Lu always said there were two pots of money, one for white organizations and another for Black organizations when it came to event funding. He'd tell me, 'Bobby, there's a pot of money that white organizations access for their events, and then there's what Black organizations are given.' I always hoped we'd reach a point where an event's funding would be based on its merits alone, not the racial background it was associated with."

"This conversation with Lu really opened my eyes. I began to notice how my own bank tended to allocate fewer dollars to Black and Latino organizations compared to white ones. One day, I decided to challenge this practice."

"I went to my boss and argued that if a Black organization needed the funding to execute a first-class event, we should provide the necessary support to make it happen. My boss simply looked at me and said, 'You do what you need to do.' From that point forward, we started allocating the kind of funding that Black organizations needed to host the events they envisioned. I credit Lu with sparking this change. Thanks to him, I realized the importance of stepping up and doing the right thing. We might have been the first in Denver to make such a shift." **- Bob Willis**

From that point, we continued to introduce significant figures to our community. We brought in Tiger Woods right as he was emerging into the public eye. He initiated the First Tee program with a clinic at the Park Hill Golf Course and also spoke at Macedonia Baptist Church in Denver. This was how my relationship with Bob developed. At the time, he was with Norwest Bank, and together we were dedicated to organizing fundraisers. We aimed to create events that were not only unique but also celebrated our Black heritage.

"I was always impressed by Lu's commitment to enriching the Black community, particularly through introducing them to new cultural experiences and high-quality events. A prime example is the Dance Theatre of Harlem, which we recently hosted for the second time. Without Lu's initiative, we might never have experienced such performances here." **- Michael A. Hancock**

STAMPS OF APPROVAL

I started showcasing the arts so that people could see these meaningful images. My interest soon expanded into collecting black stamps, tracing back from the earliest ones to contemporary issues. Initially, it wasn't popular to have black stamps. I also gathered sheet blocks of Booker T. Washington on fifty-cent pieces, a piece of history about 90% of the black population doesn't even know existed, black farm money.

I wanted to instill a sense of pride in our heritage through these collections.

When I met Valeria, her house was very sterile, like a hospital. After we got together, I began introducing her to the artifacts I collected. For instance, I owned an Aunt Jemima cookie jar that initially offended her. She couldn't understand why I surrounded myself with these 'black items.' I had to explain the significance and the stories behind each piece.

Our collecting journey together really took off after a trip to Kansas City. We visited an antique store where we found a replica of my Aunt Jemima cookie jar valued between $200 to $300. That moment changed her perspective, which led me to start collecting serious pieces, beginning with works by Romare Bearden.

When we decided to buy a new house in 1988, we were out with Odell looking at different homes. We were driving through the Piney Creek area when Lu spotted a house he liked, and I liked it too. It had a "For Sale" sign out front. Lu immediately said, "Let's stop here and check it out." Slugger was with us too.

"Odell tried to be the voice of reason and said, "You can't just walk into someone's house, I need to call the realtor and set up an appointment." But before he could even finish saying that, Lu had already jumped out of the car, walked up to the front door, and rang the bell. The owner answered, and true to form, Lu charmed his way right into the house. She ended up letting us all come in and take a look around." – **Valeria**

As soon as I saw the kitchen counter, which resembled a bar, I knew this was the home for us. Valeria and Slugger explored the rest of the house, but I stayed by the bar, chatting with the owner. That's where I feel most comfortable, either in the kitchen or on the floor.

When it was time to move in, I happened to be out of town, so Valeria and Slugger handled everything. By the time I got back, the house was completely in order.

Pictures were hung, everything was perfectly arranged, all done the "Valeria way." It looked beautiful.

I was excited to start bringing in my personal touch. My paintings, artifacts, and my Black art collection from my house in Montbello. But Valeria wasn't having all of it. She told me straight up that I wasn't bringing all those "little nigger" figurines into the new house.

After some back and forth, we came to a compromise. I was able to display some of my items, such as my prized Gold Dust Twins and the little boys eating watermelon paintings. It meant a lot to me, those pieces tell a story, our story, and history that shouldn't be erased.

The value of my collection is something I can't fully grasp. I've paid up to $25,000 for some pieces, and their worth has only increased since the artists passed away. For example, artworks by Romare Bearden are now valued between $15,000 and $18,000 each.

My 'sister,' Joyce Reynolds, also embraced the art world. She went to art school and opened a gallery. I've sent her pieces to display, including works by sculptor Ed Dwight.

My introduction to Ed happened when I first moved to Denver and was visiting Mattie Springfield's home, filled with his bronze statues. That night, she took me to a foundry where I met Ed Dwight, before he became famous for his major statues like those of Hank Aaron and Martin Luther King Jr. At one point, I even acted as Ed's agent.

The progression of collecting often starts with prints, moves to limited editions, and, if affordable, to originals. The expense of originals today is prohibitive for many.

When my third wife passed, I attended her funeral and then fell ill. My daughter Shelley came to check on me. Her first words were about the cereal boxes, something I had always told Valeria where I wanted my cereal boxes to go.

Shelley grew up appreciating black artifacts, influenced by her mother. Now, she's as passionate as both her parents about collecting. She's clear about her inheritance, she wants the cereal boxes.

Interestingly, Valeria has since developed a fondness for these artifacts. She now helps me expand our collection, which includes a special curio dedicated to Obama memorabilia and other art pieces.

Art, music, and culture. They've always been more than just expression. They're memory. They're resistance. They're healing. Everything we've endured and overcome as Black folks, our joy, our pain, our brilliance, it all lives in the art we make and the stories we tell. Whether it's the soul of a jazz horn, the rhythm of a gospel choir, or the colors in a mural on a city wall, there's wisdom in it. It's how we've passed down truth when the world tried to silence us.

I've always believed in honoring that, boldly and without apology. Being Black ain't something to shrink from, it's something to stand in. Loud. Proud. Unfiltered. Our culture teaches, reaches, and uplifts. And if I've done anything right in this life, it's using every platform I had to celebrate it.

Chapter 16 THE FEYLINE CONNECTION

After Gene and I successfully managed Fey's 30 concert dates, selling out 27 of them, my professional relationship with Barry Fey began to flourish. We retreated to the mountains, and as Gene stepped away from the entertainment industry for good, I tightened my partnership with Barry, who was based in Denver.

Before and after the Funk Fest, as well as the tour with Parliament-Funkadelic, I had already started collaborating with Barry to bring a diverse range of acts to Denver. The city was very receptive, especially at venues like Red Rocks where I produced numerous shows that year, which helped cement my ties with Barry both professionally and personally.

Working with Barry was a new chapter, but by then, I'd seen the cycle, Black promoters like me built the talent, only to watch big white promoters swoop in once the spotlight hit. We'd lived that story, and I wasn't afraid to speak on it, just like we did with Bill Graham.

But here's where Barry stood out. I didn't feel like he was trying to muscle in or push me aside. Barry recognized what I brought to the table, and instead of seeing me as competition, he saw me as a partner. He respected the communities I connected with, the talent I could bring to the stage, and the hustle that went into every show. With Barry, I never like I was being edged out, it was about teaming up to build something bigger.

Our partnership took us everywhere. We worked together to bring not just funk and R&B acts, but rock, jazz, and pop to Denver. Red Rocks became our playground.

A place where I could see firsthand how blending my experience with Barry's reach could create something special. And sure, I always kept my guard up because I knew the game, but with Barry, I found someone willing to work with me, not around me. That was the heart of *The Feyline Connection*.

Looking back on those moments, the meetings, the fights for fairness, the battles we waged not just for ourselves but for what was right, I came to realize something deeper than the business itself. It wasn't just about contracts or commissions. It was about dignity. About standing up and saying: We helped build this, and we deserve to be at the table when it's time to share the feast.

That fight taught me one of the greatest lessons of my life: If you don't claim your seat at the table, someone else will, and they'll eat your meal, too. In the entertainment world, in business, in life, you've got to know your worth, and you've got to speak up for it. That's not always easy. Sometimes it means making waves, sometimes it means being labeled difficult or demanding. But if you stay silent, you risk disappearing in the shadows of the very stage you helped build.

And it's that same truth that shaped how I worked with Barry Fey, and how I approached every partnership after. I didn't just want to be in the room, I wanted to help set the agenda, to make sure our community's contributions weren't just recognized, but valued.

This backdrop of advocacy and partnership was key in defining my ongoing collaboration with Barry. He recognized the unique challenges and opportunities in promoting Black shows and gave me the autonomy to produce these events independently whenever the chance arose. For instance, if Larry Bailey or Lewis mentioned acts passing through Denver, I would take the lead in pitching to Barry, who would then step aside to let me manage the production.

We established a mutually beneficial working arrangement based on who brought the act to the table. If Barry introduced a Black act, he would take a larger share of the profits, and vice versa. Typically, our profit-sharing agreement was split 60%/40%, depending on who secured the act. This partnership not only demonstrated a successful business model but also reflected a deeper understanding and respect for the challenges we, as Black promoters, faced in a predominantly white-controlled industry.

Becky Taylor, a well-known radio personality, reminisces about me and Barry and our dynamic partnership, *"Lu was integral to Barry, especially in bringing jazz shows to Colorado. I remember when Lu brought Stevie Wonder to Boulder, back in the late 1970s. I was working at the Events Conference Center at the University of Colorado. It was impressive to see a Black man in such a pivotal role. A few years later, in 1981, Lu organized 'Jazz on the Rocks' at Red Rocks. One memorable show featured Grover Washington Jr. and Patrice Rushen. Unfortunately, it rained out at Red Rocks, so we moved the performance to the Events Center."*

The strength of my relationship with Barry was cemented during a particularly challenging time in my life when I was struggling financially. Reflecting on this period, I thought, I was in a tough spot, having wrecked my car and being broke. In a conversation, my business partner, Linda Motely, bluntly told me to put my car in the shop. Her matter-of-fact tone made me realize the severity of my situation.

I resisted initially, confessing to Linda, I can't put the car in the shop; I have no money to get it out. She replied firmly, *"You put your car in the shop, and either you find a way to get it out, or they'll sell it."* Her words laid bare the obvious choice before me, find the funds or lose the car. It was a gamble on my ability to pull through this crisis.

Caught in this dilemma, I remember, despite my hesitation and lack of funds, I put the car in the shop. As predicted, calls from the shop soon began, pressing me for payment. With no clear solution in sight, I turned to Barry, who directed me to his wife, Sydney. I explained my situation to Sydney, promising to repay any help she could provide. She agreed and facilitated a $1,400 loan from their account after I gave her the pink slip as collateral.

This financial aid was a turning point for me. With Sydney's help, I retrieved my car, and that marked the last of my financial lows. Returning to hairstyling briefly, I managed to pay back Barry and move forward. My gratitude towards him persisted until his passing, and we shared a lifelong bond.

What those years taught me? Plain and simple. It ain't always about fighting to be seen; sometimes it's about knowing how to build with folks who see you already. Barry and I had that in common.

We liked to do things our way, on our own terms. When he opened the Rainbow Music Hall, I was managing Rose Royce, and they wrapped up their tour right there. That sealed my name. Barry didn't just notice, he handed me the keys for booking Black acts at the Rainbow.

From that point on, it was *Lu Vason and Feyline*, or *Feyline in Association with Lu Vason*. That wasn't just a line on a flyer, that was my work finally getting its due. And what stuck with me most? When folks respect what you do, don't just stand next to them, build with them. That's how you grow.

Leigh Hogan, Barry Fey's accountant, reflects on the unique partnership between Barry and me, noting, *"There wasn't really any competition between Mr. Fey and Lu because their relationship was symbiotic. Barry didn't have the connections to bring in the acts that Lu could, and Lu needed the capital and network that Barry provided. It was truly a mutually beneficial partnership."*

From a personal perspective, I view my time with Barry fondly, despite his reputation for being somewhat difficult. Barry made a lot of his friends and associates angry because he was seen as a "tyrant," I recall.

But I guess, being a bit of a tyrant myself, that aspect never bothered me. I understood he did what he needed to do to get things done. People outside of business responsibilities don't always understand that.

Barry and I shared a running joke among our regular interactions. If I called him, he'd joke, "*I don't talk to Black folks on Tuesday.*" I'd reply, Then I'll call you tomorrow, and sure enough, I'd call him the next day, often to invite him out for barbecue at M&D's, his favorite.

Our friendship extended into various dining experiences, where we'd explore different barbecue joints. During one of our lunch outings, Barry mentioned a new venture he was exploring outside of music promotions, intrigued by the theatrical production potential.

He was considering producing "Casablanca the Musical" and needed to match funding from Warner Bros., who were willing to invest between $2 million and $4 million. I brought Gene into the conversation to gauge his interest in the project, which had garnered attention even in China, though Gene remained skeptical of the authenticity of the overseas acclaim.

Just before Barry died, we were still good friends. Our routine lunches continued, and on one occasion at a barbecue restaurant, Barry's interaction with the staff highlighted a shift in his recognition. He quipped to the server, *"You don't know who I am?"* It was a revealing moment that showed me Barry wasn't as widely recognized by the newer generations as he once was.

Ironically, Barry later found himself in a financial pinch and borrowed money from me. He insisted on repaying me, but I reassured him, you don't have to pay me back. After all, Barry had helped me through numerous challenges over the years.

Eventually, Barry wrote a book and began earning from it. He was eager to settle his debt, but I insisted, "You don't have to pay me back." Our history was marked by mutual support, transcending mere financial transactions and deepening our lifelong friendship.

It was just three days before Barry passed away. We had a conversation, and he told me, *"Lu, I'm so depressed."* I was puzzled and asked, *"Why are you depressed? Why don't you work on the Casablanca musical project?"* Barry had recently undergone hip replacement surgery and wasn't feeling himself. I assumed his mood was due to the physical restrictions and the painkillers he needed to take.

"Is it your hip that's bothering you?" I asked. *"No, it's my knee,"* he replied. At the time, I didn't fully grasp it, but I think when people face such physical challenges and financial worries, they become disheartened and lose the drive to do much. That realization hits me now as I reflect back.

I told him I'd call in a couple of days; that was a Wednesday. Meanwhile, Valeria kept reminding me, *"Lu, you need to call Barry."* She must have told me three times over the next few days. Despite her reminders, I never made that call.
That weekend, Valeria and I were at Gerald Albright's house for brunch. She kept nudging me, *"You need to call Barry."* I promised I'd call him once we got home.

However, as soon as we walked in the door, the phone rang. It was LaDorria. *"I'm sorry to hear about your friend,"* she said. What friend? I asked, confused. *"Oh, you didn't know?"* she responded, surprised. Know what? I pressed, growing impatient. *"Barry Fey killed himself,"* she revealed. And just like that, Valeria's intuition about urging me to call Barry made sense. I was in shock, barely able to process the news, feeling a surge of guilt for not having called him sooner. I was overwhelmed by emotions, regretting ignoring Valeria's gentle prompts.

The only person I could think to call was Gene DeWitt. I told him about Barry, and we were both stunned. "*Not Barry*; *he wouldn't do something like that,*" we said. It was unimaginable. Looking back, we now understand that a combination of medications and depression can lead to tragic decisions. Barry had been a Marine, a tough man who had once been very prominent.

He'd even indulged in luxury, like buying a Mercedes convertible when he started driving again. However, his fortunes began to decline, particularly after investing heavily in a film project with Willie Nelson and his gambling on racehorses, which likely led to significant financial losses. Tragically, Barry never secured the matching funds from Warner Bros. for his musical, and all the props and materials for the production ended up stored away in Canada.

This loss hit me hard. I still think about Barry all the time. Valeria and I occasionally see someone who reminds us of him, and it's like he's still with us in spirit. Barry's death, much like the unexpected passing of my partner Linda Moore, who died from complications following a successful surgery, remains a profound and painful mystery in my life.

Linda was always quick to offer sound advice, even faster than Valeria at times. Her sudden loss from a blood clot was another devastating blow.

Reflecting on these events, the memories of Barry and Linda continue to impact me deeply, a reminder of the unpredictable nature of life and the importance of the connections we hold dear.

To Barry Fey and Linda Mosley, two souls who left fingerprints on my journey.

Barry, you were more than just a business partner. You were a wild spirit, a brilliant mind, and a man who saw possibility in chaos. You gave me trust when others hesitated, opportunity when doors were shut. We didn't always see the world the same, but we saw each other. That mattered.

And Linda…You were my anchor when the winds blew hardest. You showed up with grace, with strength, with that quiet kind of wisdom that can only come from someone who really sees you. You weren't just part of the rodeo, you were part of my life. You kept me grounded when I was drifting, lifted me when I was sinking.

To you reading this, hold on tight to your people. Cherish them. Celebrate them. Laugh with them. Learn from them. Tell them how much they mean to you while you can. Because it's not just the big wins that shape our lives, it's the people who stood beside us when no one else did. The memories we make with them…those are forever.

Chapter 17: WE ARE FAMILY

"When my first daughter was born. Lu was listening to it on the phone with me. He was laughing at me and I was crying. I thought I was being a big old sissy, but later on learned that Lu was a big sissy too, because he cried; he just didn't want to let anybody know that he was crying." - Jody Gilbert

I guess you could say I've got a big family, but not everyone's related by blood. You'll often hear people calling me 'Dad,' even though I'm not their biological father. And you'll hear me refer to many as my 'son' or 'daughter,' even if they aren't my biological kids.

It's not really about bloodlines. It's about the bond we share. I treat each of them like my own children. Each relationship unique, each person receiving their own respect, and each learning something special from me.

"When I first met Lu, I didn't know much about his family. I just remember thinking, 'Wow, this man has people everywhere!' Every time I turned around, it was, 'That's his daughter,' 'That's his son,' 'That's Uncle Lu,' or 'That's my Daddy.' It turned out none of these people were related to him at all, that's just how he felt about them, and how they felt about him."

"Lu had that kind of bond with many of us who worked with him. There were plenty of times, not just for me, when people got so frustrated with Lu. Honestly, if he hadn't been the kind of person he was, folks would've just thrown up their hands and walked away. But instead, whenever things got tough or frustrating, we'd just smile, shake our heads, and say, 'Well, you know Lu.''- **Lynn Dillard Wright**

Acynthia Villery learned patience and the business side of rodeos from me. We spent so much time on the road together, we became very close. When Acynthia's father was alive, he and I were tight. After he passed, it was like I stepped into that role, Acynthia always jokes she ended up with two fathers.

With Lynn Hart, it was different. He developed a deep appreciation for Black history, something he knew nothing about before meeting me. He was up in South Dakota fighting bulls when Slugger spotted him and encouraged him to join us. Back then, we didn't have any Black bullfighters, and Lynn stepped right into that role.

"I became like a son to him; he adopted both Slugger and me under his wing. Now, I call him 'Dad' and he calls me 'his boy.' He was really proud that I had won the National Martin Luther King Jr. Holiday award from Coretta Scott King for getting the first Native American Day, as well as the Martin Luther King Jr. Holiday, passed by the South Dakota legislature at the age of 30."

"Yes, Lu had his ways. He used to call me 'dumb dumb,' which really got under my skin. I told him, 'I'm not dumb; don't ever call me dumb dumb again.' He tried to brush it off, but I made it clear that calling me that was as offensive as using a racial slur. I stood up to him; after all, he was like my dad, and I felt I could say anything to him."

"Overall, I owe a lot to Lu. I worked with him for 11 years as one of his bullfighters and rodeo clowns. I can't express enough how much impact he had on me. If it wasn't for him, white America including black Americans wouldn't know nearly as much about the contributions of Black cowboys and cowgirls."

"You know, most people don't even realize where the term 'cowboy' comes from, they used to call the Black workers 'boy' when there was a cow that needed tending to, while the whites were known as 'wranglers' or 'drovers.' That's why I like to joke and say I can play Cowboys and Indians all by myself." - **Lynn "Smokey" Hart**

Boozer was one of the first. We really bonded when we brought the rodeo to Atlanta back in 1985. Slugger joined us that same year, but it wasn't until 1987 that our father-son relationship truly began.

Boozer didn't see his real father much, which is why he gravitated towards me. I became the father figure he was missing. Slugger, on the other hand, had a strained relationship with his living father, so I ended up filling that role for him more than anyone else.

Their involvement also deepened their respect for the rodeo and for Black cowboys. Like many, they hadn't grown up seeing Black cowboys in movies, so they lacked an understanding of their history. Although Acynthia and Slugger were familiar with Black cowboys from Texas, they didn't really know about the historical figures or their significant contributions.

LaDorria Jones came into the picture much later. She quickly felt like a daughter to me, especially since my own children were far away in California and Washington. LaDorria and I grew incredibly close over time.

"When I first met Lu in March 2003, he quickly took me under his wing, calling me his daughter, which really helped me feel better about myself. I'm originally from East St. Louis, Illinois, and they say you can take the girl out of East St. Louis, but you can't take East St. Louis out of the girl. I never had a real relationship with my biological father, and I never fully shared that story with Lu. But as Lu introduced me as his daughter, it helped me build a stronger sense of self-worth."

"This new family connection with Lu even helped me start mending my relationship with my biological father. In 2004, when the rodeo came to St. Louis, I stayed back in Denver, but I encouraged my father to go. He did, and he met Lu; they hit it off and started a mini-relationship of their own. That year marked the beginning of a growing relationship with my real father. Lu is my Colorado dad. That familial bond is what keeps bringing me back; I'm family now." - **LaDorria Jones**

"Linda introduced Lu to our family, and he quickly became like a father figure to us, especially after my own father passed away. Lu and Linda grew incredibly close when he moved to Denver, where Linda was working in entertainment with Barry Fey, who started referring groups to Lu for booking. Linda then bought a record shop, which became a hub for Lu to have signings for entertainers who came into town, leading the two of them to organize concerts together."

"They were like siblings and collaborated closely on the rodeo; Linda was truly an integral part of his life. They often made decisions together, and like any close relationship, they had their moments of disagreement but always reconciled. Linda was always there for Lu; they constantly communicated." Tragically, Linda suffered from an aneurysm shortly after a knee replacement in June 2010. Despite initial recovery, she endured another aneurysm and passed away on June 30, 2010, after insisting she was fine over Father's Day."

"Her loss was a profound shock; she was the linchpin for our family, and her passing deeply affected everyone, especially Lu." - **Karen Motley**

I can't emphasize how deeply I miss Linda. She was there for me in countless ways, providing emotional support, sharing in my challenges, and celebrating my successes. Her presence was a cornerstone in my life, and her absence is profoundly felt. I frequently reflect on the multitude of ways she enriched my life and the void her passing has left.

Clarence Gipson came into the picture as a bull rider, but I persuaded him to try bareback riding, during which he unfortunately got injured. During his recovery, he stayed at my home in Montbello, where Gisele looked after him with the same care she gave me, and they developed a close bond. After recovering, Clarence left Denver for a while, but returned to stay for about a year. He was always around between Texas and Denver.

Similarly, Renée Penick, who was my secretary at the time, also stayed with me for a year. She was my fourth secretary and we grew quite close, just as I had been with Cherie Hall, my first secretary. Renee came and went, but she was always there when I truly needed her, all the way to the very end. I know I wasn't the easiest boss, I upset each of them at one point or another, and that's something I wasn't proud of.

"Lu always pushed me to strive harder and taught me that when faced with challenges, you shouldn't retreat but face them head-on. He's a tough character; I've seen him be strict with others, and it used to make me cry. But standing your ground with him earns his respect more than if you're too passive. Many people overlook this. His lessons have guided me in my career and personal life, teaching me that age doesn't define our capabilities or ambitions—it's about what we choose to do with our lives and seizing the opportunities our careers offer." - **Renee Penick**

In the early eighties, September Browne joined our team and has been with me ever since, either as my assistant or as one of opening comedy acts at my shows. We've undoubtedly developed a close relationship, and I embraced her daughter as one of my own children as well. We too became family.

As I stated earlier, family doesn't have to be blood.

"We were one of the main ticket sellers for his events, selling tickets right from our restaurant. Lu and the rest of the crew, including the entertainers, often came over to our place after shows. We were like family, really close, like brothers. Those gatherings at our house were always a great time. Everyone would stay almost all night, having a blast. With Lu there, it felt just like home." - **Mack & Daisy Shead, Former owners of M&D's Restaurant**

For Andre McClain, I provided many opportunities because he was eager to become a cowboy. He was already familiar with horses, but he aspired to be a singing cowboy.

Once he joined us, he began singing and picked up rope and horse tricks. His talents blossomed into showmanship, which eventually led him to a role with the Ringling Brothers Circus.

"I've always been passionate about horses and rodeos. In the early '90s, I met Lu through Rex Purefoy, who at the time was sponsored by Coors as a contract act for the rodeo. Seeing Rex, a Black man in entertainment, perform inspired me greatly. Watching him command the arena, I knew I wanted to learn and be like him. I taught myself horse riding, fancy trick roping, and more."

"Over time, I mastered various skills: roping tricks, walking on stilts, horse riding, and animal training, and I even became a singer and announcer. In 1997, while working at Harold Penner Clothing in Denver, I presented my show to Lu Vason."

"Lu took me under his wing, teaching me the business side of rodeo and guiding me through the industry. I traveled with the Bill Pickett Rodeo for several years, performing in a one-man cowboy show inspired by Lu and Rex. My experiences with them led me to expand into stilt walking and trick roping at rodeos."

"To me, Lu isn't just Lu; I call him 'Dad.' When Ringling Bros. noticed my versatility and offered me a job, Lu initially laughed and discouraged it, knowing how much I loved the rodeo. But after realizing how important this opportunity was for me, he supported my decision. Though he never sugarcoats anything and we've had our disagreements, I've learned so much from him. He's still my dad, and that just happened naturally." - **Andre McClain**

I've also got surrogate siblings, like **Cynthia Beaty Byrd**, a high school friend who shared my passion for music. She's a singer, so we naturally connected over promotions and marketing.

Then there's Moses Brewer, who represented Coors when they were considering sponsoring the rodeo. Before that, Rae Taylor had sent him to sell me some purified water. I told him I only drink Perrier, but somehow, we hit it off and have been close ever since.

Carolyn Carter came into the picture not as a rider but with her sisters who were all into riding. Since her first rodeo, she hasn't missed a single one. After putting in 30 years, instead of a retirement watch, she wanted a saddle. So, I surprised her with a custom 30th-anniversary saddle at the 2014 finals in Washington D.C.

Joyce Reynolds and I became like siblings too. Our mothers were friends, and Joyce, who was talented in hairstyling, wanted to go to Beauty College. I offered her a job at my salon, which cemented our bond. Plus, I introduced her to my best friend, Marlon Scott, and they started dating, drawing us even closer. Joyce has been one of the longest "sisters" I've had.

I met Joyce through Belva's brother-in-law, Shelby Davis, co-producer of the Miss Bronze Pageant, around 1962 or '63. Shelby, who ran a modeling and charm school with his wife, Tonita Davis, brought me on as a judge for the pageant because of my critical eye and stage expertise. Joyce and I remained close and she later worked for me when I opened my entertainment office.

"Lu seems to know everybody in the world. I really noticed this once in Seoul, Korea. We were there when suddenly someone shouted, 'Lu, Lu!' It turned out to be members of the Jackson music family, Mrs. Katherine Jackson and Rebbie, and they knew Lu! He has a knack for knowing everyone, which means he always ends up socializing at any event we attend. Sometimes, I worried we didn't have time for all the socializing, so I would often have to step in to ensure that we stayed on track with our business commitments. This was a full-time job within itself."- **Valeria**

I've always been someone people feel comfortable talking to because I tend to listen more than I speak. I offer advice only when it's truly needed. Most of the time, people just want someone to listen. They want to be heard because they have their own ideas and perspectives.

I learned a valuable lesson from my oldest son, Ralph, when he was young. One day, while we were sitting at the kitchen table, I told him to be quiet. He responded, "Why should I be quiet? Little people have things to say too." That moment stuck with me. It taught me to listen to everyone, because everyone, no matter how small, has something important to say.

"Lu has such a kind heart. He's always been there for the underdog, always ready to help anyone in need, regardless of his own status or how well-respected he is in the community. His willingness to assist, no matter what the issue, really shows the kind of person he is. And personally, he's been a confidant for me; whenever I needed someone to talk to or sought advice, Lu was there. I'm truly grateful for his support." - **Kim Oliver, Lu's Banker**

"Dad definitely has his quirks, he can be stubborn, mean, and impatient with people. But beneath it all, he has a really good heart. He's actually quite sensitive, though he rarely lets that side show; he doesn't easily reveal when he's hurt. I remember feeling a bit upset when I saw him walking Karen Motley down the aisle at her wedding, wondering why he hadn't done the same for me. But as I watched him with Karen, I realized that if Dad didn't do it, who would? At that moment, any resentment I felt just melted away. He was clearly the right person for that role, and I felt so proud of him. Later, Karen hugged me, worried I'd be upset. I reassured her that I wasn't mad at all; I was just proud of Dad for stepping up. It made me realize that, even though things weren't perfect when I was growing up, my father has always been a pillar for the community. That pride washed away any hard feelings; I let go of all that baggage." - **LaShelle Vason**

"Dad and I did speak every day. We called ourselves the "Night Owls". We would speak late at night when everyone was sleeping. He would say, "your best ideas come late at night, in the midnight hour". Dad motivated me, he inspired me, and he believed in me. He always encouraged me to be my best self, and to not apologize for being my authentic self." - **Sheri Vason**

I've always believed that close relationships enrich us, allowing us to learn from each other. I'm not sure what Belva Davis might have learned from our time together in Oakland during the '60s and '70s. However, when she visited my and Valeria's house last year, it became clear that our interactions had been meaningful to her. I feel that it was more about mutual respect, as I learned so much from Belva myself. We were family

Mary Ann Pollar, a pioneering Black female promoter who worked with icons like Maya Angelou, Odetta, and Abbey Lincoln. They were all staunchly pro-Black at a time when it wasn't yet mainstream, long before the "I'm Black and I'm Proud" movement. I absorbed these values partly through Oscar Brown Jr. as well. I appreciate the two of them.

"It was 1991, the year my daughter was born, when I truly realized how special Lu was to me. We were in Kansas City just after a rodeo, and I got a call from my wife, Felicia, saying she was in the hospital. I rushed to the hotel across the street to use the long-distance phone, this was before cell phones. As I was on the phone, hearing about my first daughter Lorena's birth, Lu was right there with me, listening in. I was crying tears of joy, and Lu was laughing, but I later found out he was moved too, he cried as well, he just didn't show it."

"Lu made it clear that if my family ever needed anything, we could always count on him and Valeria. Whether it was a little financial help or just moral support, they've been there for us 100 percent over the years. My daughters, who are usually wary of people outside our immediate family, affectionately call Lu 'Grandpa.'"

"They know they can always reach out to him and Valeria if they need anything. Lu is truly a very special person in our lives." - **Jody Gilbert Lu's Graphic and Layout Artist**

Danny DeWitt was like a "brother" to me. We first met at my entertainment office, where we shared many poker games on Friday and Saturday nights, along with other friends. Those poker nights were what really cemented our friendship and brought us closer.

Professionally, Danny worked as Gene's assistant, and when Gene opened his clubs, Danny helped manage them. He's the reason I ended up in Colorado; he introduced me to his brother Gene. When Gene purchased a club in Denver and needed to book entertainment, Danny recommended me, saying I was the guy in Oakland who knew all the entertainers. After I met Gene, he told me, *"You've got all the power, but you don't have any juice."*

I also knew Louis Freeman back in California, although I initially didn't realize our sons were best friends. I met Louis through my promotional work and during visits to his radio station, KDIA, where he was the news director. Belva Davis, another connection of mine, was a DJ and talk show host there, long before radio talk shows gained the popularity they have today.

Louis and my relationship became even closer when he moved to Denver. We had some amazing conversations and spent some great times together as friends. He became one of my brothers.

"Why do I love Lu? It's simple, he has a good heart. He's an incredibly caring person, even though he might shield that side of himself. At times, he can come across as quite hard-core because he's very clear about what he wants and when he wants it. He's not one to be swayed or talked out of his decisions easily. But beyond that tough exterior, he truly has a heart of gold." - **Gisele McFarland**

If there's one truth I've come to hold dear, it's this: I've never done a thing alone. Not one. My life has been a rodeo of wild dreams, uphill climbs, crash landings, and triumphant returns—and through it all, I've been blessed beyond measure by the love, loyalty, and laughter of family and friends.

My *family*, by blood and by bond, have been my grounding force. They saw me before the bright lights and big ideas. They held me down when life tried to knock me out, reminded me of who I was when I almost forgot, and pushed me forward when I hesitated. Whether it was Emma showing me a better path, or my cousin introducing me to jazz, they each lit a spark that shaped my soul.

And my ***friends***, Lord, my friends have been the melody to this journey. From playing Bid Whist in the college parking lot, to raising glasses after sold-out shows, to sitting around Thanksgiving tables that weren't mine by birth but became mine by love, I have lived a rich life because I had people who stood with me, walked with me, and sometimes even carried me.

I've always said I'm a dreamer, but I'd be lying if I said I didn't borrow courage from those who believed in my vision even when they couldn't see it. To those who worked beside me, prayed for me, challenged me, loved me, you are the true backbone of this legacy. You are the thread that weaves through every rodeo ticket, every curtain call, and every dream and vision I dared to chase.

If I leave behind anything worth remembering, I hope it's not just the rodeo. I hope it's the spirit of unity, of possibility, of people from all walks of life coming together like kin. Because **we are *family***. Not just the ones who share our name, but the ones who share our dreams, our fight, our joy.

And if my story has taught me anything, it's this: family isn't just who you're born to, it's who rides with you, who roots for you, and who never lets you ride alone.

I may have done it my way, but I never did it by myself.

Chapter 18: THIS IS MY RODEO!

"I always say that it's my dream; I would like for you to live in my dream but you can't change my dream." - Lu Vason

Throughout my journey with the Bill Pickett Invitational Rodeo, I maintained a steadfast vision for what I wanted to achieve. Despite the challenges and disagreements, my unwavering commitment was clear in every board and planning meeting. "It's MY rodeo,"

I would assert, underlining my ownership of the creative direction. Over time, while I learned to soften somewhat, allowing for collaboration, I never relinquished the reins entirely, always ensuring my voice was the loudest in the room. Valeria's perspective highlights a dynamic of tension and eventual synergy.

"As Lu and I started collaborating more closely, we often bumped heads. He would assertively remind everyone, "THIS IS MY RODEO!" and honestly, that would infuriate me. Despite it being his rodeo, I felt he wasn't open to new ideas or concepts, leading to some intense knock-down discussions between us."

"Over time, however, we began to find our rhythm. I naturally took on the financial responsibilities while Lu handled the creative aspects. As I grew to understand his vision for the black rodeo and his other projects, like bringing black plays and arts functions to downtown theaters where they had never been featured, it all started to click for me."

"Lu's motivations became clear; it wasn't about making money for him. He was driven by a desire to expose his community to experiences they might not otherwise have. Realizing this, I thought, Okay, I get this now. So, I learned the ropes of the business and gradually began to take over. That's just my personality."

I've always prided myself on two things: my innovation and creativity, and yes, my perfectionism. Slugger would often say to me, *"You just pump out ideas and create them, and we have to make them happen."* It's crucial for me to set our rodeos apart from the typical ones because I have people coming from all corners of the country, and I need to keep them engaged.

Take, for instance, how I handle payments. From the very first rodeo I organized to the most recent, I have never paid any cowboy or cowgirl with checks; it's always been cash. When they're constantly on the road, checks are just impractical. Plus, there have been too many instances where they've been burned by bad checks from other rodeo promoters.

So, I've learned two critical lessons: always pay the cowboys in cash so they have something tangible while traveling, and always start the rodeo on time, a point world bull riding champion Charlie Sampson stressed to me. It's these principles that help keep everything running smoothly.

"Lu is always on the lookout for the next challenge. You really have to draw close to him, listen carefully to grasp the direction he's aiming for. Admittedly, he's not the easiest person to deal with at times; you have to really understand where he's coming from in that moment. But if you stick by his side, you'll gain a wealth of knowledge, Lu is full of wisdom. He's a graduate of the School of Hard Knocks. He didn't win every battle, but once he started winning, he just kept moving forward." - **Herbert Mims.**

Herbert hit the nail on the head with his observation, I can be tough to get along with, but that's simply because I have a clear vision of what I want. I always say that this is my dream; I welcome others to join me in it, but they can't change it. That's where the misunderstandings often rose. I know that many see me as an innovator because I consistently strive to do things that are creative and beyond the norm.

We were in Denver, at a production meeting for the Denver Stock Show, also known as The National Western Stock Show; an annual, 16-day livestock, rodeo, and horse show held in Denver, Colorado, every January, serving as a major event for the agricultural industry and a popular tourist destination. It is a big deal! When I planned the grand entrance to feature the "Obama Flag," the bigwigs at the Stock Show were hesitant. They questioned, "Well, is there anything we can do about that?"

"Lu immediately responded with a firm "No!" Silence fell over the room. They then asked, "So we have to do this?" Lu confirmed, "Yep! It's not up for discussion. We're going to do it the way Carolyn has designed it, or we won't do it at all; you can leave." - **Carolyn Carter, Grand Entry Coordinator, Co-General Manager.**

It was the same with my concerts. My first major concert on my own featured Ramsey Lewis and the Chi-lites, back in Berkeley around 1969. The show was well-received, but I got a review criticizing my stage setup, saying it looked like spaghetti because I hadn't mastered the art of organizing all the wires, cords, and cable lines.

From that moment on, I ensured my stage was always immaculate, so no one would trip over any wires. That's when Neil and Jolly stepped in, Neil as my stage manager and Jolly as my production manager. Together, we put on a ton of shows.

One of the biggest gambles I took was pairing Ramsey Lewis with Gil Scott Heron for a concert. Many thought it was an odd mix and doubted it would work. However, I ended up selling out a week in advance.

At the time, I didn't know how to add a second show; I was just thrilled we sold out the first one. And it turned out to be a fantastic event, especially with Gil Scott Heron's hit "In the Bottle" making waves at the time.

"One thing about Lu, he's a thorough business guy, always has been an entrepreneur. Whenever he comes to town, he promotes everything well and does everything a good businessman should do. If he weren't such a skilled businessman, he wouldn't have lasted this long in the industry."

"I know for a fact that Lu won't tolerate anything less than excellence. He is well-loved in Prince George County, as is the rodeo. Lu has a way of getting around and connecting with people." - **Eddie Martin**

Maybe what really cemented my "This is MY Rodeo!" attitude was a particularly tough period early in my career. Back then, I was just scraping by, and it was Linda Moore, my partner at the time who worked at the food stamp office, who helped me make ends meet.

She managed to get me food stamps, and I affectionately called her my baby because she truly took good care of me. Those food stamps were what got me through on a diet of Top Ramen noodles.

"I remember a time back in 1977 or 1978 when Dad was going through a rough patch. This was around the time of his third marriage, and he was living in Colorado. Things were tough, and he really didn't have much. He went through a few years of struggle, but even then, he resisted the temptation to just take any job. He actually went down to apply for a job at the airport once, but he came back saying he could make more money than that with just one show. He even told me once that he was down to his last 16 cents." - **Corey Vason**

Like Corey mentioned, I had hit rock bottom, lower than I had ever been before. When people say they're broke, I truly understand what they mean. I was three or four months behind on my mortgage and in really bad shape. Around that time, I was really into the jazz musician Chuck Mangione.

I remember watching him on TV, leading his band with Esther Satterfield singing alongside. He was in total control, especially during the performance of "Feels So Good." That's when it clicked for me, I realized I needed to take control. I came from the outhouse back to the penthouse.

"Dad managed to pull himself together and kept moving forward, being the determined person, he always was. I think his willpower and, honestly, a bit of his arrogance, helped him get over that tough hump. His arrogance, in a way, fueled his determination to succeed. Although he had his challenging moments, and I was in California while he was in Colorado so I didn't see everything day-to-day, I knew he was going through a hard time. But he managed to pull himself up in a big way." - **Corey Vason**

"It's truly inspiring to witness an African-American man dedicated to creating value both within and outside the community. Lu has spent his entire life doing just that. He's a man who has always stood on his own two feet." - **Michael A. Hancock**

Ever since then, I've taken control as much as I can, except when it comes to my wife. Valeria won't let me be in total control because I just wasn't a good money manager. She's the one who actually runs things and make the finances work. She lets me say I'm in charge, but everyone knows who the real boss is.

"Lu also had a "dangerous" side to him that many people don't know about. You really need to know him well to see it. I remember this one time when a guy came up, disgruntled about the payout or something. This guy walked up to Lu and started making a fuss. Right then, we saw a whole other side of Lu. Whoa, shoot! He straightened the fellow out real quick."
"Lu is a good-sized man, and he made it clear right there that he could handle himself. It's like the old saying, "I can laugh and I can joke, but I don't play." The "streets" in Lu came out real quick. We were all there ready to back him up, but it looked like Lu needed no help. I said, "Dang, Lu! That got a little western." And Lu just said, "Oh, that man ain't gonna do nothing." And he didn't." - **Glynn Turman**

That man was Cash Joubert. He was the only cowboy who ever caused a fuss at the rodeo. Honestly, I don't exactly remember what happened.

"Now, I'm not saying that Lu walks on water or crossed the Red Sea, but many times, he and his wife, Valeria had to finance this rodeo out of their own pockets because the sponsorship dollars just weren't there. It takes a strong person, mentally, emotionally, and physically, to bring these cowboys and cowgirls across the country. Often, he had to front all the money, again from his own pocket and at his own expense, to ensure they got there, because we all know that without the cowboys or cowgirls, there's no show." - **Jeff Douvel, Bill Pickett Rodeo Oakland Coordinator.**

We've always struggled, right from the start. A major challenge has been securing sponsors, as I've mentioned before. Unfortunately, we have to approach major companies, many of which still don't believe that black cowboys exist or that the rodeo can maintain a level of professionalism.

There were a couple of years where I focused solely on securing black sponsors. I wanted the rodeo to be "By Blacks, For Blacks;" that was my mission for about two years. For most of that time, it worked out. We had sponsors like Glory Foods, which was black-owned at that time, Bronner Brothers hair products, and Andy's Seasoning, all owned by blacks. As long as the company or distributorship was black-owned, we upheld our mission of being "For Blacks, By Blacks."

We still have Andy's Seasoning and some of the others, but their marketing budgets have decreased. Also, what often happens is that after a while, big companies come in and buy these smaller businesses, but usually, these larger companies are not black-owned.

Then there was the guy with the Creole Potato Salad, New Orleans Bill's Creole Potato Salad, to be exact. His product is now in stores all across the West Coast, and we've been doing our part to help Bill Washington, aka New Orleans Bill, expand out to the East Coast.

The product is still Black owned, though the distribution side isn't. But that's just the game, sometimes you've got to make certain trade-offs to move forward.

And let me tell you, starting and growing a Black-owned business, especially one as ambitious as the Bill Pickett Invitational Rodeo, ain't for the faint of heart. When you're Black, folks don't always give your ideas the respect they deserve. And getting financial support? That's ten times harder. You have to fight for every inch.

Valeria used to say I was too soft, and maybe she had a point. I never liked telling people no. Folks would come to me with all kinds of ideas, and my mind would immediately start working, trying to figure out how we could make it happen, how we could turn their dream into something real.

But Valeria was the one who kept me grounded. She knew when to hit the brakes, especially when I was ready to spend money we didn't need to. She helped channel my energy, helped protect the vision from growing too wide too fast. Still, I believed in people. I believed in what we could build together if we just had the right shot.

"Valeria often says that my dad, Lu, is too soft and doesn't make the best business choices. But I truly believe that his success stems from his ingenuity and creativity. He found a niche that no one was filling at the time. Plus, he's well-liked; he has this ability to get help from people who genuinely like him. When you're well-liked, people are willing to do things for you for free, just because they love you. He has that kind of appeal." - **LaShelle Vason, Lu's daughter.**

"Lu is a uniquely charismatic guy, almost like the driving force behind the entire rodeo scene. He has some really capable people on his team, like the general managers. Take Jesse Guillory, for example; he managed the arena side of things brilliantly, organizing the cowboys and overseeing the execution of all events. He really did a ton of work.

"With Lu, you should know that even though I was the one planning the event as the coordinator from outside the arena, he was always deeply involved in everything. He tended to micromanage, a mild way of putting it. His approach often seemed like organized chaos. He was the perfect example of this. From the outside, it might look confusing with so much going on and his roundabout ways of doing things. But Lu always knew exactly where everything was and what everyone was supposed to be doing. To him, it was all organized; for the rest of us, it felt chaotic. But that's just how he operates; it's no problem, it's all good." - **Lynn Dillard Wright, Former Los Angeles Coordinator, Sales Manager**

I've always been guided by a strong sense of vision and ownership. I held tightly to my projects, ensuring they reflected my core values and the goals I set. This wasn't just about keeping control; it was about ensuring that every aspect of the rodeo was a mirror of my dream.

Over the years, I learned the importance of balancing this firm direction with the ability to collaborate. By welcoming diverse ideas into the fold, we could innovate and expand in ways I might not have imagined alone. Yet, this journey wasn't without its hurdles. My path was often strewn with challenges, but resilience became my closest ally, helping me to persist where others might falter.

Above all, the true measure of my efforts has always rested within the community. The impact we've made there, the legacy we've built together, stands as a testament to what can be achieved when one is dedicated to creating genuine value for others. Through this all, I've strived to lead with both conviction and an open heart, aiming not only to succeed but to inspire.

I'm always looking to try something fresh and new. Take, for example, the OperaJazz concert with Angela Brown. People often tell me, "You know, black folks don't like opera." While there's some truth to that, we also have a rich history in opera. So, to make it more accessible to our community, I decided to mix in a little jazz. I thought this blend would appeal to both jazz and opera audiences.

This journey reminds me a lot of when I first set out to create the rodeo. Folks told me I couldn't pull it off, they doubted the vision, said it wouldn't work. But I did it. *We* did it. And the community showed up and embraced it. I had dreams of taking it to other cities, more hearts, but the truth is, my health wouldn't allow it. Still, I have no regrets. Like Frank Sinatra once said, and it's the one line I've always said I want on my tombstone, **"I did it my way."**

And that's exactly how I want to be remembered.

Chapter 19: ROPED INTO HISTORY

"Three generations have grown up and come to the Lu Vason/Bill Pickett Rodeo. Kids that used to be in strollers and in the arms of their mothers and fathers who came to see the rodeo have grown up and are coming and participating in the rodeo. So it's something that's really, really ours; and that's the way Lu wanted it." - Glynn Turman

We are now going into our 31st year of the Bill Pickett Invitational Rodeo. A lot of people didn't think it would last that long, much less be as successful as it has been.

"You know, Lu isn't just part of Colorado history; he's a part of Western history itself. When you step back and look at it, the things he's accomplished with the Bill Pickett Invitational Rodeo are truly unmatched. I've always believed that when you create something good, something special, folks naturally want to copy it. But nobody has ever been able to replicate what Lu built with this rodeo, nobody."

"When I think about Lu and the mark he's made, I see history unfolding. He's taken it upon himself to educate people about the contributions of Black cowboys, how they lived, how they overcame, and why their stories deserve to be recognized. Lu didn't just talk about history; he placed these forgotten heroes directly into it. In my book, Lu's efforts put him right up there with the civil rights leaders. He didn't march with signs, but he's opened minds and changed perceptions through the rodeo. That's a powerful legacy." - **Bob Willis**

When we started the rodeo, we were stepping into completely unknown territory. Most folks didn't even know what a cowboy truly was, much less that there were Black cowboys competing in rodeos. To keep things real, Black Cowboys struggled to gain recognition in the industry until Charlie Sampson won the World Bull Riding Championship in 1983.

Charlie didn't compete in our events, but Coors, our major sponsor at the time, hired him to make special appearances, which really boosted our profile. Before Charlie's win, people weren't even aware that a Black rodeo existed, despite there being plenty of talented Black cowboys out there.

Take Charlie's mentor, Myrtis Dightman, for example. He was an incredible rider but never received the proper recognition or publicity he deserved. And truthfully, even Charlie himself faced constant setbacks. He was clearly the best bull rider out there, yet somehow always ended up second. They just wouldn't let him win. Eventually, Charlie's talent became undeniable. He was so skilled, they had no choice but to acknowledge him, finally awarding him the victories and recognition he'd deserved all along.

Valeria remembers, *"You know, it was fascinating to me because before I met Lu, I'd never even heard of a rodeo. I didn't know what it was or even how to spell it! But Lu introduced me to this rodeo world. I met all his friends, and he shared with me how he came up with the idea for the rodeo, how he'd spent time with Paul Stewart down at the Black American West Museum. He even took me down to personally meet Paul."*

*"If you had asked me back then if I believed there were Black cowboys and cowgirls, I'd have said no. But when I finally saw them, when I met them, they were so welcoming. They immediately made me feel like part of their family. It just felt natural, like it was meant to be." -***Valeria**

FROM THE RED CARPET TO THE RODEO DIRT

Over the years, the Bill Pickett Invitational Rodeo didn't just draw crowds, it drew stars. Big stars. Real ones. People who understood the power of legacy, culture, and showing up for something that mattered.

I used to look out across the crowd, tip my hat, and think, Man... look who came to the rodeo.

We had legends grace our grounds like **Lou Rawls, Sinbad, Pam Grier, Stevie Wonder, Mike Tyson,** and **Gladys Knight. Danny Glover, Arnold Schwarzenegger, Glynn Turman,** Reginald T. Dorsey, Obba Babatunde, **James Pickens Jr., Jennifer Lewis,** and **Marla Gibbs** came out to show love. **Denzel Washington** and **Blair Underwood** didn't just show up, they leaned in.

We saw the comedy of **Chris Tucker,** the talent of **Jamie Foxx,** the elegance of **Vanessa Williams,** and the soul of **The Emotions & the Whispers.** Isaiah Thomas, **Howard Rollins, Delroy Lindo, Chris Rock,** and even **Tiny Lister Jr.,** they all participated in one way or the other, they sat in the stands, hung out in the VIP area or in the back with cowboys and cowgirls, taking in the experience and the power of the culture.

We were honored by icons like **Altovise Davis, Sherry Belafonte, Dawnn Lewis, Janet Hubert, Jayne Kennedy, Karyn Parsons,** and **Tina Knowles. Suzanne de Passe** even came and honored the rodeo with her presence. We struck up a great conversation that led to multiple meetings about a potential movie!

The actors, the athletes, the singers, the storytellers, and even politicians, they came from all over, Hollywood, Broadway, sports, politics, and music, all to witness something real: a rodeo where Black cowboys and cowgirls took center stage.

From **Mario Van Peebles** to **Mykelti Williamson,** from **Ashford & Simpson** to new voices like **Muni Long,** the rodeo became more than an event, it became a gathering place for greatness.

Every one of them left with a little more pride. A little more history. A little more understanding of what we were building. Because when you came to **my rodeo,** you didn't just watch a show. **You felt something.**

BOOTS, HATS, AND ALL THAT

Every city where we hold a rodeo has its own flavor. Los Angeles turns into more of a spectacle because of all the celebrities who come out and add a bit of star power. Oakland, on the other hand, fits the image most folks have of what a rodeo should be, outdoors, under open skies. Oakland also has this special ritual where we ride down from a hilltop, proudly bringing the American and African flags into the arena. It never gets old seeing those colors fly.

Washington D.C. is special because it's steeped in African-American history and heritage. People there genuinely understand and embrace the cultural value of our rodeo. It's also our finals now, but honestly, I'm not sure if the folks there come because it's the finals, or simply because it's a rodeo. The fact that it's an all-Black event is what really brings people from all over, Pittsburgh, Philadelphia, Atlanta, North Carolina, Virginia, everybody makes that trip, because D.C. is so centrally located.

Atlanta has its own charm. It's a bit smaller, but the Black community there has an extraordinary sense of pride in what we're doing. Memphis, meanwhile, is still warming up to the idea. To them, it's still basically just a rodeo, one that just happens to feature Black cowboys. They haven't fully embraced it as something unique quite yet.

St. Louis always gives us an exciting welcome. There's a real curiosity there; the folks just love seeing us come back every year. We're not necessarily out to teach a history lesson, but we definitely raised awareness and sparked interest in the legacy of Black cowboys. We aim to keep our rodeos anchored in urban areas where we can have the most impact.

And Denver is truly one-of-a-kind, mainly because we're part of the prestigious National Western Stock Show. Ever since we've joined up with them, we've held our event indoors, which has been a real blessing, considering we've dealt with some heavy snowstorms!

Before that partnership, we used to have it outdoors in Adams County, and you could always count on one day of beautiful weather, and one day when Mother Nature would remind you who's boss.

"Lu is pretty much like the Quincy Jones of Rodeo. Quincy Jones, he could not do everything, but he just made sure you have the right people around him to emulate what he was doing, kind of as an overseer. The rodeos are running just as smooth as when he was doing it." - **Howard Johnson, Singer and Performer**

There are plenty of cities we'd love to return to, but some places just didn't have enough folks, at least not in the urban communities, to consistently support the rodeo. For instance, we loved going to San Diego. It's a beautiful city, but they simply didn't have a large enough Black population or enough surrounding communities to draw in the crowds we needed. Columbus, Ohio, was another good one; it had a great venue, and the rodeo went off well there.

Now, Detroit, that was one of our best rodeos ever. Unfortunately, they tore down our venue there. Detroit is special because it's where we first launched our 'Rodeo for Kidz Sake' program. Gwen Martin, the coordinator, did an incredible job. Her sister, Lynn, was a teacher, so we had a strong connection with the local school system, similar to how Miss Kitty ran things down in Memphis. In fact, Detroit became so successful with the kids that we ended up holding two separate kids' rodeos each visit. Adults didn't always come out in big numbers, but the kids certainly did, thanks to the dedicated work Gwen and Lynn put into engaging the schools.

Sacramento was a fantastic rodeo, we absolutely loved it there. Bakersfield was good too, but we never quite got the crowds we wanted, mostly because we had to schedule it midweek. In many cities, Wednesday night is Bible study night, and that always made things tricky. But holding Bakersfield between Los Angeles and Oakland gave us an extra date, and it allowed our cowboys and cowgirls a chance to earn a bit more money on the road.

We've been to many cities across the country, but there are still several cities we'd love to visit but just haven't made it yet. At the top of that list is New York City. We actually had a chance to bring the rodeo to New York once. Representatives from Madison Square Garden were interested in partnering with us on an event. Unfortunately, the promoter already holding a rodeo there at the time made it extremely difficult. We ran into several issues we just couldn't overcome.

He already had the prime dates, Friday and Saturday, so we would've been forced into either a Thursday or Friday morning slot. Even more challenging, he didn't want us using his livestock, meaning we'd have to bring our own animals in. Madison Square Garden simply didn't have enough stalls for two separate stock contractors, and with his animals taking up all the available space, there was no room for ours. Our animals would've needed to be housed indoors, and the venue couldn't accommodate that. It would've been an incredible event, probably our biggest rodeo yet.

Still, New York remains on my wish list, and I'm determined to make it happen someday. As for Boston, we've gotten invitations, but that's just too far east for our horses to comfortably travel.

We even considered taking the rodeo overseas. At one point, we planned events in Japan, Seoul, and South Korea, aiming to do all three in one trip. My wife, Valeria and I traveled to Japan with assistance from former Aurora City Councilwoman Edna Moseley and even secured the Egg Dome in Tokyo. But once we returned to the U.S., we discovered each animal had to be quarantined for 30 days at five dollars per animal per day, which ended up killing the deal.

We explored Hawaii too. The arena there was excited about hosting a matchup of Black Cowboys versus Hawaiian Cowboys, but unfortunately, we couldn't finalize the arrangements. Later, my Atlanta coordinator, Liz Young, worked on taking the rodeo to the Bahamas. While the enthusiasm was there, the arena just wasn't large enough.

A couple of years afterward, we looked at St. Thomas, but ran into transportation issues. Getting our livestock there meant either flying them in on costly cargo planes or sending them on barges from Miami, both options were prohibitively expensive, ultimately forcing us to abandon the idea.

"The passion that Lu had, he shared it with me and everyone around us, folks like Acynthia, Slugger, Lynn Hart, and the whole crew. Lu had a way of inspiring us to always push ourselves harder, to do things differently, and never just settle for being like everybody else."

"I rode bulls for 30 years, and most of that time was with the Bill Pickett Rodeo. I was a world champion in '93 and '94 and won the Finals in Reno back in '93. Through Lu, I've had experiences with horses and rodeos that shaped my whole life. Everything we did together was built on the bond we shared over our love for the rodeo life."

"You know, sometimes I look back and still feel those moments, just sitting around after a rodeo with Lu, laughing and talking about the rides. Those were some good times." - **Clarence Gipson, Cowboy, Multi Bill Pickett Rodeo and International Champion**

Another international destination we considered was Toronto, because of its large Black population, many descended from Southern migrants via the Underground Railroad. It seemed like the perfect place, but we ran into issues with stock contractors taking animals across the Canadian border. Later, we discovered we could've taken animals to Japan through Canada, since Canada didn't have the quarantine restrictions.

England was off-limits altogether due to 'blue tongue' disease restrictions, any animals we took there would've had to stay. We'd even figured out a system for Japan where we'd rotate cattle annually before the calves got too big, but the quarantine rules ultimately ended those plans.

Finally, my stock contractor and advisor, Mr. Harry Bold, called me one day and said, *"Lu, there's enough space in the U.S. to run rodeos, Washington to Florida, Maine to California, why do you need to go overseas?* Harry had tried it himself and found it difficult, so his advice convinced me to focus on the United States.

As I started dreaming even bigger, imagining international tours, taking the Bill Pickett Rodeo overseas to places like South Africa or the Caribbean, I had to face the reality that not every road was meant to be traveled. My body, my energy, even time itself, was telling me to refocus. The vision didn't die, but it evolved. I realized the most meaningful work wasn't always out there in the world, it was right here at home. The stories, the people, the history, we had more than enough legacy to celebrate on this soil.

"Lu is absolutely a historian, especially when it comes to Black history. But beyond that, I believe his real legacy is all the incredible things he's done in the community, the way he's always reached out to help people one-on-one, sharing his kindness, wisdom, and genuine care." - **Gisele McFarfland**

"Another thing Lu did was bring the Bill Pickett name to life. If it wasn't for Lu Vason, people today wouldn't even know who Bill Pickett was. Even now, folks still ask, 'Was Bill Pickett here? Is he still alive?' Lu elevated Bill Pickett's name right alongside other legendary Black figures of the American West. He truly deserves to be remembered as one of the greatest Black promoters ever." - **Ngoma and Karina McNeal**

That's the thing about legacy, it doesn't just live in buildings or plaques. It lives in people, in stories passed down, in names remembered because someone cared enough to keep them alive. And that's exactly what happened with Bill Pickett and his family.

Bill Pickett's great-great-grandsons, especially Frank Phillips, were thrilled that I wanted to name the rodeo after Bill. That led us to host reunions, connecting over 200 of Bill Pickett's descendants, many meeting for the first time.

At one reunion, a family member asked why I was running the rodeo instead of them. Frank stood up and said, *"We wouldn't even be together today if Lu hadn't created this rodeo, we wouldn't even know about each other."*

That same family member, Bill's great-great-granddaughter Belle Gomez, and I eventually became close friends. Belle has been instrumental in preserving Bill Pickett's legacy. We traveled together to Ponca City, Oklahoma, where Bill is buried. For years, I tried to get access to the gravesite to place a proper headstone, but the property owners refused.

Recently, Belle told me they finally allowed it, putting a nice fence around the area. I haven't seen a headstone in the pictures she sent, so I'm not sure if there's one yet. The site, known as Monument Hill, originally was thought to hold both Bill Pickett and Chief White Eagle. It was later discovered Chief White Eagle was buried elsewhere. Today, Bill Pickett and his horse Spradley rest there, marked by a tall brick monument.

Bill Pickett has finally received the recognition he so rightfully deserves. His legacy is now cemented across the country. There's a marker in his honor in Ponca City Square, and his name is proudly etched in the BPIR Cowboy Walk of Fame at the Black American West Museum in Denver. He's been inducted into the Pro Cowboy Hall of Fame, the Texas Trail of Fame, and the National Cowboy Hall of Fame.

In Fort Worth, Texas, a statue of Bill stands tall in front of the Cowtown Coliseum, forever watching over the arena. One of the most humbling moments for me was when the United States Postal Service created a commemorative stamp in his honor and presented it to me. That meant everything.

"It's truly become an institution. The Bill Pickett Rodeo feels like a big family reunion, something folks eagerly look forward to every year. Families have come year after year, and we've watched entire generations grow up right before our eyes."

"In fact, at least three generations have now grown up with the Lu Vason Bill Pickett Rodeo. Kids who first attended in strollers or in their parents' arms are now grown, coming back with families of their own, and even participating in the rodeo themselves. It's a tradition that genuinely belongs to us, and that's exactly what Lu always wanted." - **Glynn Turman**

"Lu and the BPIR has outlasted the Black Circus, he's outlasted the Ebony Fashion Fair, he's outlasted the Black Expos they used to have around; they are all gone. He should be put up with some of the greatest black promoters of all time." - **Ngoma and Karimu McNeal**

"I was involved in setting up the Walk of Fame at the Black American West Museum. It's essential to keep that history alive, because, like they say, 'If you don't know where you came from, you won't know where you're going.'" - **Peggy Wortham**

"I think Lu should be remembered as the greatest promoter of Black rodeos who ever lived. He didn't just change the game for Black cowboys and cowgirls, he transformed it for sponsors too, making them see the value in investing in Black rodeos. Before Lu came along, something like that was unheard of." - **Jesse "Slugger" Gillory**

"Lu will always be remembered just as he's always been known, a cowboy with a vision." - **Landry Taylor**

Chapter 20: RIDING INTO THE SUNSET

As I look back on this incredible journey, from that sun-drenched afternoon at Cheyenne Frontier Days to decades of the Bill Pickett Invitational Rodeo. I'm filled with a sense of wonder. What began as a spark of inspiration has blossomed into something far greater than I could have imagined. I've often wondered what kept me going through all the challenges, the setbacks, and the moments when it seemed like the odds were stacked against me. Now, with the wisdom that comes from a life fully lived, I understand that it was more than just determination, it was purpose.

There's something exciting about standing in the arena, dust swirling around your boots, watching the crowds fill the stands year after year. I see families, grandparents who've been coming since our first rodeo, now bringing their grandchildren. I see the faces of young Black children light up when they witness, often for the first time, cowboys and cowgirls who look like them performing feats of incredible skill and courage. In those moments, I know that what we've built matters.

This rodeo was never just about entertainment. It was about reclaiming a piece of our history that had been erased, overlooked, or forgotten. When I first learned about Bill Pickett and the countless other Black cowboys who helped shape the American West, I felt a responsibility to share their stories. History books had failed them, Hollywood had ignored them, but we would celebrate them. Every time the grand entry begins and those cowboys and cowgirls ride into the arena, carrying our flags high, we're making a statement: we were there, we are here, and we will be remembered.

Building this rodeo taught me lessons I never expected to learn. I discovered that vision isn't enough, you need people who believe in that vision to bring it to life. I've been blessed with an army of believers, from my right-hand people like Slugger, Acynthia, and Carolyn, to every cowboy and cowgirl who traveled countless miles to compete, to sponsors who took a chance on us when others wouldn't, to the countless fans who have supported us through the years.

The most profound lesson, though, has been about legacy. We don't build things just for today; we build them for tomorrow. When I see young cowboys like Clarence Gipson or Lynn Hart find their passion through our rodeo, or watch Andre McClain take skills he developed with us all the way to Ringling Brothers, I'm reminded that what we do echoes far beyond the arena walls.

Every child who learns about Bill Pickett, every family that makes our rodeo their annual tradition, every person who walks away with a new understanding of the Black contribution to western heritage, they carry our legacy forward.

I've never been one to back down from a challenge. When people told me it couldn't be done, that just fueled my determination to prove them wrong. "This is MY rodeo!" became more than just words; it became a philosophy. It meant standing firm in my vision, even when others couldn't see it yet. It meant demanding excellence, even when compromise would have been easier. It meant creating something authentic that truly represented us.

That stubbornness has served me well, but I've also learned the value of collaboration. This rodeo wouldn't exist without Gene DeWitt believing in me enough to invest in that first event. It wouldn't have grown without Moses Brewer and Ivan Burwell championing us at Coors. It wouldn't run today without Valeria stepping in to handle the finances while I chase new ideas. Truth be told, I may have been the dreamer, but it took a community to make the dream real.

I've always believed in the power of knowing where you come from. That's why I filled my home with Black art and artifacts, not just as decoration, but as daily reminders of our heritage. The same philosophy guided the rodeo. We're not just entertaining; we're educating. Every time we introduce historical figures like Bill Pickett, Clara Brown, or Bass Reeves during our shows, we're connecting our audience to their roots. Pride comes from knowledge, and knowledge comes from seeing yourself in history.

Health scares have a way of bringing clarity. When I had my first health scare at Judy Barnes' house, or when I collapsed at the airport after my third wife's funeral, I was forced to confront my own mortality. These moments made me think about what I would leave behind. Would the rodeo survive without me? Would people remember the Black cowboys and cowgirls once I was gone? These questions pushed me to build something sustainable, something that would outlast me.

What brings me peace now is seeing how my vision has become our vision. The Bill Pickett Invitational Rodeo is no longer just Lu Vason's dream; it belongs to everyone who has made it part of their lives. It has surpassed being an event; it's become an institution, a tradition, a way to preserve and celebrate our heritage.

Looking to the future, I see the rodeo continuing to grow and evolve. I know Valeria will take it to another level, even though she isn't convinced at the moment. I envision new cities, maybe even international shows someday. I picture new generations of cowboys and cowgirls keeping our traditions alive while adding their own innovations. Most importantly, I see the education continuing, more people learning about the Bill Picketts, the Mary Fields, the Nat Loves who helped shape America, their contributions no longer footnotes but celebrated chapters in our shared history.

Through all the ups and downs, the greatest gift has been the family we've created. Not just my blood relatives, but the rodeo family that stretches across this country. From the cowboys who call me "Pop" to the coordinators who treat me like a brother or father, from the sponsors who became friends to the fans who return year after year, we've built something special together.

A community bound not just by a love for rodeo, but by a shared commitment to honoring our past while creating our future.

If there's one thing I hope people remember about me, it's not just that I started a rodeo. I hope they remember that I saw something missing, Black representation in an iconic American tradition, and I did something about it.

I hope they remember that I believed in the power of seeing yourself reflected in history, in entertainment, in achievement. I hope they remember that I tried, in my own way, to make sure no child would ever have to wonder if people who looked like them helped build the American West.

To everyone who has been part of this journey, **Thank you.** To the cowboys and cowgirls who risked life and limb in the arena, you are the heart of this rodeo. To the staff and volunteers who worked tirelessly behind the scenes, you are its backbone. To the sponsors who believed in us, you are its foundation. To the fans who filled the stands, you are its soul. And to my family, especially Valeria, who stood by me through it all, you are my strength.

As for me, I did it my way. I followed my vision when others couldn't see it. I built something that celebrates our history, our culture, our excellence. I created a space where we can be authentically, proudly, unapologetically ourselves. The road wasn't always smooth, but it went exactly where it needed to go.

They say the cowboys ride off into the sunset at the end of the story, but our story isn't ending. It's still being written, with each new rodeo, each new cowboy, each new child who learns about our heritage. The Bill Pickett Invitational Rodeo isn't just my legacy, **it's ours.** And as long as there are people who care about preserving our history and celebrating our culture, that legacy will continue to ride on.

So here's to the next thirty years, may they be filled with the same spirit, determination, and pride that brought us this far. And may we never forget the trail we've blazed together.

"I did it my way."

Lu Vason

EPILOGUE

As I turn the final page of this incredible journey, I find myself filled with both awe and gratitude. Special thanks to Gordon Jackson, Jr., who helped lay the groundwork for this book, having conducted the original interviews with Lu Vason, along with over 50 of Lu's family, friends, and associates. Hearing Lu's story in his own words from the recordings by Gordon Jackson, made the story real, authentic and impactful.

For me, telling Lu Vason's story has been more than just a writing project, it's been a spiritual experience, a masterclass in resilience, vision, and unapologetic authenticity. This has been a ten-year project for Valeria, and I'm honored that she gave me the opportunity and trusted me to tell his story and carry it across the finish line.

Being a generation younger than Lu, I didn't just study his path, ***I felt it***. I felt the weight of his decisions, the burden of breaking barriers, and the fire behind every bold move he made. Through triumphs and trials, Lu didn't just build a rodeo, he built a movement, one that reclaimed history, redefined identity, and gave voice to the voiceless.

What struck me most was how Lu always made space for others. He wasn't just telling his story, he made sure *you* heard about Clara Brown, Bose Ikard, Stagecoach Mary, Bill Pickett, and so many others who shaped the soul of the West. He knew his success meant nothing if he didn't bring his people with him. And that's exactly what he did.

Lu's life was far from perfect, and he never pretended otherwise. He made mistakes, lost things that mattered, and weathered more than his share of storms. But through it all, he never folded. He faced life head-on and did it his way.

That's what makes his story so powerful and so human.

I love that Lu chose Frank Sinatra's "I Did It My Way" as his anthem. Because if anyone lived that truth, it was him. From the modeling runways to jazz clubs, from hair salons to horse arenas, Lu Vason walked into every room, no matter how unfamiliar, and left his mark. Bold. Brilliant. Unapologetically himself.

He taught me that your story doesn't have to be perfect to be powerful. That your legacy isn't built on applause, it's built on purpose. And Lu's purpose was clear: to lift up the culture, shine a light on forgotten heroes, and create something that would live far beyond him.

Lu passed away on May 17, 2015, but trust me, his legacy will never die. It lives on in every young cowboy and cowgirl who puts on a pair of boots. In every girl who watches a rodeo queen and sees herself. In every family who sits in the stands and sees their history on display, alive, proud, and undeniable.

Lu, thank you. Thank you for your voice, your courage, and your relentless commitment to honoring our people. Thank you for telling your story and insisting on telling theirs too. Thank you for showing us what it looks like to stand tall, dream wide, and *ride hard* for what you believe in.

Your story and this book is your victory lap.

With respect, admiration, and deep gratitude,

Anton Cunningham
Author | Forever a Student of Your Legacy

Made in the USA
Columbia, SC
03 July 2025